ATLANTIS LOST

U.S.–European Relations after the Cold War

CONTRIBUTORS

STANLEY HOFFMANN
RONALD STEEL
JAMES CHACE
ZBIGNIEW BRZEZINSKI
SEYOM BROWN
DAVID P. CALLEO
EDWARD L. MORSE
ANDREW J. PIERRE
EARL C. RAVENAL
NICHOLAS WAHL

ATLANTIS LOST

*U. S.-European Relations
after the Cold War*

Edited by
JAMES CHACE
and
EARL C. RAVENAL

A Council on Foreign Relations Book
Published by
New York University Press • New York • 1976

Copyright © 1976 by Council on Foreign Relations, Inc.
Library of Congress Catalog Card Number: 75-15128
ISBN: 0-8147-1361-0

Library of Congress Cataloging in Publication Data
Main entry under title:

Atlantis lost.

    Includes bibliographical references.
    1. Europe—Relations (general) with the United
States—Addresses, essays, lectures. 2. United States—
Relations (general) with Europe—Addresses, essays,
lectures.   I. Chace, James.   II. Ravenal, Earl C.
D1065.U5A93   301.29′4′073   75-15128
ISBN 0-8147-1361-0

Manufactured in the United State of America

COUNCIL ON FOREIGN RELATIONS BOOKS

Founded in 1921, the Council on Foreign Relations, Inc. is a non-profit and non-partisan organization of individuals devoted to the promotion of a better and wider understanding of international affairs through the free interchange of ideas. The membership of the Council, which numbers about 1,600, is made up of men and women throughout the United States elected by the Board of Directors on the basis of an estimate of their special interest, experience and involvement in international affairs and their standing in their own communities. The Council does not take any position on questions of foreign policy, and no person is authorized to speak for the Council on such matters. The Council has no affiliation with and receives no funding from any part of the United States government.

The Council conducts a meetings program to provide its members an opportunity to talk with invited guests who have special experience, expertise or involvement in international affairs, and conducts a studies program of research directed to political, economic and strategic problems related to United States foreign policy. Since 1922 the Council has published the quarterly journal, *Foreign Affairs*. From time to time the Council also publishes books and monographs which in the judgment of the Committee on Studies of the Council's Board of Directors are responsible treatments of significant international topics worthy of presentation to the public. The individual authors of articles in *Foreign Affairs* and of Council books and monographs are solely responsible for all statements of fact and expressions of opinion contained in them.

The members of the Board of Directors of the Council as of September 1, 1975, are; Robert O. Anderson, W. Michael Blumenthal, Zbigniew Brzezinski, Douglas Dillon, Hedley

CONTENTS

CONTRIBUTORS

STANLEY HOFFMANN is Professor of Government and Chairman of the Center for European Studies at Harvard University. Among his publications are *Decline or Renewal?*, *Gulliver's Troubles*, and *The State of War*.

RONALD STEEL is currently engaged in writing the biography of Walter Lippmann. As a Foreign Service officer, he served in Washington and the Middle East, and is the author of *Pax Americana, The End of Alliance*, and *Imperialists and Other Heroes: A Chronicle of the American Empire*.

JAMES CHACE is Managing Editor of *Foreign Affairs* and Visiting Lecturer in Political Science at Yale University. He has been Managing Editor of *Interplay* and *East Europe* magazines, and is the author of *A World Elsewhere: The New American Foreign Policy*.

ZBIGNIEW BRZEZINSKI is the Herbert Lehman Professor of Government and Director of the Research Institute on International Change at Columbia University, and is Director of the Trilateral Commission. His publications include *Between Two Ages: America's Role in the Technetronic Era* and *The Fragile Blossom: Crisis and Change in Japan*.

SEYOM BROWN is a Senior Fellow in the Foreign Policy Studies Program at the Brookings Institution, Washington, and Adjunct Professor of Foreign Policy at the School of Advanced International Studies, Johns Hopkins University. He is the author of *New Forces in World Politics* and *The*

Faces of Power: Constancy and Change in United States Foreign Policy from Truman to Johnson.

DAVID P. CALLEO is Professor of European Studies at the Johns Hopkins School of Advanced International Studies. He is the author of *The Atlantic Fantasy: The U.S., NATO, and Europe* and co-author of *America and the World Political Economy.*

EDWARD L. MORSE is a Senior Fellow of the 1980s Project at the Council on Foreign Relations and Visiting Jacob Blaustein Professor of International Organization at the Johns Hopkins School of Advanced International Studies. Formerly he was Assistant Professor of Politics and International Affairs at the Woodrow Wilson School of Public and International Affairs, Princeton University, and he is the author of *France and the Politics of Interdependence.*

ANDREW J. PIERRE is a Senior Research Fellow at the Council on Foreign Relations and was formerly with the Brookings Institution, the Hudson Institute, and the Department of State. His most recent book is *Nuclear Politics: The British Experience with an Independent Strategic Force, 1939–1970.*

EARL C. RAVENAL is Professor of American Foreign Policy at the Johns Hopkins School of Advanced International Studies. He was the Director of the Asian Division (Systems Analysis) in the Office of the Secretary of Defense, 1967–69, and is the author of the forthcoming *Beyond the Balance of Power: Foreign Policy and International Order.*

NICHOLAS WAHL is Professor of Politics and Director of European Studies at Princeton University. He has been a visiting lecturer and fellow at the University of Lyons, the University of Paris, Nuffield College, Oxford, and the Fonda-

tion Nationale des Sciences Politiques, Paris. He is the author
of *The Fifth Republic: France's New Political System*.

INTRODUCTION

James Chace and Earl C. Ravenal

To say that Atlantic relations are in state of transition, or confusion, is to express a dominant and perpetual theme. In fact, disarray has been a constant property of the alliance since its inception. But in another sense, there have been several distinct turning points—or challenges—in the history of the Atlantic relationship since the period 1947-49, which also marked the beginning of the cold war.

One turning point was 1956, the crushing of the Hungarian uprising by the Soviets and the Suez adventure of Britain and France. Hungary confirmed the limits of the American commitment to altering the division of Europe. Suez disclosed the essential divergence of American and European interests— though its lessons were taken in opposite ways by Britain and France. For Britain, the thrust of foreign policy would be to repair her "special relationship" with the United States. For France, a program of independence from Atlantic entanglements was begun, which included the development of an independent nuclear striking force.

Another turning point was 1962-63. The Cuban Missile Crisis and the ensuing Test Ban Treaty marked the realization of stalemate at the strategic nuclear level. The shadow of this stalemate spread over all preparations and instruments for the defense of Europe, prejudicing Kennedy's Grand Design for binding Europe and America in an Atlantic community as well as successive schemes for sharing nuclear defense, such as the Multilateral Nuclear Force (MLF).

Now the Atlantic relationship appears to be at another turning point—or perhaps not so much at a point as in the midst of an extended transition. Most of the contributors in this volume, while they differ widely in their prognoses and prescriptions, would characterize it as the most significant transition since the post-World War II sequence that led to the construction of the relationship.

This transition might be more serious, because it coincides with, and is reinforced by, a major shift in the structure of the international system beyond the bipolarity of the 1950s and 1960s (though important elements of duality and a predominant axis of confrontation persist). The U.S. opening to China, the policy of détente with the Soviet Union, and the collapse in Vietnam indeed moved the world away from the rigidities of the cold war to an era in which less ideological power politics predominate.

The foreign policy of Nixon and Kissinger—the thrust of which continued, quite naturally, into the Ford Administration—came to be based on a conception of a balance of power, not, of course, the "classic" eighteenth- or nineteenth-century version, but in a sense appropriate to the last third of the twentieth century; that is, it recognized and accepted some ideological motives from the preceding era of confrontation, some of the rigidities of a bipolar nuclear balance, and some allegiances to existing alliances. But the policy of Nixon and Kissinger emphasized the direct approach to adversaries and the institutionalization of summitry, bypassing the more cumbersome mechanisms of alliance consultation. It moved, under the rubric of the Nixon Doctrine, to shift many of the burdens—and some of the risks—of defense to allies. It applied the diplomacy of linkage in commercial and security areas—as in the 1973 "Year of Europe" initiative—to reassert U.S. predominance over longtime friends. Its drift toward economic nationalism was expressed in the unilateral and sudden moves that resulted in the suspension of gold convertibility in August 1971 and two subsequent dollar devaluations. And its cultivation of détente, with bilateral arms control, trade, and other functional arrangements between the superpowers, inspired the fear of condominium and crass global dictation.

In particular, the rolling crisis that developed after the 1973 Arab-Israeli conflict posed the sharpest challenge to European-American relations since Suez. The Atlantic alliance staggered under the impact of events originating in the Middle East: the Yom Kippur War, with its conflicting demands on, and divergent responses by, the allies; the Arab oil embargo of the winter of 1973-74; and the drastic rise of oil prices by the OPEC cartel. These events worsened the economic condition of all the Atlantic nations, both absolutely and vis-à-vis the rich segment of the Third World, and even the Communist world. But they also redistributed the relative advantages of the United States and various European allies—again, as before, in favor of the United States.

While the essays in this book were written in the shadow of the critical events of 1973-74, several authors are skeptical of the attribution of the current troubles of the alliance to Middle East war and oil. Edward Morse, for one, insists that these pressures merely accelerated a more fundamental crisis that had been patched over, and that "the current set of tensions in the industrialized world reflect long-term trends, which are both inescapable and intractable." Seyom Brown sees the present crisis in a perspective which views centrifugal pulls in the Atlantic relationship as effects of the emergence of new functional issues that cross-cut and confuse the previous parallel objectives of the Atlantic partners.

For many reasons, therefore, the Atlantic relationship is in flux and under challenge. All the difficulties—both economic and strategic—that were latent, or suppressed, in the original relationship have asserted themselves in the keenest form. It is like a prophecy come true.

But the present challenge to the coherence and utility of the Atlantic relationship results not only from those structural flaws that were built into the relationship from its inception, but also from some entirely new factors: the emergence of new centers of power as well as a shift in the very meaning and components of power. And underlying this change in the structure of the international political-military order are vast, still poorly understood, movements in basic global functions relating to population, food, the environment, and the resultant turbulence transmitted to economic institutions—international, national, and private.

The authors of these essays are, in general, quite sensitive to the salience—perhaps even dominance—of these new issues. They are the substance of Zbigniew Brzezinski's "global agenda," the challenges and positions to be found on Stanley Hoffmann's "other chessboards." But it remains for the European commentators, in the "Bellagio Colloquy" that concludes this volume, to exhibit the peculiar poignance of these issues, as they wrestle with the interaction of these problems with the more familiar—though no more tractable—ones of regional integration.

No wonder, then, that the rhetoric generated by the present disorder differs from the traditional discourse between Europe and America. Previously, the talk was about institutions, instrumentalities, different shapings of the alliance (the "dumbbell," the "two pillars"); there were schemes to improve the collective functions of the participating states; there were complaints, on the one side, about the burden-sharing and, on the other, about American dominance, or "hegemony." Most of the commentators here would agree that such "hegemony" exists, to some extent, and has impeded European initiatives toward integration and autonomy. Not all would agree that it deserves opprobrium. Edward Morse contends, for example, that "no one can be certain that [the new pluralism] can work as efficiently as the system of American predominance in providing both military security and a framework of economic prosperity." But if blame is to be apportioned for Europe's lack of political strength, David Calleo, for one, would sympathetically echo European recriminations, while Ronald Steel would cite the Europeans themselves for using NATO to cloak their own "abdication."

But this time, there is a widespread feeling that more is at stake than the means of cooperation. And this time, though there is no common prescription—indeed prescriptions diverge more widely, and more fundamentally, than ever—there is the common belief that "more of the same" is no solution; that deeper understandings must be achieved about the nature of the challenges, and that prescriptions must be even more wide-ranging among the possibilities for response. In this volume alone, there is an extraordinary range of prescriptive responses: Stanley Hoffmann's encouragement of a "European voice"; David Calleo's sympathy for a European bloc in a world of blocs; Zbigniew Brzezinski's broadening of Atlantic instrumentalities into "trilateral" cooperation, including Japan; Andrew Pierre's advocacy of a devolution of defensive responsibilities to a "European Defense Community"; James Chace's toleration for a "Concert of Europe," even though it is not likely to turn into the coherent partner envisaged by the earlier Atlanticists; Edward Morse's reaffirmation of pragmatic policies of American leadership, subject only to certain specific negative injunctions—"thou-shalt-nots"; Seyom Brown's acknowledgment that underlying functional currents will fragment the present alliance into diverse coalitions; Nicholas Wahl's accommodation of the constrained domestic structures of individual European nations; Ronald Steel's inclination to use an attenuated American presence to shock "Europe" into a sense of responsibility for "its" fate; and Earl Ravenal's acceptance of the alternative of American disengagement.

In all this, there may be a double irony: while many states in Europe—particularly of course France—several years ago professed to resent American "hegemony" and intensively sought diplomatic independence, recently they have felt strategically more naked toward any possible Soviet threat. Now Europe fears American withdrawal and dissociation from the common fate; it invites the United States to remain committed; it renews hopes for American leadership of the alliance. But in the wake of the Vietnam debacle, the United States is seriously constrained by its domestic procedures and attitudes, and uncertain in its responses, despite the professions of steadfastness by its leaders and the continuing sympathy of its people for Western Europe.

And while, during the 1960s, the European Community seemed ever more prone to unite and to flex its newly acquired economic muscle, by the mid-1970s it was weakened by oil prices and vulnerable to possible embargoes—items that are not merely economic nuisances but threats to the vitality of each nation. And yet, because of the differential distribution of the penalties and opportunities of the oil situation, the United States attained a new lease on its economic position. Now Washington has offered the Community the choice of accepting American direction, in financial recycling, emergency sharing, and economic bargaining—which some countries, notably France, have interpreted as a new assertion of dominance—or of being condemned to weakness and danger.

Several of the authors comment on this seeming reversal of status. Hoffmann is skeptical of the long-term significance of the recent economic crisis. Calleo expatiates on the effects of "America's rejuvenated hegemony" but, in the end, forecasts its transience. Morse welcomes the re-establishment of firmer American leadership, reversing an incipient tendency (if indeed it really existed) toward alternate centers of power. Chace sees the relative weakening as an ironic blessing, disabusing the United States of essentially unfounded fears of European economic dominance. Ravenal would discount America's temporary recovery of dominance, stressing instead the inherent strategic contradictions in the alliance that tend to its inevitable dissolution.

Whatever the weight of present economic factors, one novel feature about them in the context of the European-American relationship is that they now cut *across* security ties; they are no longer perceived as running parallel to them—a central point in the analysis of Seyom Brown. The very notion of linkage demonstrates this. When linkage is broached, as it was in Kissinger's "Year of Europe" speech of April 1973, it can only be taken negatively, that is, in the sense of a trade-off. The United States indicated that it would continue to "sacrifice" security resources and undertake risks for its allies, but only if they abandoned preferential and protective bloc trading practices and agreed to modify the international monetary system to provide greater trade advantages for the United States. But it is obvious that threats to allies, tensions among functional areas of bargaining, and the insistence on their linkage will create less stable alliance structures. Linkage bargaining is bound to complicate, rather than facilitate, agreement among parties with multiple and naturally divergent interests.

Several authors are, to varying degrees, critical of the *uses* to which linkage has been put by the American government. In Pierre's diagnosis, the failures of the Atlantic relationship—specifically the aborted integration of Europe—are the result of America's overplaying its considerable advantage, as well as its inability to see where its true longer term interests lie. Morse, though he is receptive to continuing American leadership, cautions against "potential abuses of interactions among the industrialized societies." And Hoffmann points out that Europe's problem with linkage bargaining is simply that it has little to link, in return.

The strategic question centers on the "coupling" of the

American nuclear arsenal with the defense of Europe and, in a larger sense, the coupling of the fates of both sides of the Atlantic. In situations of "nuclear plenty," parity, and now "essential equivalence," some implicit decoupling has inevitably occurred. The fact that this issue is timeworn only attests to its perennial significance. It is true that these implications are potentially inherent in the situation of *any* alliance of sovereign powers. And it is true that not only all the arguments, but virtually all the types of strategic dispositions, have been run through at some time: massive retaliation, resting on American nuclear monopoly and then superiority; tactical nuclear reliance in the late 1950s and early 1960s; the stout conventional defense, the "pause," and the flexible response; the full spectrum of deterrence promised by the incoming Nixon Administration; and most recently the selective intermediate use of the American strategic nuclear force, and a renewed interest in tactical nuclear weapons and dispositions.

But the novel feature in the strategic area at this juncture is that the strategic context now really approximates the condition of parity between the superpowers foreshadowed two decades ago. Thus the question is no longer focused on the way alliance burdens and benefits might be most fairly shared. The essential question is raised to the surface: where, and at whose expense, would a war be fought? Would the two superpowers make their homelands sanctuaries by tacit or even semi-explicit agreement, planning to fight a limited tactical nuclear battle in Central Europe? Or would they plan to escalate quickly to general nuclear war? What should inspire some reflection is the fact that *every* move, in *any* direction, by the Americans has provoked suspicion and unease among the Europeans. The irony of this is noted by Pierre: "Current changes in American strategic doctrine [i.e., the 'Schlesinger retargeting doctrine'], in emphasizing limited and controlled nuclear response, may come to be seen as downgrading the automatic response, thereby weakening deterrence in Europe."

What this indicates is that, under the surface of these shifts in weapons, postures, and strategies, lies some logic that might elude solutions. Perhaps it is a logic inherent in the very nature of nuclear weapons and the overarching strategic balance they have created between the two superpowers, a logic that might inevitably corrode alliance structures. The vulnerability of the superpowers to central damage from each other might be too much of a strain for contemporary alliance structures to bear. The contradictions in the strategic postures of the United States and its allies have inspired, among other solutions, schemes of "devolution" of nuclear capabilities and responsibilities. Such schemes are advocated by Pierre, and considered the "more likely alternative" by Calleo.

Conceivably no solution—none of the possible postures—would satisfy all the strategic demands of the situation. Certainly none seems to satisfy the psychological and political demands of the alliance partners—a question more important, perhaps, for the integrity and continuing sense of purpose of the alliance. Simply muddling along might, in such circumstances, be the likely course; but that tends to immobilism on the surface, while turbulent currents stir in the depth below. As in an Arctic ice pack, sudden disintegration could occur. If the Atlantic community ever does fracture, it might well be over the divergent logics of defense—not over the different economic preferences of the allies.

Moreover, efforts to repair or strengthen the European-American relationship will test political capabilities at several levels:

(1) The "legitimacy" of the individual governments. Few of the ruling groups of European countries have enough political scope to pursue the most effective arrangements for defense in collaboration with the United States, or to project sufficient strategies for their own collective defense, or for that matter,

to construct the most rational economic nexus. This in-capacity stems mainly from their diverse and powerful constituencies, which might exercise a veto on international actions by elected parliamentary governments, particularly fragile coalitions, that are not in their immediate parochial interest. A further inhibiting factor can be found in the ex-panded expectations for domestic welfare that national governments are now committed to fulfill.

The subject of the "legitimacy" of Western European governments—and indeed of the governments of every con-temporary industrial democracy—engenders a good deal of argument in these essays. Brzezinski cites the problems of the post-industrial age that are descending on Europe a decade later than on the United States, exacerbating historical cleavages and complicating the task of government. Perhaps his "nongovernability" is a more neutral and more significant term than Kissinger's celebrated epithet, "lacking legitimacy." Morse refers to a "crisis of legitimacy," but attributes much of the current problem more specifically to "the combination of economic stagnation and double-digit inflation." Wahl con-ducts perhaps the most extended discussion of the problem of limited governmental license for foreign policy activity, a problem he considers the fundamental obstacle to "a return to the old-time Atlantic religion"—though he takes the most benign view of the phenomenon. He claims that what some call "illegitimacy" is simply the normal—or at least expected —operation of European national political systems, which Americans—particularly the self-styled "friends of Eu-rope"—are unwilling to recognize, let alone accommodate.

(2) The potential for European unity. Europe is at a cross-roads in its own conception of its coherence. David Calleo asks whether the European Community is only a "fair-weather construction." Stanley Hoffmann talks about the stubborn-ness and the parochial nature of the national bureaucracies. Several other authors—notably James Chace—remind us of the strength and persistence of Europe's historical thrust toward

unity (from the time of the Carolingian empire) but caution that it will never take the form simply of a larger nation-state. He warns against an American attempt to play on Europe's elements of disunity, particularly an attempt to wean Germany away from "Europe" to a special relationship with the United States.

But it remains a question whether Europe will attain the requisite political unity—the true homogenization of will, beyond the French vision of a concert of independent national states—for both nuclear sharing and true economic union. Nuclear sharing is the key to a European initiative in defense that might make Europe a fit receptacle for the increased security capabilities and responsibilities that could significantly reduce the American role. Certainly, Pierre's concept of orderly devolution depends on a certain degree of political integration.

True *economic* union includes, prominently, monetary union. This step is continually postponed, because it *depends* on authoritative and binding decisions across national borders for the apportionment of the costs of adjusting the entire system. Counterbalancing some hopeful signs of increasing post-Gaullist French participation in the mechanisms of NATO and the European Community are the chronic disability and doubts of Britain. Even Britain's decision to stay in the European Community, in the June 1975 referendum, might actually weaken the Community by implanting Britain's specific problems in the Community framework. The case of Italy may be analogous. Morse comments extensively on the economies of Britain and Italy. Calleo even speculates that the European Community might benefit from their dissociation.

(3) The consistency of the Atlantic community. It is increasingly doubtful that functional relations will again be aligned and composed, rather than traded off in some constantly threatening linkage bargaining. Morse talks about the original "bargain" of security for economics becoming "unglued," and the alliance partners, in a sort of "new mercan-

tilism," pursuing competing, rather than mutually compensatory, goals of full employment and current account surpluses. Brown, however, considers this behavior as more the inevitable concomitant of a change in the shape and nature of the international system.

But if a parallel approach to issues is not achieved, the Atlantic community may disintegrate, in effect, into a mere series of *ad hoc* and bilateral arrangements, thinly covered by the fossilized façade of NATO and other Atlantic institutions.

These speculations, of course, are not definitive. But their effect is to raise for the United States in the most severe form since the foundation of the alliance the question of the premises of American involvement in Europe. In these circumstances, choices that had been outside the pale of consideration come into the debate—at least as points that must be contemplated and against which more comfortable solutions must be measured.

This expansion of basic choices coincides with the first fundamental shift in the international system since the construction of the Atlantic relationship of collective defense and economic cooperation in the late 1940s, after the demise of the brief hopes for a more universal organization in the form of an effective United Nations. The essays in this book are permeated by a sense of the shifting distribution and use of power and, more than that, the shifting *nature* of power. In particular, economic instruments have been elevated, if not to primacy, at least to strategic decisiveness. And, as a result, new and potent actors have entered into the international system. Some authors sound a corrective note of skepticism; perhaps we are too much in the sway of the events of 1973-74. But most stand by their premonitions of fundamental change —though their precise diagnoses differ, and their policy conclusions diverge even more widely.

The possible results of such a power shift are many. A future balance of world power might even consist of: a United States that was relatively invulnerable to vicissitudes and pressures of an economic or strategic nature; the principle raw-material-producing (particularly energy-exporting) states, especially those that are populous, militarily potent, and less subject to internal instability; and the Communist world, which, with its managed economies, disciplined populations, and determined governments, is also relatively immune to international economic dislocations and social disabilities. Under those possible circumstances, both sets of allies—Europe and Japan—might even seem less central and indispensable to U.S. concerns.

At least the sense in which the United States "needs" Europe would be different. It would no longer be for the same obvious strategic reasons, in view of long-range and more diffused deterrence, as well as the global mobility of our forces—though Europe, of course, continues to be the key meeting place of Soviet and American spheres of interest. As Brown succinctly puts it: "North Atlantic relationships are losing their pivotal role in United States foreign policy." Chace refers to "the reduced importance of the U.S.-European connection in the context of changing global power relationships." And Brzezinski, while reaffirming the cardinal importance of Europe for American policy, puts this importance on a different ground: Europe is a "crossroads" where "the two principal alternative concepts of modern society most directly compete"; it is the focal point of the U.S.-Soviet rivalry; and, above all, it is the linchpin for a concerted response to "the novel and global problems—especially those confronting the developing world." Thus, ironically, the "centrality" of the U.S.-European relationship may have been devalued," and America "may now need a truly united Europe less."

Understandably, various European commentators take exception to suggestions that Europe either will, or ought to, lose its priority in the American scheme because of our envelopment in global issues; if anything, Christoph Bertram judges, Europe's importance for the United States will increase.

In general, we can say that what "happens" in Europe

continues to be a most powerful indicator of the "state of the world." As a specific economic nexus, the European-American relationship is central among American interests today. There is the body of sunk investment and the stream of returns that our economy derives from that investment. And, of course, there is the trade connection, profitable in both directions.

In any case, some special European-American relationship will undoubtedly persist, because it is confirmed by a fact which is perhaps the basic raw material of political association—the general sense of a common fate that derives from our overlapping history, shared values, and compatible social forms.

In reconstructing the European-American relationship to meet new conditions, the questions now—that might not have existed in such acute form in its first twenty-five years —are: will the United States and Europe have to settle for a series of "second-best" alternatives? Or are there adjustments that will work and essentially justify the continuance of the present forms and institutions? Or finally, in a new burst of "creativity" (to use Henry Kissinger's ubiquitous term), might the nations even be able to summon the political will—that is, find it desirable and then enforce such a judgment on their constituencies—to strengthen the alliance and deepen the association?

How does this book relate to this situation? Why "Atlantis Lost"? After all, "Atlanticism," though outrun by circumstances, is far from dead. Indeed, as Pierre remarks, "the preservation of Atlanticism would be the most comfortable policy for many persons in the United States as well as in Europe." Wahl, too, notes the persistence of old Atlanticist notions in American attitudes and among American elites. He also points out that the range of respectable political debate on the status of Europe and the character of the Atlantic relationship has always been much wider in Europe than in the United States. So the present time of challenge and subversion of familiar presumptions suggests not a premature coalescence around some forced common viewpoint—something that, in any case, has been tried again and again in academic exercises as well as in alliance declarations. Rather, it is a moment to break the crust of conformity, to cast the net as widely as possible, to collect a diversity of assessments of the current state of affairs, including the most pessimistic estimates that at least might shatter unpromising molds and clear the way for the proposals of others who feel the times are ready for more specific and positive initiatives.

It is in that unencumbered, frank, open-ended spirit that this book was conceived, these essays first solicited, and these discussions undertaken, among American scholars and analysts (convened at the Council on Foreign Relations in New York during the winter and spring of 1973-74), and between Americans and a group of Europeans (assembled at Bellagio, Italy, in the fall of 1974).

Instead of the traditional functional distribution of subjects—security, economics, etc.—each author attempts his own analysis of the problems and prospects of the European-American relationship. The result is a set of different "visions" of the future of the relationship. The final chapter distills the discussion, in the Bellagio conference, with the European participants. The American authors are greatly indebted to these European commentators for their painstaking and serious critiques of our drafts; many of their critical points have been accommodated in the chapters presented here, revised by their authors up to the late winter of 1975-76.

The two editors acknowledge with gratitude the sponsorship of the New York meetings and the essays in this book by the Council on Foreign Relations, its President, Bayless Manning, and its Director of Studies, Richard H. Ullman. We also express our appreciation to the Rockefeller Foundation for granting the use of its Study and Conference Center at Bellagio, Italy; to the Chairman of the Center's Program Committee, Ralph W. Richardson, Jr.; and to the Director of the Center, Dr. William C. Olson, and his wife, for their unmatched hospitality. And we are pleased to recognize the early and significant encouragement and help of the German Marshall Fund of the United States, and its President, Benjamin H. Read; and the generosity of the Fritz Thyssen Foundation of Cologne, Germany, and its Chairman, Dr. Kurt Birrenbach. We hope that all will feel their support rewarded in some measure by this book.

James Chace
Earl C. Ravenal

New York and Washington, February 1976

Chapter 1
NO TRUMPS, NO LUCK, NO WILL:
GLOOMY THOUGHTS ON
EUROPE'S PLIGHT

Stanley Hoffmann

The contributors to this volume have been asked to be forward looking and normative. They all share the conviction that the postwar era has indeed ended. The world spirit, as Hegel would have called it, or God, as others would say, decreed with a fine sense of irony that what should have been the Year of Europe would become the Year of World Crisis. With the fading away of the "Atlantic generation," with new leaders in several West European countries, with a new world agenda dominated by the "struggle for the world product," a massive transfer of wealth to the oil-producing countries, and the continuation of inflation and recession among the industrial nations, isn't a normative exercise indispensable? Isn't that great "act of creation" Henry Kissinger had demanded in his famous speech of April 1973 even more necessary now than when he asked for it?

Two caveats are in order. First, European-American relations have been the realm of prescriptive designs par excellence. We have had, over the years, the Atlantic design, first, with the Marshall Plan, NATO, and the early steps toward the integration of the West Europeans into an entity bound to the United States, later under the name of Atlantic partnership, used in order both to bless the development of that entity and to stress its true destination: playing its part in America's orchestra. We have had, on the European side, a variety of separatist designs à la de Gaulle, or in its Third Force or neutralist variants. We have had, on this side, either reactions against or amendments to the Atlantic design: schemes for sharing nuclear defense, such as the Multilateral Nuclear Force, schemes of disengagement (going back to Kennan's Reith lectures) or schemes of devolution to a uniting Europe, all opposed to U.S. overcommitment or to the overbearing character of Atlanticism; and the more recent trilateral scheme, a grandiose enlargement of Atlanticism aimed at incorporating a third "pillar," Japan, and at enlarging the common agenda. There are splendidly convincing, or at least eloquent, arguments for each of these normative constructs. Many are presented in this volume. Isn't there something disturbing about the abundance and persistence of these schemes—as if the stablest "structures of peace" were the grand designs, coexisting far above the realities?

This observation leads to a second question: if European-American relations have become a graveyard of grand designs, isn't it because all of these assume the existence or the growth of a European entity, either as a junior partner in the Atlantic or trilateral enterprise, or as a force with its own identity to which power can be "devolved," or which would be left standing should the United States "disengage"? Isn't the flabby nature of the European entity what makes most of the normative designs really academic? What if American hegemony were clearly both the cause and the effect of this flabbiness—and thus required no normative dressing up, being a massive, brute fact of life anyhow?

Thus the *préalable* to any prescriptive and forward-looking exercise ought to be a backward glance. And it should focus on the Europeans. In any of the designs, they are the missing link or the fatal flaw. Moreover, among the Europeans, the French will receive special attention, because they have played a decisive role both as initiators and as obstacles, as European idealists and as nationalists. The purpose of this retrospective is to assess the significance of the present apparent return to harmony: how much does the new state of European-American relations differ from the past? What is its import for the European entity? Only after one has reached some conclusions on these points can one suggest some directions for U.S. policy.[1]

The advent of Helmut Schmidt and Valéry Giscard d'Estaing led many commentators to talk about a new chance for West European unity *and* for friendly European-American relations. The signing in Brussels, in June 1974, of a new Atlantic declaration meant that the bickering which had marked those relations, especially between France and the United States, was now behind us. The first meetings between the new German Chancellor and the new French President suggested that the threat of a disintegration of the European Economic Community was being overcome and that a new *relance* could be expected. The European summits of December 1974 and 1975 vindicated these hopes, at least in part, thanks to a series of compromises on institutions, regional policy, and British demands. There also was a Franco-American compromise on energy policy, which reconciled the French approach with that which had been chosen by Washington and by France's eight partners.

A little history would do no harm. If European unity were in search of a myth, I would suggest Sisyphus, the unhappy symbol of all international organizations. European unification has been a succession of initiatives, followed by fiascos, followed by *relances*, followed by new crises. The European Sisyphus got to work in 1950. After the disasters of German rearmament he tried again. After the fall of the Fourth Republic, de Gaulle undertook a new *relance*, which ended with the failure of the Fouchet Plan in 1962. Then Pompidou tried anew until the intra-European and Franco-American rift at the beginning of 1974.

Thus we are at the *fifth* new dawn. Two recurrent crises have kept the West European Sisyphus at work. One has been crisis in France herself: the politico-financial crisis of 1958, the unexpected balance of payments reversal that followed the oil crisis and forced France's *de facto* devaluation of January 1974. The other has been a recurrent crisis in Franco-American relations. This does not mean that there couldn't be other causes of breakdown in the future (for instance, a major British economic and financial crisis). But it suggests that for the rock to move upward again, and stay at its new plateau, there would have to be at least, on the one hand, greater harmony of economic and financial policy among the EEC members and, on the other, a *lasting* rapprochement between France and the United States, i.e., a *major* change of policy either in Paris or in Washington: either the Americans must accept the French thesis of a distinctive West European identity (in association with, but without subordination to, American global designs); or else the French must endorse an "Atlantic" Europe taking its place in what Jobert has called Washington's cosmogony—a vision which France's European partners more or less explicitly prefer. In order to understand why none of these conditions have been met before, the trends of the past decade need to be re-examined.

Bad Trends, Old and New

Ten years ago, at a time when many social scientists on both sides of the Atlantic were predicting an "end of ideology" and a gradual alignment of European political and social systems on the American model, I tried to argue that this was a far too simplified and deterministic view. Differences between European institutions, legacies, and attitudes and American ones in political matters—the word political being used in its broadest sense, i.e., "concerning the polity"—were too deep to be erased quite so easily. I mentioned in particular the weight of a troubled past in each European polity, and contrasted it with American faith in political harmony and in the institutions that had survived so well since 1776. Obviously, much has happened since to puncture *that* analysis. First Vietnam, and later Watergate, have provided millions of Americans with the unsavory spectacle that seems so normal for Europeans, yet so scandalous here: deception and self-deception in the government, massive abuses of power and criminal acts in high places, the revelation of official cynicism mixed with incompetence—hence a serious crisis of public confidence in *both* political parties and in *all* branches of the government (save, perhaps, the judiciary), especially among the young, and the spread of cynicism in the electorate as well. There is a second way in which the American scene has come to look more "European": the mid and late 1960s have been marked by the prevalence of conflict between blacks (or other racial minorities) and whites, the young and their elders, the poor and (especially) those who had finally acceded to some ease, if not affluence. At the same time, and despite such upheavals as May 1968 in France, the political systems of Western Europe were gaining in legitimacy, and in a multitude of ways the weight of historical memories was lightening on a generation that was raised in the new conditions of mass education and economic growth. And yet these changes—which played havoc both with the original thesis of inevitable "Americanization" and with my refutation of it—did not mean that the two sides were meeting halfway. For the main trends of 1964-74 can be divided into two categories, both of which explain what I will call, in shorthand, the European semi-fiasco (semi, since there *is*, whatever its weaknesses, a Community of the Nine): those trends which continued from before 1964, and the new ones that have contributed to the difficulties or made them even worse.

A first persistent trend has been the tendency of each West European polity to remain locked in its own priorities and problems. Both European integration and the involvement of the EEC countries in the world economy have fostered interdependence, in the sense of increased sensitivity *and* vulnerability of each of the nations' economies to fluctuations and decisions outside.[2] But the nations of Western Europe have maintained the autonomy of their reactions and of their outlooks. Also, their situations have continued to be uneven, both with respect to domestic performance (cf. the British rate of growth vs. that of Italy, Germany, or France; the rigidities, habits, and demand pressures making for inflation in France, vs. the greater capacity for restraint and efficiency in Germany) and with respect to their dependence on the outside world (cf. the huge size, composition, and stability of German exports, as compared with the French, but also the far greater German dependence on the U.S. market; the lesser German dependence on outside energy sources, etc.). The combination of *unevenness* and *autonomy* has made further progress toward economic and monetary union an ordeal, as the sad story of the European currencies' "snake" between 1971 and the present has proved. The arcane debate between "economists" and "monetarists," about the proper method of economic unification, reflected largely the difference between the position and interests of Germany (fearful of having to subsidize, in effect, the inflationary economies of its partners) and the policies and concerns of France (eager to preserve her domestic priority to growth and full employment, and to create a European monetary bloc capable of challenging eventually American practices and privileges under the dollar exchange standard). The theoretical debate ended with the victory of the "economists," but the political debacle of the European Monetary Union in 1974 meant the practical frustration of both schools. For unevenness to lead to harmony (or harmonization), one would have needed either a quiet international environment in which an attempt to reach economic union through monetary coordination alone would have had a chance of success, or else the capacity of the political systems to reverse rather than accentuate the effects of unevenness. Actually, even the monetary road supposed a far greater pooling of reserves, a shared attitude toward the value and role of gold, and a determination to prevent, through credit, tax, and social policies, the national rates of inflation from becoming too different: none of this was forthcoming, for reasons having to do both with the U.S. obstacle *and*, above all, with the desire for domestic autonomy.

Domestic autonomy refers, not simply to the obvious fact that the "member states" are still pursuing their own separate courses in all areas which the EEC has not succeeded in regulating, but to the fact that each government remains responsible and responsive to *its* electorate, guided by its own electoral necessities and priorities, and inspired more by the need to devise a strategy that will support *its* presence in power, than by the need for compatibility with its foreign partners. Thus the economic policy followed by the team of Pompidou and Giscard d'Estaing between 1969 and 1973—full employment and laxity toward inflation—made sense given the domestic design and political strategy of Pompidou—until the oil crisis derailed it altogether. But it did not help the economic union, with a German partner whose priorities were exactly the reverse, and it had put a heavy strain on the common float even before the oil disaster. Ironically enough, in the period 1964-74, the only government that shaped its domestic policies according to an external design rather than to internal calculations was that of General de Gaulle until May 1968. But *his* external design happened not to be that of his partners, and his efforts were geared to maximizing French, not European, influence in the world. Moreover, the explosion of May 1968, although not a revolt against the gist of his foreign policy, was a rebellion against its domestic costs; de Gaulle's successor learned his lesson, and shifted priorities.

Thus even when a government is strong—in the sense that it

has a safe and coherent majority—its framework of calculation may be narrow: cf. all the British governments' inability to regulate industrial relations or, in France, the problem of the shrinking base of the majority's electorate. When the governing majority is not homogeneous (cf. the German coalition), or perpetually in danger of fragmentation (Italy), autonomy may well mean even greater difficulty in escaping from the domestic inhibitions or imperatives, i.e., *less* freedom to "harmonize."

For autonomy means, not freedom of independent action, but distinctive ways of acting, or of not being able to act. The same economic problem—inflation, the rise in energy costs, or labor troubles, for instance—will be handled in different ways, depending on such factors as the importance, efficiency, structure, and habits of the bureaucracy; the degree of politicization and militancy of the unions and of other interest groups; the presence and strength of extremist ideologies; and of course the constitutional authority of the Executive. Contrary to earlier hopes, the combination of bureaucratic politics on top and "querulous satisfaction," or piecemeal dissatisfaction, below, the prevalence of bargaining about bread-and-butter issues, the process of incrementalism, even the interpenetration of elites, have not made integration easier. For each political system bargains in its own style, must be on guard against its own brand of divisive or ideological politics, and has to worry about its own set of parochialisms.

A second element of continuity has been American foreign policy, in a double sense: actual *moves* and actual *weight*. To be sure, there appeared two factors that seemed, for a while, to mark a drastic change, favorable to greater European unity. Henry Kissinger had been an eloquent critic of the tendency of past administrations to want a united Europe only if it does not "challenge American hegemony in Atlantic policy," and to speak to the Europeans with omnipotent paternalism and complacent arrogance. In 1969-70, preoccupied above all with Vietnam and preparing for its "breakthrough" with the two main Communist powers—SALT and the opening to China —the Administration seemed to be following Kissinger's academic recommendations: far greater friendliness toward France, no commitment to any preferred form of European unity, indeed no grand designs. The scene changed after August 15, 1971, but the American economic offensive, in the eyes of many experts, seemed to be both a sign of and a reaction to something that Kissinger had forecast in his writings: the loss of U.S. hegemony, at least in the economic realm, due to a combination of events—the crisis of the "dollar exchange standard" collapsing under the weight of U.S. balance of payments deficits, superior productivity in Western Europe and Japan, and the slowdown in the U.S. rate of growth, et al. Insofar as American imperiousness on the one hand, American de facto predominance on the other had, in the past, made European unity more difficult by dividing Europeans into the meek and the unruly, wouldn't those two new factors, and even the American economic challenge, actually prove helpful?

Neither ultimately did, because neither meant what it seemed to mean. As some writers, like Raymond Vernon, had cautioned, the U.S. economy was still the "rogue elephant in the forest." [3] The United States, in its days of trouble, still had one possibility open to no one else—that of changing unilaterally the rules of the game and of obliging everybody else to pay a price for the creation of new rules acceptable to Washington. The measures of August 15, 1971, the two devaluations of 1971 and 1973, the *de facto* establishment of a floating rate system, amounted to just that. They resulted in a spectacular turning around of the U.S. balance of payments (and thus considerably lessened American interest in a formal new international monetary system). Then came the completely unexpected and paradoxical help of the Middle Eastern oil-producing powers to the United States. Far less dependent on Middle Eastern oil than its economic rivals, less troubled than they by the quadrupling of the price of oil, more capable of providing opportunities for investment as well as technological aid to the "new rich" developing countries, the United States has reasserted both its economic and its monetary predominance. At the same time, it was becoming clear that the "new" foreign policy of Dr. Kissinger, so different from the old in its tactics, in its overall design and flexibility, in its tone and its process of decision, was remarkably *like* the old one insofar as Europe was concerned. Two key notions of the April 23, 1973, address—Europe's merely regional interests, and European unity having to be subordinated to broader goals: those of the Atlantic alliance (enlarged to Japan) so as to be properly "outward-looking"—were weapons borrowed from the old Atlanticist arsenal, ideas still couched in George Ball language. They meant, as before, that the United States, the only power in the non-Communist world with global responsibilities, would set the directions and the framework in which the Europeans could move. Just as, before 1964, the Atlantic bond had never prevented the United States from dealing directly with Moscow over nuclear arms, or from adopting its own policy toward the underdeveloped countries, the neo-Atlantic commitment requested by Dr. Kissinger was not designed to limit U.S. freedom of action, but aimed at circumscribing the Europeans' sphere. The Europeans could unite "as long as, insofar as," etc. The speech gave a long list of "common" objectives; but the American approach to Moscow, from 1971 on, was made without any prior reorganization of intra-Atlantic relations. The fact that NATO remains organized exactly as before (except for the existence of the Eurogroup); that the United States still dominates the weapons procurements of its allies (despite, and indeed partly through, the Eurogroup); that the year 1973 also marked the adoption of one more American strategic doctrine, unilaterally and peremptorily proclaimed by Secretary Schlesinger, and not too clear in its implications; that the U.S. notion of consultation oscillates from mere information to total eclipse —all this also demonstrates continuity in practices which are precisely those that, in the past, had produced discord not only in the Atlantic pseudo-community but also in the European quasi-community.

In the past, the great objector had been France. Here we find the third element of continuity in 1964-74. Partly, this could be attributed to Gaullism: our ten-year period, after all, divides into two halves, with the General in power five years, Pompidou five more, the Gaullist party dominating the majority coalition and in control of both the presidency and the premiership throughout. But is it just Gaullism which explains why France has been the champion of resistance to the United States even when she has, for a while, tried (in Giscard's new Foreign Minister's words) to "dedramatize" her relations with Washington in order to make a European consensus easier? If this were the case, how would we explain the battle over the European Defense Community, or Suez? That France's stance is sharper and makes compromises that paper over basic antagonisms more difficult when "orthodox Gaullism" reigns is sure. But a "more courteous" stance—to use a Giscard term—and an aptitude for paper compromises are not necessarily the same as a substantive shift (recent European summits have been rich in such paper agreements). To explain France's disposition, we must turn to a multiplicity of factors:

(1) A general approach to foreign policy, molded by the style of French education, by French analytical and conceptual reasoning, by the "lessons of history" as learned in school: international relations is a battlefield of national designs, where the stakes are survival, domination, power and wealth. Thus policies are seen as deliberate, calculations of national advantage as permanent, compromises as temporary, alliances and enmities as changing.

(2) The legacy, among the elites—especially those over forty-five—of the humiliations of dependence on another power in the interwar period, in the days of the Nazi occupation and even in the Fourth Republic (many of the centrists and rightists in power today were colonial "hawks").

(3) A strong, if somewhat contentless, patriotism and desire for "cutting a grand figure on the stage," in the public at large. I have tried to analyze this rather elusive force elsewhere,[4] and to show that, at present, it provides little policy guidance. But it is there. It did contribute to Mitterrand's defeat in 1974, for the voters sensed the incoherence of the Communist-Socialist alliance in foreign policy. And it *limits* even if it does not *inspire*; i.e., it precludes abrupt reversals of foreign policy and makes of the "European idea" a welcome concept rather than a driving emotion.

(4) What could be called the external configuration or situation of postwar France. France was not, like Italy, a nation that had tried a policy of aggressive grandeur and had had to pay dearly for it (if anything, France had had to pay for timidity, appeasement, and internal divisiveness). She was not, like Germany, a pariah and a divided country, condemned to pursue a chimera (reunification) and to live a nightmare (security). Like England, France was an impoverished ex-great power in full external retreat. But unlike England, she had no "American connection" or "English-speaking peoples" illusion; and unlike England, she showed extraordinary economic dynamism and imagination, despite the poor performance of the Fourth Republic's political institutions. All the other factors listed dictated a search for an active foreign policy (i.e., the opposite from Italy's search). Now, French foreign policy could not be active *and* entirely pro-American: not only because, after the experiences of 1918-45, few wanted really to play *brillant second* to another power anymore, but also because the United States had already two such *seconds*, in London and in Bonn. Hence a field of forces limiting French choices exactly to two: either a *deliberate* challenge of the United States (but she could not go too far, for security reasons above all, and because of the abyss that such a policy would dig between France and all her neighbors) or a *deliberate* "construction of Europe" concentrating on common interests. (But sooner or later Sisyphus reaches the Sphinx's

riddle, if I may scramble my Greek myths: does "common" mean common to the Europeans *and* the Americans, in which case what is Europe's distinctiveness; or does it mean those interests which distinguish Europe from America, and in this case what happens to European unity?)

(5) An internal configuration that corresponds to, and fits into the external one. There are two main elements here. One is the constellation of political and social forces. As in Italy, there exists a French bourgeoisie—in industry, in the professions, in the armed forces—which sees in the United States a *feste Burg* against communism, not only abroad but at home. But this has never been either the *dominant* view of French bourgeois (anymore than the "rather Hitler than Blum" view had been, earlier), or the *only* view of those bourgeois who held it (they often criticized the United States for its anti-colonialism, for instance). The desire to use foreign policy as an instrument of domestic protection against the far left, so overwhelming in the Italian case, was far more spotty in France, whose grande bourgeoisie, even in the late 1940s, felt far less unsure of itself than its Italian counterpart.[5]

On foreign affairs, the French political scene shows two different and partly overlapping alignments: a pro-European one, which includes most of (not all) the Socialists, the centrists, the right, and some of the Gaullists, leaving out other Gaullists (unless Europe had become France writ large) and the Communists; and one that should be called not anti-American but "anti-American hegemony," which includes the Communists, most of the Socialists and the Gaullists, and leaves out centrists and rightists. Thus an "anti-American hegemony" policy could not be openly disdainful of European unity, since the coalition behind it could not rule together on domestic affairs, and a "pro-European" policy cannot be too meek and mild about the United States, for the very same reason. Should the left finally come to power (in legislative elections followed by a new presidential one), the common denominator of its two fractions would have to be a policy not unlike that of the past. Should the present coalition break up, one could imagine two scenarios: a majority composed of rightists, centrists, and Socialists, or one composed of the left plus the Gaullists. In both cases, one remains within the same foreign policy perimeter, *à des nuances près;* and at present, both scenarios are unlikely.

(6) The other internal element brings us back to the first of the three factors of continuity: national autonomy. What is distinctive about the French nation-state is *le phénomène bureaucratique.* This means, first, that France, like Britain and no other major state in Western Europe, has a bureaucracy with a long, strong, and self-perpetuating tradition of activity in foreign affairs; second, that French bureaucracy is also the matrix and the motor of French economic and social development, to a degree that is unique among liberal societies. Hence both a formidable resistance to its dismantlement, and a propensity to define Europe in "French" terms, i.e., to want it to be a network of rules and programs (and where should these come from, if not from the one civil service with the richest experience in that proliferating field?).

The Past Decade

Let us turn now to the *new* trends of the period 1964-74, and to the reasons why they have worsened the European predicament. The first one is the displacement of the center of gravity of world politics, from the diplomatic-strategic field to the chessboards of economic and monetary relations; or if one prefers, the grand entry of economics into the realm of high politics. In the previous period, as Richard Cooper has shown, economic and monetary relations within the developed members of the world economy had been largely separated from political and military relations, and ran on a distinct, largely depoliticized track. (As Robert Gilpin, in turn, has shown, this in itself resulted from a political decision or deal

—a U.S. decision, a U.S.-Western Europe-Japan deal—and was therefore reversible.) [6] This separation had served as a shield behind which European integration was able to progress. In early 1968, the failure of General de Gaulle to rally the Six behind a common stand opposing the American-sponsored Special Drawing Rights (SDR) and demanding a reform of the Bretton Woods system was a forerunner of things to come. After 1971, the European Community was buffeted by two major storms, both of which are too familiar to be recounted in any detail. The first was the American offensive against the Common Agricultural Policy (CAP), the preferential agreements, the burden which the cost of American troops in Europe added to the U.S. balance of payments deficit, the "trade diversion" resulting from Britain's entry, and the American moves toward a new monetary system. This was of tremendous significance, not because such policies expressed an American "decline," but because they meant that the one area of autonomy granted by the United States to the Europeans in the past was now being revoked. In the early 1960s, the Europeans had divided over the issue of whether to *extend* the realm of cooperation from economics to diplomacy and defense, to which the United States clearly objected. This time, the United States was making rather self-righteous demands in the economic area, and promoting monetary policies that were bound to play havoc with the CAP (each change in rates resulting in a new painful round) and with the financial surpluses of creditor countries. In effect, Washington was, first, demanding that the Europeans help the United States reverse its global trade and payments deficits, and indeed help the United States return to a surplus position that would finance continuing American investments in Europe; second, the United States was resorting to monetary practices that were bound to complicate the life of the fragile European monetary union. Under these circumstances, the Europeans had only two possibilities. One was to resist, at the cost of straining their relations with the United States, and without being able thereby to impose their views about a stable monetary system to which the key remained the United States. But, as usual, resisting beyond a certain point meant splitting: there was a common will to protect the CAP, at France's intransigent insistence, but not to say no on all other points. The other possibility was to yield, as was done on several such issues.

At least this did not affect Europe's relations to the developing countries. European cooperation, and the expansion of the European economies, had taken place in a world of low energy costs and low raw materials prices. The sudden reversal, at the end of 1973, in addition to raising the specter of possible worldwide recession, to wrecking the balance of payments of all West European nations save West Germany, and to destroying the six-nation joint monetary float, once again posed in the sharpest terms the oldest dilemma: whether to seek redress in the shadow of the United States, or whether to argue that there was enough of a difference in position and interests between the United States and Western Europe to justify a separate European policy and a separate approach to OPEC. As is well known, at first the French said no to the first alternative, and the other Europeans said yes to both. By the end of 1974, everything was declared compatible with everything else, but as we shall see below, European unity was not the winner. To conclude: above all an "economic animal," the European Economic Community could not fail to be the victim of the sudden appearance of high waves on the previously quiet international economic ocean.

A second new and damaging trend has been conspicuous in both of the episodes in which the first one had unfolded. The consistency of U.S. policy toward Europe, noted earlier, nevertheless takes on a completely different meaning when the *context* is no longer that of the 1950s and early 1960s. I do not believe that Dr. Kissinger, by contrast with his predecessors, decided that European unity was no longer in the U.S. interest. I think that, unlike his predecessors, he was always skeptical of its chances; more than they had been, he was impatient with the slow and rigid procedures of decision-making in Brussels, and prone to see in them a pretext for European provincialism and pusillanimity. Like his predecessors, he does not want European unity *at the expense of* U.S. interests; but unlike theirs, his conception of the U.S. interests that should be protected is huge. This sounds paradoxical, since he had denounced earlier policies as overextended and as straining U.S. psychological and physical resources. And yet, there has been a triple change.

(1) A change in substance: the United States is no longer primarily the leader of a grand alliance (which also has a vested interest in preventing a large-scale war); it is the builder of a "structure of peace" which entails a transformation in the nature of all major relationships, alliances as well as antagonistic bonds, and the creation of a complicated system of worldwide balance and regional balances. This means a high *priority* to dealing with Moscow and Peking, a considerable amount of attention spent on defusing powder kegs in Southeast Asia or the Middle East, and, more recently, a heroic effort at coping with the problem of economic interdependence: energy, recycling, food, etc.: in other words, global *movement* rather than worldwide *containment*. But with the emphasis shifting from manning the barricades, especially in Europe, to building a planetary framework, U.S. policy becomes much more *confining* for the Europeans: the same old tendency to circumscribe their moves now shrinks their compound into a cage.

(2) A change in style: in its switch from stolidity to maneuver, the United States has shifted from its "free world partnership," "common interest of the West" style, not to one but to two others: a pure "national interest" style, manifest not only in brutal Connally-isms but also in subtler Kissinger "linkages"; and a neo-idealistic style, but on a *global* scale, and so far largely reserved for speeches. The latter does not overtly conflict with a European entity; yet it stresses the latter's confinement by fitting the entity into the global "struc-

tures." [7] The *Realpolitik* style actually hits at the European entity, for it is both more *blunt* and more *divisive* than the earlier style: it both invites a test of strength with the less than cohesive European Community over every contentious issue, *and* suggests bilateralism as a perfectly conceivable, even desirable, alternative, should the confrontation yield no sufficient concessions. For it makes it quite clear that politics aims at rewarding the good and punishing the rambunctious.

(3) A change in tactics. In order to achieve the necessary breakthroughs (toward the "stable structures" as well as the consolidation of U.S. interests) Kissinger has carefully chosen pivots on which to lean in order to turn stalled situations around. Thus he has leaned on China in order to change relations with *both* major Communist powers; on Moscow in order to break the long deadlock with Hanoi; on Egypt in order to break the Arab-Israeli impasse; on Saudi Arabia—less successfully—to regain leverage on OPEC. This virtuosity has been triply damaging to the Europeans. First, it reinforces their confinement: for it is not, for Kissinger, merely a matter of setting a global framework, it is a question of doing it oneself, *first* and in one's own way. This means in effect telling Brandt that he can have his *Ostpolitik*, but only after Washington has pushed its own; or telling the EEC it can have its dialogue with the Arabs, but only after the United States has made its own deals; or showing the Europeans that for the time being the Middle East is a *chasse gardée* of the superpowers (indeed of the United States); or demonstrating that Mutual Force Reductions (MFR) is above all a Soviet-American appendage to the great powers' détente. Second, it exacerbates the tensions between Washington and the Europeans, as long as Kissinger finds no pivot in Western Europe: France is too hostile or concerned with her own game, West Germany has been too reluctant to appear as having a privileged position, Britain remains too troubled and marginal, and Brussels seems devised to make the quest for a pivot fruitless. Without a pivot, yet with the need to keep the

monopoly of initiative, Kissinger has been led to demand a say in the process of intra-European consultation. Third, should Bonn (which under Helmut Schmidt has played a highly visible role of go-between trying to harmonize domestic economic policies and energy policies both between the United States and the Europeans and within the EEC) become actually Kissinger's pivot, what happens either to European unity, should the others (and especially the French) balk, or to European distinctiveness if they don't?

Now whereas the change in the scenery of high politics is obviously here to stay, the triple shift in U.S. policy may not survive the eventual departure of the new Bismarck. But while he may not have made his actions durable, he may well have transformed the stage enough to make any alternative more favorable to European unity harder to achieve after him. This is so especially because of the third new trend.

It could be called a subtle regression of the European enterprise. I call it a subtle regression because—after the blockage of the years 1965-69—there was, after all, some motion: three new members, four summits, the Werner plan, the joint float, an embryonic regional fund, the common stands of the Nine on the European Security Conference, in November 1973, on the Arab-Israeli dispute, later on Cyprus, the beginning of serious talk on how to reconcile France and the Eurogroup countries over defense. And yet, against all this, there were three disturbing factors.

One was the fact that Britain's entry, and the negotiations that brought it about, in a way diverted the members—precisely in the years of the exceptional combination of Pompidou, Brandt, and Heath—from other tasks; and once Britain joined, it became clear that, far from bringing the grand new impetus which many had expected, she introduced into the EEC a new source of heterogeneity, due to her economic performance and the mood of her public opinion. Thus there was *more* acrimony.

Second, a new and dangerous phenomenon developed: the

long lists of common endeavors adopted at summit meetings were not followed by any corresponding advances (with the partial exception of the monetary attempt). There was therefore a remarkable failure to progress *enough*, at a time when the centrifugal forces, described above, were exerting sharp pulls on the Community. To meet and defeat them, *more* progress would have been necessary, in matters such as economic and tax policies (so as to keep the rates of inflation and growth within common limits), social and regional policies, foreign investments, transportation, and of course energy. Only through such cooperation could the disruptive effects of short-term capital fluctuations and speculations against the weaker currencies have been dampened. But it was precisely the old prevalence of domestic priorities and habits that prevented such advances, then led to increasing discrepancies between national performance and policies, now that international economic issues were at the heart of world politics. Previously, in quieter days, it had merely led to a certain complacent failure to move beyond the free trade and CAP achievements. This time, the leaders knew they could hardly afford such complacency, and they solemnly adopted their lists and their calendars—yet nothing positive happened.

This also pointed to a third disturbing factor: despite the fresh blood provided by the new members, the Brussels institutions operated in a vacuum. Without a genuine impulse from the national governments and bureaucracies, the EEC Commission could only contribute to the impression of a car stuck in the sand with wheels turning in vain and merely throwing dust around: it too could, slowly, grind out its lists of suggestions and draft fine plans—but nothing would happen, or, as in the case of the monetary union, much less than the commissioners had hoped. This was a far cry from the days when the Commission had played a major role in shaping the CAP and the original association agreements. These symptoms of decline may have been overlooked, because of the relative solidarity of the Nine in the face of various U.S.

demands, and because of the progress of the Davignon procedure. But a common stand on the European Security Conference meant little, given the limited significance and opportunities provided by that interminable charade, and the common stand on the Middle East was no more than a joint deploration—except that it determined Dr. Kissinger to ex-communicate any further such statements of European autonomy, however ineffectual. And during the crisis provoked by the Arab embargo, the members of the EEC were unwilling or unable to express publicly their solidarity with Holland: it was the multinational companies which practiced what the Community failed to preach.

One could, again, argue that there is no need for this new trend to last. Haven't the dangers of regression, indeed the destructive moves made by several members since January 1974, instilled in all a desire to pull away from the brink? Such a desire exists, as the Paris summit of December 1974 and subsequent ones showed. But there are powerful reasons that make it difficult to be too optimistic.

The Present Predicament

It could be presented in the form of a paradox: we are witnessing the end of the "Atlantic system," and yet this marks the demise of the "European Europe."

By Atlantic system I mean the postwar, interstate, and transnational system of economic and monetary relations, "Atlantic-centered, United States-protected, and New York-financed"; a system whose agenda consisted above all of issues *among* the non-Communist industrial states, whose transactions were taking place in the framework of a "liberal and self-adjusting free trade system" (for industrial goods) "based on stable and fixed monetary rates," and on the assumption of "steady access to relatively inexpensive raw materials." [8] As long as this system worked, the debate between partisans of a

"European Europe" and champions of an "Atlantic Europe"—on both sides of the Atlantic—was largely a debate on issues of interest only, or primarily, to the two sides of the Atlantic: how much autonomy for European defense, given the inevitable reliance on U.S. strategic nuclear forces, the recognized need for U.S. troops in Europe? How much agricultural protectionism for the EEC? Should the allies of the United States be obliged to absorb unlimited quantities of dollars? Also, even though the Europeans were divided over the *goals* for which European economic resurgence and cooperation should be used, there was no doubt about such resurgence and the need for such cooperation. The grand designs evoked in the beginning of this essay all address themselves to these kinds of issues and all assume Europe's resurgence and internal cooperation.

Now the system has indeed broken down, but *not through Western Europe's doing, and indeed at the expense of Europe*. Despite the similarity between the current and past "new dawns," Sisyphus is facing something radically new. This is not the place to analyze that breakdown in detail, but in short it can be attributed to two principal forces. One is the United States' playing sorcerer's apprentice, first in provoking the collapse of the international monetary system, and in exporting inflation through its deficits of the 1960s and early 1970s, but also through its post-1968 diplomacy aimed at creating a new international order. The other is the OPEC group's raising the price of oil and imposing, so to speak, a huge tax on the citizens of the consuming countries. There are, to be sure, other factors, especially the increasing demands made by developing countries for a greater say in world affairs, either in the form of massive armaments or in conferences such as the one on food and those on the law of the sea. As a result, the new agenda which faces Americans and Europeans concerns not issues *between* them but *global* issues. The *contentieux* of American economic grievances that occupied commentators and conferences from 1971 to mid-1973 is gone. This, in turn, loubly increases the discrepancy between the two sides. For the United States is used to operating in a global system even f the new turbulent world in which it finds itself differs both from the "Atlantic system" of the recent past and from the rather classical scheme of world order Kissinger had originally envisaged. But for the Europeans, the end of the Atlantic cocoon exposes their inability to face global issues, after almost thirty years of concentration on either domestic affairs, or decolonization, or "community-building," or defining relations with the United States. This discrepancy in outlooks is bolstered by a discrepancy in usable power. I have already referred to it, in connection with the impact of the oil crisis. Whether we think of American opportunities for investments in OPEC countries or for OPEC investments in the United States, or of America's military trump cards, either in the form of arms sales to OPEC countries or as residual threats; or of America's capacity to "recycle" money—on its own conditions—to needy industrial or developing victims of the new cost of imported oil; or of America's technological and industrial advantages in the scramble for substitutes for oil; or of America's "bargaining chips" in dealing with the Soviets over military issues in Europe; or of America's possible uses of food aid—we find that its assets are everywhere formidable. This does not mean that the old belief among the Europeans in the necessity of their cooperation is gone, but that their common faith in Europe's resurgence has been badly hurt.

Moreover, another consequence is the increasing discrepancy within Western Europe. Between West Germany and all the others, the gap is growing, insofar as the balances of payments, success in the battle against inflation, and the strength of the currency are concerned. The division of the EEC into essentially three classes of states—Bonn, with its huge export potential, its strong Deutsche mark, its trade and payments surpluses; Italy and (at least until the North Sea oil comes to the rescue) Britain, at the low end; France and the Benelux countries in between—makes cooperation and internal cohesion far more difficult. It puts Bonn in the unhappy position of having to act either as the constant rescuer of partners in trouble or as a kind of Shylock. It puts several other European nations before the choice of having to be in debt to the OPEC countries—through borrowing or by allowing massive foreign investments—or to be in debt to Bonn or, indirectly, to Washington.

In other words, now that the agenda is filled with global issues, the West Europeans face it with a house that is not only not in order, but increasingly heterogeneous. In theory, precedence should be given to putting that house in order so as to be able to face those issues coherently. Before the EEC can move forward again and adopt all the joint policies it has avoided for so long (including a less flimsy monetary unification), it must take two series of painful measures. First, there must be greater harmony among the internal economic policies of the members. Without aggravating a recession that could become cumulative and politically unbearable, they must bring the national rates of inflation down to a comparable, reasonably low level; otherwise, there will be no possibility of monetary coordination, and a further degradation of the commercial position of the states most exposed to inflation, with dangerous consequences for the CAP *and* the free trade policy. Second, there must be a coordination of the measures that the members have to take in order to cope with the enormous rise in the price of imported oil and other raw materials. Not all of them can simultaneously overcome this ordeal by increasing their exports massively, and by attracting Middle Eastern investments or providing technology or weapons to OPEC countries. Should they try, cooperation would be replaced by cutthroat trade competition, by a race for bilateral, barterlike deals with the oil or raw material producing countries, and probably by measures aimed at forcibly reducing imports, thus violating GATT and the Treaty of Rome.

In other words, the first priority is to arrest disintegration

—with measures which the persistence of national autonomy will make difficult to streamline, with publics which, everywhere except in Britain, had come to expect a continuing high rate of growth as a natural right, and at a time when all the governments, for different reasons, are in a somewhat precarious condition. Again, this does not mean that disintegration *won't* be reversed by emergency measures of cooperation. But it means that the progression toward a full panoply of common policies will once again have to wait—and that the will to stay out of the abyss is not the same as the will to unity: once inflation and recession are tamed, or the balance of payments problems are eased, will the impulse to unite be overpowering enough, or won't the habit of national muddling-through prevail again? Recent compromises leave a strange taste: some, like the agreement on regional policy, or France's return to the joint float, are small steps forward; others appear more symbolic than substantive; others read like agreements to reweave Penelope's tapestry.

Another major factor intervenes. The *relance* of 1969 was made easier by the relative indifference of the United States to most of the issues that were then being discussed among the Europeans, by American sympathy for British entry, and by the Europeans' careful avoidance of the one subject that would have proved divisive because of the "American connection": the problem of military security. But today, most of the subjects that a *relance* would have to cover—further coordination of foreign policies, defense and armaments, monetary cooperation, a common energy program (whether it deals with oil or with enriched uranium), recycling, the regulation of foreign investments, a revision of the CAP, a common space program—are subjects in which the United States is not only interested but involved, and about which it tends to make its position brutally clear. Thus the road to unity goes through U.S. consent, as was demonstrated by the difficult bargaining that led to a re-evaluation of the price of gold—on terms drafted by Washington—as well as by the episode of the

EEC-Arab conference plan. Theoretically, of course, there is another course: collective defiance. But here, indeed, there is nothing new under the sun—on the contrary. After more than twenty-five years, the habit of dependence has become second nature: it leads most Europeans to insist on their own identity, to support French attempts to have it defined or acknowledged, to criticize U.S. high-handedness—and yet to be satisfied with soothing words of respect, with the token of consultation, with the shadow of identity, and to leave the ultimate worries and decisions and the substance of power to Washington. Dependence breeds abdication and irresponsibility on one side, arrogance and exasperation on the other: Kissinger had warned about it most eloquently—ten years ago.

The course of events at the end of 1975 shows this: now that the Atlantic system is collapsing, it is Atlanticism that prevails in Europe, because the only choices open to the Europeans seem to be two: either, through division, they fall into the kind of paralysis and bickering that would compromise whatever has been achieved within the EEC in the past. Or else they cooperate for the solution of the global issues, but under American leadership, with the EEC playing the role of a subcontractor. It is the United States, today like yesterday, which controls the escalatory process in European deterrence, and whose decisions on its troops and weapons in Europe determine the security of Western Europe. It is the United States and the U.S.S.R. which decide how much leeway West European diplomacy can have in world affairs. It is on the U.S. economy that the future of the West European economies ultimately depends, for a large and lasting recession here would push them even farther down. It is the United States which has the decisive voice in any recycling scheme of adequate proportions. Hence the extraordinary reversal between the beginning and the end of 1974. At the beginning, when American pressure for a common approach to the oil crisis began, Jobert first sought an agreement among the Nine, and only then consented to go to Washington—where that agreement to rule out any new agency promptly exploded. At the end, eight of the Nine had joined the International Energy Agency, endowed it with a majority-vote procedure far more compelling than anything in EEC, and adopted sweeping plans proposed by Washington; and the French, without joining it, had agreed to cooperate with it. As a result, the common energy policy of EEC is likely to be little more than the execution, by the European members of IEA, of the policies adopted, not by the EEC, but by the IEA, and the locus of coordination with France.

In other words, having had to choose between disintegration and "Atlantic" integration, the Europeans have chosen the latter. In the days of the Atlantic system, they had already made the same choice in the realm of security. On the defensive against the OPEC revolution, just as against the massive Soviet presence in the heart of Europe, the Europeans have had to adopt the United States as their protector and, to a large although not exclusive extent, as their intermediary.* But whereas the EEC had never tried to extend to the military realm, energy is within its domain, and is not exactly unconnected with issues such as trade, or money, in which it has in the past attempted to make its distinctive mark. Thus, by a cunning twist of history, the rather petty issues that had crowded the inter-Atlantic agenda in the early 1970s have indeed been transcended by a new Atlanticism, due not to

---

* In both cases, France is more resigned than convinced, and can be said to accept, *faute de mieux*, the overall situation, if not the specific institutions. France can have her own defense scheme and nuclear force, and her own energy policy and bilateral oil deals; but she has to cooperate with NATO and with the IEA (or U.S.-led recycling schemes) because she cannot ensure either her military or her economic security by herself: détente with the U.S.S.R., cooperation with OPEC, two major French objectives, require the shields provided by NATO and by oil-consumer agencies, given both the dependence of Western Europe on the United States, and the other Europeans' preference for "Atlantic" schemes.

that lofty act of creation that Kissinger could not quite
conjure up, but to the world-shaking consequences of the
energy crisis, which Kissinger has masterfully exploited.

It is hard to escape the conclusion that the long-term trend
in Western Europe has been a kind of renunciation, both of
fuller, distinctive unity and of a world role. The reversal
of Europe's economic fortunes, the revolt against the costs
of defense or against conscription, the centrifugal pulls of domestic politics, all these factors rule out a sudden mutation
Europe today deserves Acheson's old judgment of England: it
has lost an empire, but not found a role.

Twelve Propositions for One Predicament

I have no intention of doing a pastiche of Ronald Laing's
Knots (although the study of schizophrenia and of double
binds is an excellent introduction to that of Western Europe
since World War II). And yet, the twelve propositions that
follow all tend quite naturally to read like dilemmas, para-
doxes, and vicious circles. They try to condense past experiences—and to explain why the future will be tough.

(1) France wants to assert her independence. But France by
herself has not got the weight. Therefore she needs Europe as
a supplement to her power and as the true focus of independence. And yet a "European Europe" capable of action, i.e.,
not paralyzable by vetoes, and functioning with some form of
majority rule, might not assert *its* independence, since most of
the members either give priority to their ties with Washington, or want to make sure that the common policies are compatible with and satisfactory to Washington.

Thus there is some truth in Karl Kaiser's assertion that
"substantial progress on the internal development of the
Community and its assertion to speak with one voice in international affairs are not possible without a change in French
policy." [9] What he means by that is a willingness of France to

'submit to the Community as a group"; which, to the French, means giving up the goal of independence, or defining European commonness in "Atlantic" terms and accepting, in effect, the priorities set, and the confinement decided, by Washington. That particular knot may, at times, *appear* untied: when Washington stops pressing, or when the issue is too minor to affect American interests, or on the contrary when U.S. demands seem to go beyond what even the more pro-American Europeans are willing to grant, i.e., to hit at the very foundations of the EEC. But on the whole, Washington has been clever enough not to go too far, and imperious enough not to let Europe go too far. Behind the smooth communiqués and soothing comments of past months, one can find this knot drawn more tightly than ever. Giscard's reasoning after the Jobert phase and fiasco is exactly the same as Pompidou's after the end of de Gaulle's drama. As a French official cleverly puts it, France must use cunning with the superpowers as Prussia did with Napoleon between 1807 and 1813: "By accepting lesser ambitions for the external policy of the Europe of the Nine, and at the cost of a modicum of benign Atlanticism, France would above all seek, discreetly but firmly, the internal reinforcement of the Community from the triple viewpoint of economics, politics, and military affairs." [10] But what made sense, first in the days of America's own benign neglect, then at the moment when U.S. pressures on the EEC's cement and European fears of a superpower condominium seemed to provoke the birth of a "European identity," makes very little sense today. For the "triple reinforcement" is now either emptied of substance by, or subordinated to, the priority France's partners chose to give to their Atlantic connections, once the energy crisis appeared to jeopardize their interests far more dramatically than America's pressures and methods had done before. Today, "reinforcement" dwindles into the seasonable striking of compromises between petty, rapacious national demands, and the Community becomes a transmission belt which allows

Washington to jerk Paris back closer to Atlantic orthodoxy thanks to the friendly persuasion of France's eight partners and the mediating skills of Schmidt. Between the IEA and other grand Kissingerian schemes on the one hand, the understandings that link Bonn and Washington on the other, Europe, the last field of maneuver for French diplomacy, becomes both a shrinking vest and a straitjacket.

(2) The recent shift to economic and monetary issues has resulted in a displacement of power within the EEC, toward Bonn, the one remaining surplus country, with the best record on inflation, exports that have survived four re-evaluations of the DM, and the most solid currency. And yet, despite Schmidt's assertiveness, Bonn continues to be the most inhibited of the West European "Big Three" (Italy—the fourth —isn't inhibited: it has opted out).

Thus (and this is one of the factors of the worsening European crisis) there is a discrepancy between economic might and political power. Because of "knot" No. 1, the French would-be motor often tends to behave as a brake. But the German dynamo is no motor. Some years ago, certain writers believed that once the Federal Republic accepted the division of Germany, it would be freed of the inhibitions Bonn had observed as long as restraints on national autonomy could be rationalized as prerequisites to reunification. But the forces that inhibit Bonn go deeper. There is the continuing concern with improving relations with Moscow and Pankow, so as to "humanize" the condition of the East German people; the continuing desire for West European cooperation, despite its financial cost to the "main provider of finance for the Community";[11] the continuing reliance on the United States for military and economic security; the new determination not to be financially drained by partners and clients —so that "national autonomy" for West Germany means little more than the obligation to juggle all four balls, and not to let any one fall to the ground. This explains why the advocacy of a Bonn-Washington axis, i.e., the overt choice of Bonn as Wash-

ngton's European pivot,[12] is pointless: as Kaiser, again, puts
t, "the choice would be deeply regretted, if not resented" in
Bonn.[13] Paradoxically, it is only if Bonn serves as a go-between
or buffer that it can play the pivot's role: a naked attempt to
ead the Community—even if it is toward Washington—would
be rejected by Bonn's partners. Bonn can, at best, serve as
Washington's transmission belt to Paris and to that other,
arger belt, the EEC. This means, in effect, that Bonn's economic might, which increasingly constrains its European
partners' choices, ultimately serves Washington's political
power far more than its own. Once more, the potential leader
appears as a brake.

(3) Each of the major actors on the American-West European stage wants something, and wants the opposite also—or,
if you prefer, puts impossible conditions on getting what he
wants.

Thus the United States has often complained that the main
obstacle to true partnership is the absence of a European
partner: nine middle and small nations do not one partner
make. And yet, it does not want them to "gang up on the
United States," as Mr. Nixon delicately put it, i.e., to join
except on U.S. terms. And when they get together, Washington complains about the rigidities of the intra-European process of decision, insists on taking part in it, denounces its
outcome when it differs from American preferences, tries to
split up the collective "partner" when he does not behave, or
else makes what could be called ransom demands in the name
of the U.S. global responsibilities and under the heading of
linkage.

Thus it is not too surprising if the result in Western Europe
is a babble of voices, not the one voice allegedly preferred by
Washington. Similarly, France wants a world role for Europe,
but only on condition that Brussels follow the French line,
and Paris refuses—even if it does so less abruptly and absolutely than from 1958 to 1973—either to grant to the EEC's
central institutions powers that could be used in directions not

previously agreed to by France, or to endorse (for instance in Euratom, or by joining the Eurogroup) common policies that could curtail French freedom of maneuver: all of which limits the effectiveness and the scope of the European entity in world affairs. West Germany wants to be anchored in Western Europe, and tied to France, but on conditions that deprive the former of any specificity (e.g., in defense and diplomacy), and that recurrently antagonize the latter. And Britain, clearly, has not resolved her own ambivalence: the Tory government used to behave in a way remarkably similar to France's; the Labor-ites seem to want commitments from their partners but noth-ing much in reverse.

(4) An unorganized and splintered Europe is unfit for the "global partnership" offered by the United States. But Amer-ican insistence on subordinating European unity to global concerns keeps Europe from organizing except within Ameri-can-designed frameworks.

This goes back to the argument I presented years ago about the centrifugal effects of the involvement of each European nation in the international system: the more turbulent the latter, the more disruptive its effects on the European enter-prise, which needs a kind of protective barrier of calm to allow it to concentrate on its own development. First the strains of decolonization, later the global designs of de Gaulle, now the global acrobatics of Dr. Kissinger accompanying the world economic storms, have interfered with "community-build-ing." One reason why the Year of Europe (seen by Dr. Kis-singer as a kind of gift to the Europeans, a generous reply to their call for attention) did evoke more resentment than grat-itude among them is that, at a time when they were trying both to "absorb" their new members and to withstand the gusts of monetary fluctuations and speculations, they did not want to be distracted by having to cope with the planetary agenda of Dr. Kissinger. And precisely because there are al-ways enough such storms and stresses occurring at any time, America's adding to them under the pretext of helping forge an "outward-looking" Europe can hardly be deemed anything but disruptive. In this instance, the last months of the constellation of Pompidou, Brandt, and Heath had to be spent largely meeting, resisting, or arguing with American demands, protests, and excommunications.

(5) An unorganized and splintered Europe is not the mistress of its fate. But one reason, perhaps, why its efforts at uniting have been so halting may well be a gnawing awareness of the fact that a united Europe would not make that much of a difference.

This has to do with a variety of factors. Even a united Europe would be at a disadvantage, by comparison with the United States, in the economic dimension of its security (i.e., the high level of dependence on outside sources of energy and raw materials and on outside markets—even with the prospects of the North Sea oil reserves). Western Europe will, whatever its own efforts, continue to depend on the United States for the military dimension of European security. It faces multiple obstacles should it want to regain influence in parts of the world now dominated by one or the other or both of the superpowers. Moreover, the solution of many problems that afflict Europe cannot be found in Europe, and has to be sought at a higher level (so that it becomes a choice between a "neo-Atlantic" framework and a "North-South" one, as in the oil imbroglio, or else there is no choice at all). To be sure, a "Europe speaking with one voice" might speak more firmly at those higher levels, or to its tutors—but those tutors would still keep the gates, Europe would still be squeezed between other powers and blocs, and the "single voice" might anyhow not be very clear.

A reflection on what could be called the scope and consequences of genuine European "autonomy" is urgently needed. There was such autonomy in the realms of internal trade and agricultural policy. There could be also in areas such as social or regional policy. But over energy, foreign investments, the world monetary system, defense, i.e., global, or inter-Atlantic, or East-West issues, a "West European focus" can be at most an *element* in a solution or a *complement* to a solution. A European monetary union may strengthen the hands of the Europeans in future bargains with the powerful dollar; it can not impose a new world scheme. Now, attempts at devising common European policies and positions may theoretically be the best way of affecting the solution of the problems that exceed Europe's own grasp. But it is not clear that the European *framework* always makes most sense for the Europeans own interest (in the case of oil, they are a group of states highly dependent on OPEC's goodwill, for instance), nor is it always obvious to each member of the Community that a joint position that will be no more than a contribution to a distant outcome is worth paying the price of decreasing national freedom of action. For the tighter the geographical focus, the heavier the constraint: to search for a solution in a larger framework—NATO rather than EDC, a "new Bretton Woods" rather than EMU—may actually allow a good deal more freedom of action, especially the freedom to pursue one's own domestic priorities.*

(6) Western Europe has an obvious interest in preventing a Soviet-American "duopoly" that would keep it (and Eastern Europe) a stake, not an actor, in political and military affairs, or in thwarting a *de facto* alliance between the United States and the richer developing countries (eager for industrial and military equipment), which would squeeze it out of economic influence and even perhaps welfare and wealth. Yet the actual dependence of Western Europe on the superpowers for security, on the "new rich" for energy and raw materials (and markets to earn the money for buying these), makes it extremely difficult, even futile, for the Europeans to assert their

---

* One reason why the "spillover" theory of functional integration proved far too optimistic was its failure to distinguish between issues over which autonomy existed, so that common mastery seemed to justify paying such a price, and issues over which it didn't.

"independence." They could not, at the European Security Conference, obtain more than paper concessions from the Soviets, given Moscow's obduracy and Washington's reluctance to press too hard on this point. With respect to the developing countries, nobody wants to brandish too big a stick, and the French are those who advocate the softest speech. With respect to the U.S.S.R., first the Germans, later the British talked tough, and the French, the Italians, later the Germans tried to charm the minotaur. Being treated as a "nonperson," to use Jobert's expression, is a humiliating experience, and in 1973—the Year of Europe—Europe was so treated, first (at the summit in the Middle East) by the Big Two, later—and how contemptuously—by OPEC. But when one depends on the humiliators, one rarely dares behave like a real person, for one might get not merely humiliated but trampled.

Which brings us to a corollary: it is obviously in the interest of a dependent Europe to consult broadly with the United States, or with the U.S.S.R. or with the oil-producing countries, since it is when the outside world is least stormy that internal progress is most likely. But the more one consults with the mighty, the easier it becomes for the consulted ones to hint that such and such a move by their consulters would be deemed unfriendly. (Do not undermine my peace efforts in Egypt! Do not plan a West European defense system, for it would be a new military bloc and might oblige me to tighten the screws in Eastern Europe! Do not gang up with the United States and other oil consumers, for we might have to raise our prices and cut production!) And the more paralyzing such friendly advice becomes.

(7) Europe is the victim of everybody else's linkage. But it cannot play "linkage" in return, for it has precious little to link.

Kissinger and Nixon can state that the American military shield, and American economic grievances, are not unrelated. Moscow can link détente and economic cooperation. Middle

Eastern nations can promise oil against nuclear reactors or Mirages. What can Europe do? I do not mean to suggest that it has no assets. France, Britain, Italy have weapons to export. Most of the European nations have industrial know-how to sell to countries that do not want to be locked into monogamous embraces with Washington or Moscow. The poorer developing countries need foreign aid from Europe. But Europe suffers from two terrible deficiencies: no monopoly of anything (by contrast with the OPEC stranglehold), and not enough of what it has. Ultimately, in military as well as in economic terms, nobody's security is dependent on Europe: the ultimate guarantee is either in oneself, or in one or the other superpower.

(8) There can be no coherent Europe without effective (i.e., both legitimate and "performing") central institutions. Yet their effectiveness presupposes an agreement on purposes.

This is the old "Monnet dilemma." He and his supporter hoped that once the general goal of a united Europe was set and common institutions were established, they would then gradually decide on the directions and move toward the goals. But there have been two catches. One is that *none* of the members has been willing to let the institutions proceed toward objectives that he did not approve. It is a grave mistake to believe that France has been the only obstructor. Holland has consistently objected to a common energy policy (which would have regulated the multinationals). Germany has blocked a regional policy within EEC, and been most reluctant to envisage a European defense system outside NATO. Nobody except Mr. Spinelli has seemed to want much of an industrial policy. Without a clear agreement on purposes, the existing institutions can grind out proposals, not policies. The second catch has been that recurrent temptation, the fling into wishful thinking: if Europe doesn't progress, it must be because its institutions are too weak; let us therefore strengthen its institutions, have its parliament elected by universal suffrage, extend the scope for majority rule in the

Council of Ministers, multiply the meetings of heads of governments, increase the powers of decision of the Commission, and so on. Institutions are indispensable to prevent a consensus on goals from disintegrating, and to give it precision and follow-up. But they are no substitute for that consensus.

(9) Even for merely preserving and protecting the past accomplishments of the Community, the present institutions of Brussels are inadequate. But merely to "reinforce" them would not be the answer.

Their real deficiencies do not reside in the weakness of their *powers*, but in two other sources. First, with the exception of the CAP (a painful exception that confirms the rule), the EEC is based much more on an economic liberal model than on a planning one: there is an internal free trade and free capital movements area, but no common industrial or investment policies. Even the Werner plan led, not to economic coordination or even to a joint monetary policy, but merely to a joint float, unaccompanied by measures that could have saved it from the storms that blew in from the outside. This means that the institutions of Brussels have found themselves floating above those formidable regulatory machines, the national bureaucracies. Insofar as the nation-state is still in control, Brussels has the crippling disadvantage of either leaving to the members whole areas connected with, and partly decisive for, the internal free trade area, the CAP, and the monetary union; or else producing its own proposals which end up in dusty folders; or else carefully bargaining with the separate bureaucracies in order to reach compromises that might have a chance of success, yet not so paradoxically turn out to be both too little and too much (cf. the experience of industrial and of scientific policy). Second, insofar as *each* nation-state actually experiences a loss of control, for all of the reasons which have put economic sovereignty at bay—the role of the multinationals, the way in which the international economy carries inflation or recession, the divagations of capital movements—the problem is the same in Brussels as, say, in

Paris or Bonn: reactive regulation in self-defense means essentially cutting oneself off from the world economy, with serious political and economic penalties. Moreover, whereas one or the other country, pressed by its own momentary priorities, can face such penalties for a while and take its own measures, an agreement by all of them to adopt common measures to regain control has never been possible, if only—once again—because of the "American connection," as well as because of differences in economic philosophies between planning countries (like France even under a right-wing coalition) and more liberal ones (like Germany even under Socialist rule). Thus in neither set of cases is institutional reform the solution: we are back at knot 8.

(10) Should there be an agreement on new goals and policies, stronger central institutions would be necessary. But they would not suffice.

I have insisted throughout this essay on the resilience of those politico-administrative containers, the nation-states, even when they have similar economies and comparable social systems. We are not dealing here with relatively flimsy or lightweight political systems such as those of the states of the American union, at the time when federalism became a reality. This suggests that it will not be enough to cap those tight national networks with a supernetwork in Brussels, or (depending on the subject matter) with several "central" networks, such as the one in Brussels for the economic realm, and another one for defense and diplomacy. For to have two levels of strong institutions is to plan either conflict or paralysis. At best, there will be the introduction of one new and formidable layer of delay, more bargaining, more splitting of responsibility (cf. the addition of a "regional" level to the communes, cantons, and *départements* in France). Any devolution must entail a dismantling, any addition must be a replacement. In institutional matters, one can say both: *on ne détruit que ce qu'on remplace* (A. Comte), i.e., the states will last as long as there is no substitute for them, and *on ne remplace que ce qu'on détruit*, i.e., the new central institutions will remain ineffective unless the national bureaucracies are deprived of powers and lines and programs and personnel, the old networks are disrupted or bypassed, and new ones are built around the central institutions. This is both different from, and even more difficult than, a transfer of allegiance. Hence one more cause for pessimism.

(11) There has always been most progress when the Europeans were able to preserve a penumbra of ambiguity around their enterprise, so as to keep each one hoping that the final shape would be closest to his own ideal, and to permit broad coalitions to support the next moves. And yet there always comes a moment when a terrible clarifier calls for a lifting of ambiguities, at which point deadlock is more likely than resolution.

The clarifier may be a statesman. First it was de Gaulle, in his questions to the other Five and to Britain, summoning them to accept his view of a "European Europe" and dismissing as nefarious the ambiguities of Monnet's conception. Then came another demand for clarification, in the shape of Henry Kissinger, who requested an "Atlantic," or neo-Atlantic, commitment from the Europeans. The clarifier may also be an event, a challenge that forces a clear choice. The oil crisis (exploited by Kissinger) has been such an event. A Soviet-American deal, for instance at MFR talks, or even a unilateral American withdrawal of tactical nuclear weapons, that would tend toward a partial denuclearization of Central Europe, might be another. Most of the Europeans have always resisted demands for clarification, not out of cowardice, but out of an instinct for survival: to clarify, to choose, means to cut some possibility off. Yet not to clarify, when one is summoned to, means both, in effect, to accept internal division, and to prefer the hedgehog's tactic to any bold advance.

(12) It is unlikely that the European enterprise will make

rapid progress, reach full federation, or even lead to a full economic monetary, diplomatic, and military confederation. But it is equally unlikely that it will unravel.

Americans have always tended either to salute European unity too soon, or to bemoan European disintegration too fast. There are huge material and psychological reasons why some modicum of unification is in everyone's interest. The scope of economic interdependence between the members of the EEC is such that they have no other choice. The absence of a purely national alternative, or its costs, or its insufficiency, in diplomatic and military affairs, make it advantageous for each of the members to present himself as both a free agent and as part of even an embryonic and faltering Community. None of this may be sufficient to reverse the trends gloomily described above, and to make of a European entity the fifth side of the pentagonal "structure of peace." Nor does it mean that some unexpected great shock inflicted by Washington, Moscow, or some OPEC, may not once and for all sweep away all the doubts, obstacles, and factors of inertia (although it would have to be a delicately calibrated shock: large enough to threaten the survival, not merely the security or well-being, of Western Europe, but not large enough to kill). Yet if one had to hazard a prediction, it would be that the "European idea" will stay alive, that the European enterprise will continue, gropingly and painfully, and that thanks to it the nations of Western Europe will play in world affairs a role slightly less modest than that which they could otherwise perform.

What Is There to Do?

Normative exercises of this sort have a certain built-in hubris, in that they tend to exaggerate the extent to which American policy can determine European behavior. I have myself indicated how much importance Washington's moves have had, both as an integrating and as a disintegrating factor

in Western Europe. But even if ultimately the fate of Western Europe is in the hands of others, the Europeans' capacity
to affect that fate, and to set limits to the capacity of others to
shape it, remains. The United States cannot "build" a West
European entity: neither exhortations to unity nor pressures
on the EEC have resulted in sufficient coalescence among the
Europeans. "What is there to do?" is therefore first of all a
question to be asked *of the West Europeans*. Even in a world
of global issues which somehow devalues the autonomy of
Western Europe; even with the power disadvantages mentioned throughout this essay; even with the the formidable
obstacles of bureaucratic inertia, pressure group politics, self-
perpetuating domestic parochialisms, and weak governments,
do the West Europeans want to try to overcome or at least
minimize their handicaps, and play a common and distinctive
role? Even if they cannot, by themselves, solve their own
problems, and make more than a modest contribution to the
solution of the common problems of an interdependent
world, do they have the will and ability to devise their own
contributions and partial solutions? Or will they use the new
globalism as one more alibi: will what Giscard has called the
shift from a civilization of groups to a worldwide civilization
become an excuse for not behaving as a group? There is one
more paradox here: those Europeans who turn to "outward-
looking" solutions, and to vast frameworks in which Europe's
distinctive voice cannot emerge, are often in reality the truly
inward-looking ones, for they leave the answers to others.

Narcissism,[14] abdication, and a retreat from a concern for
power on the world stage (often disguised as a concern for
residual power to maneuver at home) are symbiotic here. To
be sure, the United States cannot be ignored by the West
Europeans—especially when the skill of its Secretary of State
and the recent trends of history have put so many threads into
one weaver's hands. But America's might and weight have
become a justification for European faintness. De Gaulle's
analysis remains valid, whatever one may think of his policy:

without a federator within, Western Europe is either incapable of adequate progress toward unity, or prone to let the United States be the federator. My own analysis leads me to the conclusion that this will not change, unless highly dramatic circumstances—a new and far more explosive war in the Middle East, an American attempt to resolve the energy-and-payments problem by force—literally oblige the West Europeans to dissociate themselves from the United States without, however, falling into that other form of sloth or cowardice, "Finlandization." One can build scenarios of that kind. At present, they seem unlikely. One can neither rule them out—nor hope that they would come true.

We are thus left with, so to speak, the American side of the "dumbbell." A full discussion of what Washington ought to do will be undertaken elsewhere. A few suggestions are, however, in order. First, the old "solutions" proposed for European-American relations are inadequate, both because they assume a European entity that simply isn't there and because they do not fit the new global issues. Even when they were offered in reaction against the "Atlantic system," they envisaged a very different end to it from the one that brought it down. Thus disengagement—essentially a military formula—fails to take into account both the obstacles to the emergence of a West European military organization in the aftermath of American withdrawal and the unraveling effects a military disengagement might have on the rest of the network of American interests in Europe. Similarly, devolution was not devised primarily for economic issues. Should one try to expand its meaning, and for instance advocate a "neo-mercantilist" solution—a world of regional economic and monetary blocs replacing the broken-down Atlantic system—one would still have to prove that one would really stabilize economic relations in the world by restoring national economic autonomy, and that there would be self-restraint among the blocs; and one would have to show that Western Europe is able and willing to be such a bloc. As for trilateralism, it is inadequate to cope with the problems of the Third and Fourth Worlds and—in contrast with the other two schemes—pays scant attention to the issue of military security.

Are we thus left with nothing better than the present policy, a perpetuation of the grandiose American attempt to preserve what I have called indirect primacy, and to shape the solutions of all the issues? The present reassertion of American preponderance over Western Europe, the fact that *at present* the United States has become more important than ever to the West Europeans both for their military and for their economic and financial security, should, however, not create illusions. In the long run, the "globalization" of issues will tend to make the United States less decisive and relevant to Western Europe, because of a gradual, uneven, but unmistakable shift of wealth from the industrial world to large parts of the developing world, and because of the increase in military power of the Communist nations as well as many of the developing countries. The Atlantic reflex of the dependent consumer nations of Western Europe should not make one forget that for several years already they have been defining their positions—or refrained from defining positions—with an eye on Moscow as well as one on Washington. And the rush to the International Energy Agency is due in large part to a desire for being in a better position to negotiate with the "new rich," and to convince the United States that—to use the clichés of the day—conciliation, not confrontation, must be the objectives in "North-South" affairs.

If this is so, then the question for the United States is double. Should—miraculously enough—the West Europeans resume the quest for their own "personality" and take initiatives which, given the issues, cannot fail to concern the United States, what should Washington do? Should America encourage or discourage that quest? The reasons I have given in the days of the Atlantic system for American encouragement remain valid: I continue to believe that in the long run a policy of primacy is doomed, that given the similarity of values and the broad range of common interests between the Europeans and the Americans, the risks involved in such a policy are outweighed by its advantages, and that in those areas where the interests and assessments differ, greater European assertiveness would actually be helpful. Should Washington opt for encouraging the European quest, it could begin by not objecting to West European initiatives even if they seem, in the short run, to run against or to delay more global or "Atlantic" approaches; and it could, in military affairs, prod the West Europeans toward "devolution," at least in the conventional realm. Should the United States, however, prefer to discourage European distinctiveness, all that would be needed would be a continuation of its policy of 1973-74.

If there is no "European" *relance*, what should American policy be? Merely to say that the United States would have no choice but to exert its leadership is no answer, for the key questions are leadership toward what, and with what intensity. Three issues would have to be examined—each one affecting the fate and future of Western Europe. First, what should be the institutional framework of U.S. policy? Would we prefer to operate essentially through institutions that we dominate, and oppose the establishment of institutions that could constrain our freedom of maneuver or that of our "multinational" corporations? Would we systematically prefer bilateral relations to multilateral bargaining, or would we try to build more truly pluralistic and constraining ones? Second, what should be the style of U.S. policy? Third, what should be the substance of U.S. policies? On the answers depends the degree to which the West Europeans and the EEC, despite their timidity and troubles, would still have breathing and political space to pursue the reality, not merely the appearance, of step-by-step, bargain-by-bargain unification. The United States has, broadly speaking, a choice between a policy of hegemony that would clamp a lid on the Pandora's box of the European movement and a policy of initiative toward common actions in a far more fluid and plural world. But that is another story. . . .

NOTES

[1] For earlier assessments, see the author's "Europe's Identity Crisis," *Daedalus*, Fall 1964; "Obstinate or Obsolete," *Daedalus*, Summer 1966 (new version in the author's *Decline or Renewal?* [New York, 1974], Chapter 12).

[2] On these dimensions of interdependence, see Robert O. Keohane and Joseph S. Nye, "World Politics and the International Economic System," in C. Fred Bergsten, ed., *The Future of the International Economic Order: An Agenda for Research* (New York, 1973), pp. 115 ff.

[3] Raymond Vernon, "Rogue Elephant in the Forest: An Appraisal of Transatlantic Relations," *Foreign Affairs*, April 1973.

[4] *Decline or Renewal?*, Chapter 13.

[5] Cf. my essay on Italian foreign policy in S. Graubard and F. Cavazza, eds., *Il caso italiano* (Milan, 1974), pp. 379 ff.

[6] Cf. Richard Cooper, "Economic Interdependence and Foreign Policy in the 70s," *World Politics*, January 1972, and Robert Gilpin, "The Politics of Transnational Economic Relations," in Robert O. Keohane and J. S. Nye, eds., *Transnational Relations and World Politics* (Cambridge, Mass., 1972).

[7] Cf. Kissinger's interview to James Reston, *State Department Bulletin*, November 11, 1974, p. 634.

[8] Zbigniew Brzezinski, "Recognizing the Crisis," *Foreign Policy*, Winter 1974, p. 63.

[9] K. Kaiser, "Europe and America: A Critical Phase," *Foreign Affairs*, July 1974, p. 730.

[10] J.-G. Leroy (pseudonym), "Le petit homme, la France et l'Europe," *Contrepoint*, No. 15, 1974, p. 83. We may note that the "Prussian analogy" was a favorite of the Vichy politicians trying to justify their *Collaboration d'Etat* with Germany.

[11] Helmut Schmidt, "The Struggle for the World Product," *Foreign Affairs*, April 1974, p. 451.

[12] For a rather brash argument in favor of such an axis, see C. Fred Bergsten's testimony, *American Interest in the European Community*, Joint Hearings before the Subcommittee on Europe and the Subcommittee on Foreign Economic Policy of the Committee on

Foreign Affairs, House of Representatives, 93rd Congress, November 8, 1973, pp. 89 ff.

[13] Kaiser, "Europe and America," p. 739.

[14] Cf. Jacques Freymond, "Europe Atlantique—Europe européenne" (mimeo), pp. 17-18.

Chapter 2
THE ABDICATION OF EUROPE

Ronald Steel

The Atlantic alliance was built on a reality and marketed on an illusion. The reality was that the United States could not let Western Europe fall into Russian hands, and that the Europeans wanted American protection. The illusion was that the alliance would lead to a true partnership of equals with virtually identical interests. The illusion has dissipated. The reality remains.

Despite striking achievements in economic cooperation and expansion, Western Europe remains a congeries of independent nation-states with different, and often conflicting, foreign policies. There is no single European will. Political union seems more elusive today than it was a decade, or even a generation, ago. Unable to achieve a common currency, a common defense, or even a common policy on such crucial matters as energy, Western Europe remains in a state of military and political dependency.

If Europe has not achieved unity, neither has it attained communion with America. Because Europe is neither unified nor strong, the relationship is not one of equals, but of clients and their protector. To speak of "partnership" in such a relationship is to engage in euphemisms. Europe's role in the alliance is to keep its house in order, to be a good customer for American products, and a safe haven for investment dollars.

The decisions over war and peace are made elsewhere. This may be the basis for a convenient political relationship. But the proper word to describe it is not "partnership," nor perhaps even "alliance." As Walter Lippmann wrote in the early days of NATO, "As between a global power and a regional power, a complete two-way alliance is impossible—that is to say, if the regional power is not a dependency or a satellite."[1]

For the United States the Atlantic relationship has been strikingly successful. It has held the line against the expansion of communism beyond Eastern Europe, provided an economic trading bloc that financed American investments in Europe and American interventions abroad, and confirmed for Americans a global sense of mission. That it has simultaneously been able to achieve all of these objectives has greatly enhanced its desirability.

There are good reasons for this. First, the alliance seemed an inspired response to a military necessity. To American leaders, and to many Europeans as well, Stalinist Russia appeared bent on dominating the entire continent, whether by conquest or by penetration and subversion. This perceived threat to Western Europe was strengthened by the extinction of democracy in Czechoslovakia and confirmed by the Korean war. By the 1950s it took on global dimensions.

Through a line of continuing development, a foreign policy consensus was created in America: first the Truman Doctrine, then NATO, and finally global "containment." By its possession of the atomic bomb, by a vast rearmament program launched by Truman and Acheson, and by forging an integrated military alliance with Western Europe, the United States would meet its new "responsibilities" to hold back communism. NATO became the indispensable finger in the dike.

The second virtue of the alliance was that it did provide a vast protected market for the products of America's farms and factories. From the late 1940s until the early 1960s the United States exported twice the value of goods to Western Europe as it imported from those nations. Even though the creation of the Common Market reduced this surplus, a favorable trade balance continued through the 1960s and helped defray the cost of maintaining American troops in Europe.

Because they were willing to underwrite the overall American balance of payments deficit by accepting unlimited amounts of dollars minted lavishly by the U.S. Treasury, the Europeans helped finance such costly adventures as the Vietnam war. In the same way they also facilitated, much to their eventual dismay, the take-over by American firms of a good many European industries. This condition of "monetary hegemony" was the price that Europeans were expected to pay for American protection, as Washington made clear in the unilateral decision to end dollar convertibility of August 1971.

Third, the alliance, in addition to its military and economic virtues, was flattering to American pride. It confirmed that the mantle of Western leadership had passed from the Old World to the New. The child of Europe and for nearly two centuries its dependent, the United States had become the protector of its parents. This was not only an American perception. The British, particularly, but also the French, urged the United States to assume the imperial responsibilities they found increasingly difficult to manage: Greece, the Middle East, Indochina. After the Truman Doctrine, to be sure, Washington needed little prodding. But even those who questioned the self-assumed global "responsibilities" found a flattering sense of power in the American protectorship over Western Europe.

That all of these conditions have now changed is obvious. Restored to prosperity, if not to full self-reliance, Western Europe feels less threatened by the Russians and less acquiescent under American protectorship. The themes first sounded by de Gaulle have now been picked up as a generalized European litany. There is resentment at the take-over of European industries with inflated American dollars, irritation at pronunciamentos from Washington over political and economic matters affecting Europe no less than the United States,[2] and mounting anxiety over a superpower entente that seems to involve the denuclearization and political impotence of Europe.

From an American perspective the changes are no less striking. It is no longer "international communism" that is seen as the enemy, but rather, in Kissinger's world view, political instability. Thus there has been a new flexibility, and a new uncertainty, in American foreign policy. Not only has the Sino-Soviet rivalry finally been officially noticed, but it has been the precondition of the triangular balancing act undertaken by Kissinger with the blessing of Nixon and then of Ford. Soviet Russia remains an adversary, but also an accomplice in the effort to maintain a global status quo that is congenial to the interests of both superpowers.

Now that the cold war has been transformed from a life-or-death struggle into an old-fashioned contest for influence in the hinterlands, it is difficult to generate public or congressional enthusiasm for the old alliances. With security being more narrowly defined than in the past, the cost of maintaining foreign garrisons and a global network of military bases is beginning to seem a dubious luxury. After Vietnam it will be a long time before any President can send American soldiers to fight a protracted land war. Given this revision of military objectives, the cost of maintaining the American garrison in Europe is increasingly hard to justify.

Even more important than cost in the new equation is the change in the relationship between America and Western Europe. Throughout most of the cold war, Europe was an acquiescent political partner of the United States and a profitable commercial one. With only minor misgivings the allies, except for Gaullist France, accepted the military strategy that was chosen for them and provided a profitable market for American exports.

But when the allies demanded a voice in how and where American nuclear weapons would be used in the defense of Europe, they tread on ground that directly involved America's own security interests. Deterrence, in Washington's view, depended on absolute control by the United States over these weapons. To share control with the Europeans could force the United States against its will into a nuclear war with Russia. This is so because the Europeans have generally favored a strategy that threatens early recourse to nuclear weapons as a form of deterrence. The United States seeks to prevent a conflict in Europe from escalating to the nuclear level. Thus it has emphasized reliance on conventional weapons, and has even favored the withdrawal of some of its tactical nuclear force. While some Europeans have favored such a strategy because it seemed to reduce the risk of nuclear war on the continent, many now express alarm that it means a reduced American nuclear commitment to Europe. Thus, despite changes in strategy, the anxieties remain because they are built into a system resting on an inequality of power and decision-making.

Together with these differences over strategy has come a change in the economic relationship. By the end of the 1960s America's trade surplus with Europe had shrunk by 80 percent. The very success of the European Economic Community—with its booming exports and its demands for controls on the inflated dollar—transformed Europe into a powerful economic competitor. The Marshall Plan worked brilliantly in restoring Europe as a market for American products. But the process went too far for Washington when it resulted in European attacks on American "monetary hegemony."

In the early 1970s all these factors came together: the détente with Russia, the opening to China, the disenchantment with cold war alliances, European resistance to American nuclear strategy, and the growth of economic competition among the Atlantic allies. The result was a fundamental change in American foreign policy. The United States would emphasize its military security through a policy of nuclear deterrence based on intercontinental strategic weapons, and seek to contain the weapons race by arms-control negotiations with Russia. This new policy sharply reduced the military importance of allies, who were informed that they would be helped in proportion to their willingness to help themselves.

This, of course, was the so-called Nixon Doctrine. While it was originally thought to include only such client states as South Vietnam, Cambodia, and South Korea, its logic applies to Europe as well. Its purpose was to assuage domestic opposition to costly interventionist wars through a limited military retrenchment, yet at the same time remain politically engaged throughout the globe. The United States would retain its dominant world role by maintaining bases and by providing military equipment for client regimes. But it would intervene far more selectively, leaving the fighting of peripheral wars to its allies and clients.

The Nixon-Kissinger "structure of peace" was based on three assumptions: that after Vietnam the American public would no longer support direct military interventions, that China and America had a mutual interest in the containment of Soviet power and influence, and that a modus vivendi could be reached with Moscow based on mutual restraint and respect for spheres of influence.

The effect of this new strategy on America's cold war allies is only now beginning to be felt. In Southeast Asia it will mean the neutralization of the area, as de Gaulle had urged in the early 1960s. In the Middle East it will mean recognizing that a settlement between Israel and the Arabs can be achieved only with the cooperation of Moscow. The contest for influence between America and Russia has fed the Arab-Israeli quarrel and hardened positions on both sides. Inheriting Britain's classic role, the United States has sought to exclude Russian influence from the Middle East. But this policy long ago became obsolete with Russia's rise to superpower status. However even-handed the United States may be in its efforts to bring about Arab-Israeli settlement, it cannot hope to succeed without Soviet acquiescence. Such a settlement will be difficult at best. But it is virtually impossible so long as the superpowers see the Middle East as a staging area for their own competition.

In Europe the new strategy means providing a nuclear cover, but insisting that the major share of the conventional defense of the continent be assumed by the Europeans themselves. An American garrison would remain in Germany both as a symbol of American involvement and as an element in the conventional defense of Europe. But its primary purpose would not be to serve as a nuclear trip-wire, as it has been explained to many Europeans and as they prefer to believe. American strategy precludes such a role since it seeks, in the event of conflict, to confine the defense of Europe to conventional weapons for as long as possible. The role of the American forces thus becomes both symbolic and political: a symbol of the American nuclear guarantee, a manifestation of the political influence that America exerts over Europe through NATO. Such a role could be satisfied by retaining American forces on the continent at only a fraction of their current level. A reduction of these forces can be delayed, however, so long as this method of assuaging European anxieties does not become too expensive.

Inherent in the concept of the Russo-American détente is the determination that the dialogue between the superpowers will be conducted directly and not by proxy or through intermediaries. Each, of course, will remain dominant within its own alliance. The United States would no more allow Russian interference in NATO decisions than Moscow would allow Americans to interfere in the Warsaw Pact. The détente nonetheless affects relations within the alliance as much as between the superpowers. The European allies will be informed, and even consulted. But the critical issues will be decided by those with the power to do so. Insofar as the Europeans complicate or impede an agreement, they will be circumvented. This was dramatized by the Soviet-American accord of June 1973 on mutual force reductions, which was worked out between Washington and Moscow without a European voice being heard.

With the replacement of containment by a policy of guarded engagement between the superpowers, it is essential that allies be kept in line and Third World crises defused. In the new Washington-Moscow relationship, allies play a distinctly subsidiary role. They can impede or even sabotage détente. But their contribution to America's physical security is greatly reduced. From a military perspective the cold war alliances are becoming an historical anachronism.

This does not mean, to be sure, that they are unimportant. To the contrary, they are useful militarily for the bases they offer—although the European allies, as the last Middle East crisis revealed, are resistant to allowing them to be used for anything but their own defense. They also serve political purposes as levers for political influence and the exercise of economic power. On a psychological level they serve as confirmation that a great power has attained the global status to which it aspires. Since security is rarely defined in military terms alone, alliances provide for the extension of influence and the creation of an orbit congenial to the perceived interests of the dominant power. So long as America and Russia remain great powers, each will feel compelled to keep the other locked out of its sphere of influence.

All this does not mean that alliances are irrelevant, but it does mean that the alliances forged during the cold war have lost much of their original *raison d'être*. They were the product of a bipolar world, a stage of military technology, and an Armageddon psychology that no longer exist. As America's key alliance, NATO has been profoundly affected by these developments. Yet its structure remains rooted in an earlier world. That it is in a state of confusion is axiomatic. That it cannot persist in a form consistent with its rhetoric has now become unavoidable.

There are a number of routes the Atlantic alliance could

take. First, it could be transformed into a true political community linking America and Western Europe. This is the dream of the old Atlanticists, and it is an inspiring vision. But the price would be higher than either America or Western Europe is now willing to accept. For the United States it means giving Europeans a share in the nuclear deterrent and subjecting America's global military and economic policies to a measure of European control. For Europe it means abandoning any hope of reuniting the continent or of protecting Europe's economy from disappearance into an Atlantic trading bloc under American direction. If such an Atlantic union did not occur during the worst days of the cold war, it is highly unlikely today.

Second, the alliance could simply disintegrate. Whether it would be formally dissolved, whether various states would exercise their exit option and leave one by one, or whether it would remain a decorative object housed in a Brussels suburb is not really important. Yet such a disintegration is unlikely within the foreseeable future for the simple reason that it would leave the Europeans dangerously exposed to Russian power. While they complain about American dominance of the alliance, it is infinitely preferable to being left alone with Russia while still militarily weak. If NATO simply collapsed without a European organization to replace it, the individual members would go scurrying for cover. Most would seek refuge under an American umbrella in a series of bilateral arrangements; a few might even try to bargain an accommodation with Russia. In either case their position would be weak and their dependency intensified. That none of the Europeans want this, and that they have labored over the past three decades to prevent it, is the best argument against it happening.

Third, NATO could split in two as the divergence of interests intensifies. As Henry Kissinger observed, in reminding the Europeans of their proper place in the alliance: "The United States has global interests and responsibilities. Our European allies have regional interests." [3] This was an accurate, if blunt, assessment of the situation. Should the Europeans choose to act on it, they could decide to reduce their military dependency on the United States. This would require the creation of a strong conventional army subject to a single European command. It would also mean building a credible European nuclear deterrent based on the French and British forces. Such a nuclear force is clearly within Europe's economic capabilities. But at the moment it remains far beyond Europe's political capacities. Except for a handful of Gaullists on both sides of the Channel and the Rhine, few Europeans care deeply about the ability to stand alone—particularly when the benefits of a benevolent American hegemony are so obvious and so relatively cheap.

Fourth, the alliance could settle into an institutionalized American hegemony over Western Europe. This would be the simplest alternative, since it would require no significant changes in the present state of affairs. The Europeans would have to acknowledge that the price of American military protection is economic dependency. This would mean refraining from building a monetary union, for such a union would likely diminish the role of the U. S. dollar and the ability of the United States to dominate economic policy in the West. The Europeans would have to maintain a liberal, rather than a mercantilist, economy and subordinate their own internal needs to those of a transatlantic economy dominated by the United States. On a practical level, the Europeans would be expected to pay the cost of maintaining a garrison of GIs on the continent, although at considerably lower force levels than at present, and to cover, if necessary, the deficit in the U.S. balance of payments by the purchase of military equipment and Treasury notes.

In addition, one could enumerate less stark alternatives, such as a gradual erosion of American leadership and a heightening of European influence, or compartmentalized security relationships between the United States and various members of the alliance.

However, there are choices that can be made. Europe does not necessarily have to follow a policy either of dependence or of drift.

If Europeans want to change the balance of forces, they must choose a path of action. The United States does not have to choose, for the current situation is quite favorable to its interests. Europe is dependent on America for security and prosperity, for protection against the Russians, and for access to Arab oil. America is not dependent on Europe in that sense, even though the two economies are tightly interwoven. There is a reason why Europeans complain but Americans make declarations.

Washington can remain impervious to the complaints of its allies about its economic policy, or its military strategy, or its private deals with Moscow, because it knows that there is little the Europeans can do about it. Whenever the complaints become unduly shrill, the Europeans are reminded that the piper calls the tune. Nixon made the links quite clear in the spring of 1974 when he warned the Europeans that they could not have "cooperation on the security front and then proceed to have confrontation and even hostility on the economic and political front." [4]

However heavy-handed such a statement may be, it is an accurate assessment of the balance of forces within the alliance. The choice is clear for the Europeans. Either they forge a political union capable of providing for their own defense, or they accept the fact that America's economic and political hegemony is the unavoidable price of military protection. They cannot have it both ways.

Even sympathetic Americans find it tiresome when Europeans complain about Washington's domination of the alliance but shrink from undertaking the steps that would be necessary to end it. Choices are made by default as much as by design. So far the Europeans have chosen abdication and grumbling rather than initiative and resistance.

The United States, to be sure, is not making the road to independence easy for its allies. Washington periodically declares its support for a self-reliant European Community. But what it means by that is a Europe that will pay for its own defense yet continue to allow the key decisions to be made across the Atlantic. Whenever the Europeans have tried to act independently, as in the oil crisis of 1973-74, American officials reacted indignantly and even issued guarded threats. As it turned out, the EEC cracked under the Arab oil boycott, as each nation tried to save its own skin. It was a performance that showed not only how divided the Europeans were, but that the real decisions over their energy sources lay outside their control.

Although Washington claims to favor a politically unified Western Europe, such rhetoric may be deceptive. By its own actions the United States has consistently sought to impede the creation of any European entity that would not be fully integrated into an American-directed Atlantic system. "We cannot be indifferent to the tendency to justify European identity as facilitating separateness from the United States," Henry Kissinger scoldingly declared in 1973.[5] The Secretary of State presumably assumed that his listeners would not remember his pleas, before he entered the U.S. government, for a greater American understanding of European sensibilities. "A separate identity has usually been established by opposition to a dominant power," he had written only a few years before. "A United Europe is likely to insist on a specially European view of world affairs—which is another way of saying that it will challenge American hegemony in Atlantic policy."[6]

What was true then is true now. But the pleasures of hegemony are such that the view is rather different from the top. American policymakers are not necessarily insincere when they call for a strong Europe. It is just that they suffer from mixed motives. This is the built-in paradox of Atlanticism. The United States is verbally committed to the creation of an independent Europe that can be built only in opposition to American hegemony. This independence Washington has sought to block whenever it has become manifest.

There is, to be sure, a good case for "devolution," the gradual turning over to Europeans of military decisions hitherto held exclusively in American hands. This could provide a much needed spur to European unification, and relieve the United States of responsibilities that the Europeans are perfectly capable of bearing.

But it would also reduce American influence over Europe. To a greater degree than we have been generally willing to admit, our definition of security has been based on our ability to influence and to serve as an example to others. Without these psychological factors much of American postwar foreign policy makes little sense. Viewed narrowly, neither economic influence nor military security dictated either of the two major wars of intervention: Korea and Vietnam. It was only in the wider perspective of maintaining the perimeters of an American sphere of influence, and of behaving (as Henry Kissinger later explained of the proxy intervention in Angola) as a superpower is presumably expected to behave, that these were justified by their advocates.

Thus, to concentrate on the security aspect alone—or at least to define security exclusively in military terms—is to miss what much of NATO is about. For this reason American policymakers find good reasons to maintain the alliance indefinitely in its present form. Even though NATO may be militarily outmoded or even superfluous, it is extremely useful for the exercise of American influence over Europe.

In the absence of any real European initiative, which, considering the present balance of forces within the alliance, seems unlikely in the foreseeable future, there are three possible courses of action open to the United States.

First, it can continue present policies. Most of the American troops would remain in Europe and a good part of their cost would continue to be covered by offset arrangements. The Europeans would complain about changes in American strategy over which they have no control, or about nuclear and political arrangements reached between Washington and Moscow. But they also insist that they want the troops as a symbol of America's willingness to become involved in nuclear war on their behalf. The price of these hostages is a hegemony they find distasteful, but apparently not yet intolerable. Tensions will no doubt increase, and eventually the whole alliance could break down under the impact of rivalry and recriminations. But that time is not yet, and skillful diplomacy could probably patch over differences for another decade.

Second, the United States could dramatically reverse field, seize the standard of NATO's most acerb European critics, and actively encourage the creation of a politically unified Western Europe with its own nuclear deterrent. This would, presumably, reduce complaints of U.S. dominance and eventually eliminate the conditions that Europeans have so resented and Americans have found so profitable. In the long run, such a course may be unavoidable. It is far from certain, however, that a nuclear-armed Western Europe with a territorial grievance against the Russians would be a source of stability in the world. Nor is it clear that the virtues of equality would exceed for the United States the pleasures of hegemony. Why relinquish unnecessarily a position that provides such benefits? An abdication of such proportions is usually imposed by circumstances; rarely is it offered gratuitously. In any case, the situation has not reached a state of crisis grave enough to make such an American offer necessary.

Third, Washington could downgrade the alliance without ending it. This would mean pulling out its forces, rather as was done in France and Greece, while still maintaining a political commitment. The purpose of this would be to reduce the danger of America's being drawn into a European war against its will. Some have seen this as the ulterior meaning of the

1973 Russo-American treaty on nuclear weapons and believe that accord implies the denuclearization of Europe. There are some seven thousand tactical nuclear weapons in Europe. Many of them are only nominally controlled by the United States and pose a considerable political danger.

Were they deprived of American hostages and the tactical nuclear weapons, Europeans might well fear that the American guarantee would not be fully honored in time of crisis—or that Washington would prefer to confine any future war to European soil. But since the United States has compelling reasons to prevent Western Europe from falling into Russian hands, any rational Soviet diplomacy would have to assume that the guarantee might well be invoked in the event of attack.

Nonetheless, it is possible that a formally denuclearized Europe would feel cast adrift and might try to establish some form of modus vivendi with the Russians. For many this evokes fears of "Finlandization," that is, independence subject to Soviet scrutiny and goodwill. Naturally most Europeans find this unacceptable. For this reason alone they might be driven to build their own nuclear force, thus spurring the political integration that has so far been blocked by their dependence on the United States.

A nuclear or self-reliant Europe would, to some degree, mean a more neutralist Europe. This need pose no threat to American security. But the economic and political hegemony that Washington has exercised over the continent would be greatly reduced. Many Americans, particularly those who associate the nation's well-being with the national security apparatus, would find it hard to adjust to this situation. Having found a flattering identity in the role of Europe's spokesman and protector, many would resent the "loss" of our richest dependency. This may be the most important factor of all. It is the fear of losing influence, of playing a diminished role on the world stage that lies at the heart of America's imperial diplomacy.

In the long run this loss of influence is unavoidable—at least the kind of influence that has been exerted during the cold war. It is a product of the détente with Russia and the accommodation with China. It has been powerfully affected by events over which the United States has no effective control: the recovery of Europe, nuclear proliferation, the oil crisis, the disintegration of the world monetary system, worldwide inflation and depression, and the inability to prevent the Soviet Union from playing a political role in areas traditionally considered to be under Western influence—such as the Middle East and Africa.

For America the path is clear, though not always straight. It will pursue détente with its adversaries—despite pitfalls, detours, and setbacks—because it is clearly to its advantage to do so. Toward its allies it will continue to exert hegemony—which it will define as "cooperation" and "interdependence"—until it is forced to abandon this by drastically changed circumstances.

Those circumstances could take one of two forms: first, from a European withdrawal into neutralism and an accommodation with Moscow; second, from the creation by Europeans of a political union that would permit them economic and military independence. In either case the United States would find that it had lost its role as Europe's protector, along with the economic and political advantages that have gone along with that role. Should Europe choose independence and power, rather than subservience and accommodation, this would also dramatically transform the world balance of power—as would Japan's decision to acquire nuclear weapons.

In any case, the writing is on the wall, although there is a good deal of time in which to indulge in hegemonic privileges. Interdependence may be an illusion, and alliances may be of declining military importance for the United States. But the prerogatives of hegemony are real. They are institutionalized in the structure of the Atlantic alliance. They are likely to persist so long as the Europeans continue to fear in equal measure the Soviet Union and an independent power role for themselves.

NATO is neither a prison nor a partnership. It is a symbol of Europe's will to abdicate.

NOTES

[1] Walter Lippmann, "Today and Tomorrow," (syndicated column), May 17, 1951.

[2] American officials have shown little patience with Europe's anxieties. During the 1974 oil crisis Kissinger referred to the behavior of Europeans as "craven" and "jackal-like." He told a group of Congressmen's wives that the "biggest problem" for American diplomacy was the relations with Western Europe, and that "the deepest problem in Europe today which we still see is that there have been, very rarely, fully legitimate governments in any European country since World War I." One wonders which allies the Secretary of State had in mind, the British, the French, the Germans, the Italians, the Dutch, the Belgians, the Norwegians, the Danes? Cited in *The New York Times*, April 9, 1974.

When asked by an interviewer why Europeans were hostile to American policy, particularly in the Middle East, the Secretary of State responded, "I think they suffer from an enormous feeling of insecurity . . . they know that we're essentially right in what we're doing. So the sense of impotence . . . produces a certain peevishness." Cited in *The Washington Post*, January 3, 1975.

[3] Henry Kissinger, address to the Associated Press, New York, April 23, 1973. Cited in *The New York Times*, April 24, 1973.

[4] Richard Nixon, Chicago, March 15, 1974. Cited in *The New York Times*, April 9, 1974.

[5] Henry Kissinger, address to the Pilgrims, London, December 12, 1973. Cited in *The New York Times*, December 13, 1973.

[6] Henry Kissinger, *The Troubled Partnership* (New York, 1966), p. 40.

Chapter 3
EUROPE: IS THERE
A PRICE TO BE PAID?

James Chace

Thirty years after the great European civil war that began with the guns of August in 1914 and ended with the Americans and Russians on the Elbe River in 1945, there is still no "Europe" as such for Washington to deal with. Writing in 1965 in an aptly titled book, *The Troubled Partnership*, Henry Kissinger warned that "the European sense of identity . . . could well be to insist on a specifically European view of the world . . . which is another way of saying that it will challenge American hegemony in Atlantic policy. This may well be a price worth paying for European unity; but American policy has suffered from an unwillingness to recognize that there is a price to be paid."

Since Europe has neither united nor disintegrated, the United States has never been called upon fully to pay this price. The question of costs thus remained unanswered, while new questions have arisen. First, in Washington's view, is European unity desirable at all? Second, are the costs as important to U.S. policymakers as they appeared to be a decade ago? And finally, is European unity available at any price?

It is in the light of these questions that American policy in the post-cold-war era should be judged. There could be no greater misapprehension of American purpose than to confuse American withdrawal from an untenable situation in Southeast Asia to the notion of a general U.S. withdrawal from global strategies and engagements. If anything, America's global concerns have never been more evident than in the 1970s. Maneuverability and flexibility have largely replaced the rigid alignments of the "era of confrontation." And the proclivity of Washington to project regional situations on a global stage increased under the stewardship of Henry Kissinger. Thus, when the Arab-Israeli conflict broke out in the fall of 1973, Washington seized the initiative to try to establish a piecemeal Pax Americana in the area, and an assertion of a U.S. hegemonic claim that it had not insisted on since the early 1950s.

A disposition to impose hegemony over an apparently fragmenting Europe was also evident in the wake of the unexpected Yom Kippur War which dramatized European weakness. America's previous postwar policies had been couched in the rhetoric, if not of equality, at least of being no more than *primus inter pares* within the Atlantic alliance. For this reason it is wise to recall that whereas the American hegemonic drive in the Western world during the cold war had most probably been unintentional, the behavior of America toward the Community during the Nixon-Kissinger period may well have been a deliberate attempt to retain and, indeed, reinforce a hegemonic role in the West. To grasp the continuity of a policy which both voiced support for European unity and distrusted the monster Europe that might emerge, some recent chronology might prove useful. For as Europe's disarray in the 1970s appeared more evident, America saw new occasions for insisting on a dominant role over a fragmenting collection of nation-states.

II

Throughout the tenure of Richard Nixon, Europe had been constantly startled by the new, nonideological character of American foreign policy. The démarche toward China, begun almost immediately after Nixon took office when he visited General de Gaulle in 1969 and spoke of a new receptivity toward a U.S. opening to China, suggested that the American leadership now agreed with the General that ideology was much overrated. The apparent adoption by Washington of Gaullist viewpoints, including settlement of the Vietnam war and détente with the Soviet Union, might have signaled a new understanding and possible tolerance for French policies, thus easing tensions between the Community and America. But such was not to be. When the policy of benign neglect, exhibited toward Europe during the Johnson Administration, was finally abandoned, what resulted was what West German political commentator Theo Sommer called "malign attention," an attitude that became manifest with the proclamation by Washington in 1973 of the patronizing term "the Year of Europe," and the subsequent crises that were triggered by the Yom Kippur War.

The focus on Europe was dramatically announced by Henry Kissinger's Atlantic Charter speech of April 23 of that year. It was a curious document. Did the sloppy phrasing portend what his rhetoric proclaimed, i.e., that "the Atlantic Nations" (now including Japan despite geography) "join in a fresh act of creation, equal to that undertaken by the postwar generation of leaders of Europe and America"? In short, as some commentators believed, was this a speech comparable to General Marshall's commencement address at Harvard in 1947, a speech which inaugurated the Marshall Plan? If so, the response was certainly far different from what Nixon's foreign policy adviser must have expected. The Europeans reacted with suspicion, for the speech contained disquieting phrases. Most worrisome to the Europeans was the Kissinger linkage of economics and defense; unless concessions were forthcoming in the trade and monetary fields, he implied, America might scale down her defense effort on the continent. Finally, the Europeans were troubled by Kissinger's assertion that while the Europeans had regional interests and responsibilities, America's were global.

While the latter statement was arguably true in regard to security considerations, it was quite wrong as far as economic matters were concerned. Problems of trade, monetary reform, defense strategy, costs, and offset agreements in NATO—these were already dealt with or being discussed within existing institutions. What became apparent was that the Nixon Kissinger apparat, in its passion for "conceptual break-throughs," desired new institutions; and if such institutions did not materialize in a fashion acceptable to, if not favorable to, the unarticulated desires of Washington, it might mean that yet another American "agonizing reappraisal" of the alliance was in order.

They were not, in fact, forthcoming. Under French pressure, the neo-Atlantic Charter was stillborn; the European response was divided into two parts in order to prevent any linkage between economics and defense. A so-called Declaration of Principles by the European Economic Community was agreed to in September 1973, branded by Kissinger as "lacking in substance." A year would pass before a NATO declaration would be issued. And when it did appear, in June 1974, it failed to resolve the substantive issues which had consistently bedeviled the alliance.

III

How long ago it seems to have been since the European leaders at the Paris summit of 1972 committed themselves to political union by 1980 and economic and monetary union before then! It was another age; it was another world. But then, as so often happens in a world where contingency gravely affects the determinants of policy, the Arab-Israeli conflict broke out in September 1973. Like the Suez crisis of 1956, this war brought to the fore certain tendencies that had been inherent in the U.S.-European relationship since the death of Stalin. Indeed, Suez and the 1956 Hungarian uprising were surely watersheds of the postwar era, as the Yom Kippur War may turn out to be for the 1970s.

The American decision not to intervene in Hungary not only revealed the emptiness of the rhetoric of "rollback" in Eastern Europe, but suggested the idea that America and Russia might seek a modus operandi at the expense of Europe—both East *and* West. Of even greater import was the fact that Washington sided with Moscow in the matter of Suez against London and Paris in the U.N. Security Council. For this brought into the open the question of American credibility in the defense of Europe's perceived interests.

From the realization by Western Europeans that the United States would not automatically support London and Paris, the two major European powers drew opposite conclusions. To London it seemed essential that the wartime "special relationship" between America and Britain be repaired so that the interests of these two powers should never again so dangerously diverge. To Paris, on the other hand, it seemed that France must pursue an independent nuclear deterrent, for just such times when American policy collided with French vital interests. Moreover, a year later, the Treaty of Rome, establishing the Common Market, which was to become the embryonic European Community, was signed. (All this occurred, it must be remembered, before General de Gaulle returned to power in 1958.)

Six years after Suez, the Cuban Missile Crisis caused Europeans to once again reassess their American connection. At this time, when the Russians and Americans confronted one another "eyeball to eyeball" and the Russians blinked first, many believed that the United States would risk a nuclear war, into which Europe might be drawn, over a situation which the Europeans did not regard as vital to their interests.*

The Middle East war of 1973 once again broke down the façade of the alliance, whose fissures had already been deepened in the aftermath of the Atlantic Charter speech. To begin with, it was evident that neither the United States nor the Soviet Union would regard the conflict as a local matter and that the United States insisted on alliance solidarity while Washington moved to impose a settlement. The United States called a worldwide military alert without either consulting or adequately informing its European allies. Though the "alert" was a response to possible armed Soviet intervention in the area, to the Europeans it seemed an overreaction to Russian threats and certainly dangerous to Europeans, who once more were held in jeopardy against their judgment. Moreover, the U.S. support of Israel exposed Europe to new and frightening risks. The Arabs invoked the oil embargo to gain leverage for their demands, and the Europeans, dependent on the Middle East for 80 percent of their oil, stood to lose far more than did the United States, which imported only 5 percent of its oil from the area. Under the circumstances, the Europeans resisted cooperation with the Americans.

To the Europeans the Arab-Israeli war was essentially a regional conflict and, acting on their own perceptions of world politics, they refused to cooperate with Washington. There were declarations of neutrality from Greece, Turkey (and Spain), which did not allow an American airlift to Israel from

---

* The story is told that when former Secretary of State Dean Acheson was sent to enlist General de Gaulle's support for U.S. actions in the missile crisis, the General asked his distinguished emissary whether he had come to consult or to inform. When told it was for the latter purpose, the General replied to the effect that he approved of a nation acting independently.

bases on their territories; Turkey did grant overflight rights to the Soviet airlift to the Arabs; other European countries restricted movement of U.S. military supplies from stockpiles in Europe.

This irritated prominent Americans both in and out of government. The American columnist Irving Kristol stated: "The plain fact is that the United States found itself on the brink of a confrontation with the Soviet Union and in this circumstance our European allies deserted us." [1] When West Germany refused to allow further shipments of military supplies to Israel from German ports, Secretary of Defense James Schlesinger declared, "We maintain our forces in Germany because it provides us with enhanced readiness. Can those stocks of U.S. military supplies be used only in Germany and NATO? If they are not available to use for other uses, then maybe we'll have to keep them some place else." [2]

In an excellent summary of the consequences of the Middle East war, the International Institute for Strategic Studies survey for 1973 commented in response to the Schlesinger statement:

On such a view the military balance could be increasingly seen as a bilateral superpower one, the maintenances of regional balances—for example, in Europe—being of lesser importance, since strategic deterrence would stabilize those regions of potential military confrontation. If properly organized, supplies and forces could be moved rapidly in the case of a crisis, as the massive American airlift to Israel demonstrated. However, regional events, while affected by overall strategic deterrence, should not be permitted to determine global action—a long-standing American (and Soviet) expression in the Agreement on the Prevention of Nuclear War signed by Nixon and Brezhnev on 22 June [1973].[3]

If détente did not produce the global cooperation envisaged by Nixon and Kissinger after the June declaration with

Brezhnev, neither did it evaporate during the stresses of the Yom Kippur War—at least in Washington's view. Kissinger always aimed at an entangling of Soviet and American interests when necessary in order not to permit exclusive Soviet spheres (with the exception of Eastern Europe), and he saw regional conflicts as affecting relations between the two global powers whenever Russia and America were on opposite sides. This policy was as evident in his handling of the 1971 India-Pakistan war as in his posture toward the Marxist government of Salvador Allende in Chile.

Kissinger's affinity for dealing with adversary relationships was shown by his handling of the Arab-Israeli disengagements of early 1974, which allowed the United States to play the leading role while at the same time keeping the Soviet Union both informed and quiescent. Russia was no longer the paramount power in the area, but its role, like America's, was global and would remain so.

In allied relations, however, the atmosphere became increasingly embittered. Most evident in the months following the Arab-Israeli conflict was the spectacle of the advanced industrial nations scrambling in an unseemly manner to pursue *sauve-qui-peut* policies by concluding bilateral deals with Arab sheiks. This was not what Washington wanted. Not only had the United States shown itself the dominant power in a region considered vital to European interests; now Washington demanded that the Europeans follow America's lead in dealing with the oil-producing nations. In the wake of the oil squeeze, the push-pull relationship that had always existed between America and Europe gravely strained normal alliance tensions, with the Secretary of State privately describing the Europeans as "craven, contemptible, pernicious" and "jackal-like." [4] What the policy of the United States appeared to be in the aftermath of the war and the European response to it is to define in no small measure the likely direction of U.S.-European relations for the future.

The definition, as provided by Kissinger, seemed bound to a

past that had long since been altered by events. Was it not possible that Europe might take another step forward, this time in the direction of political coordination, because of the European perception that America was the new adversary? Secretary Kissinger certainly displayed this adversary approach—hardly that of a diplomatist—when he declared in the London speech: "The attitude of the uniting Europe . . . seems to attempt to elevate refusal to consult into a principle defining European identity." He further stated: "To present the decisions of a unifying Europe to us as faits accomplis not subject to effective discussion is alien to the tradition of U.S.-European relations. . . . To judge from recent experience, consultation with us before a decision is precluded, and consultation after the fact has been drained of content. For then Europe appoints a spokesman who is empowered to inform us of the decisions taken but who has no authority to negotiate." [5]

Kissinger had identified precisely the area of greatest difficulty for the Europeans, that is to say, the difficulty Europe had in coordinating policy. Angry at lack of consultation, unable to respond coherently to Kissinger's call for a new Atlantic Charter, the Community's Council of Ministers affirmed in December 1973 that "the growing concentration of power and responsibility in the hands of a very small number of great powers means that Europe must unite and speak increasingly with a single voice if it wants to make itself heard and play its proper role in the world." [6] But such a brave new world was not to be.

Despite rhetoric proclaiming the U.S. commitment to European unity, in many Europeans' minds the American stance implied that Europeans should dance to an American tune. European unity—if it meant divergence from American interests—might no longer be a palatable policy for the U.S. government—if indeed it ever was.

Further events were to bear out this notion. On March 4, 1974, the European Community agreed to a meeting with Arab leaders from which the United States would be excluded. Here was a perfect example of the Europeans making public a decision only when such a decision could not longer be influenced or modified in the light of U.S. interests. The irritable response of Kissinger in the wake of this announcement was to ask the Europeans just what they meant when they spoke of wanting to be a "distinct and original entity . . . in their relationship with the United States." Kissinger also declared on March 11 that "the biggest problem American foreign policy confronts is not how to regulate competition with its enemies . . . but how to bring our friends to a realization that there are greater common interests than simply self-assertiveness." [7]

The public irritation of the U.S. government reached its apogee on March 15, 1974, in a speech delivered by President Nixon in Chicago. At this time, the President explicitly underlined the linkage between security—as provided by the United States—and economic and political cooperation, which he demanded be aligned to U.S. interests:

> The Europeans cannot have it both ways. They cannot have the United States participation and cooperation on the security front and then proceed to have confrontation and even hostility on the economic and political fronts. . . . The day of the one-way street is gone. . . . We are not going to be faced with a situation where the Nine countries of Europe gang up against the United States which is their guarantee for their security. That we cannot have.[8]

Given the previous statement along these lines by Kissinger, the Chicago speech should not be regarded as a Nixonian aberration; rather it highlights factors endemic in the U.S.-European relationship. Certainly, after Chicago, the rhetoric cooled. A few months later the Europeans were able to piece together a ramshackle contraption that allowed any member of the Nine to bring up an issue that might require consultation with the Americans. If the other members of the Community were to agree, then the Nine would consult with Washington. But if there is no such agreement, then those countries who wish to can consult with the United States and, in so doing, hold up a decision by the Nine on that issue until such bilateral discussions are over. *Faute de mieux,* Washington seemed disposed to accept this loose method. Similarly with NATO. Reaffirmations of solidarity—dull but obligatory—were all Washington could obtain. Thus the "fresh act of creation" called for by Henry Kissinger took the form of a rather stale rehash of alliance principles.

In any event the slate cannot be wiped clean. And the departure of Richard Nixon from the scene is not likely to affect significantly the inherent conflicts within the alliance. Those who have believed that the U.S.-European disaccord was more a question of style than of substance are likely to be proved wrong.

IV

In postwar European politics, both fragmentation *and* unity have had their own rhythms. Certainly, those who proclaimed the death of the nation-state were premature; indeed, in the latter half of the twentieth century, both in the advanced industrial nations as well as in the newly independent states of the Third World, the renewed vigor of the nation-state is unquestioned. But the quest for regional unity has also continued. At times the thrust toward unity has been functional. Organized state systems such as the European Economic Community (rightly called the Common Market), countries seeking joint rules to govern foreign investment and to coordinate disparate centers of production such as the Andean Pact—these patterns of functional unity have seemed to promise a system that would someday go beyond a customs union toward the federated state so dearly beloved by the functionalists.

But functional unity is severely inhibited by the desire of the nation-state to resist the submergence of its national consciousness into a larger goal—a goal which could most likely become paramount only as a response to an external threat. In this instance, if functional integration cannot serve as the motor force of this larger unit, perhaps the European consciousness may find its vocation, its source of strength, indeed its identity, in defending itself against the potential hegemonic ambitions of the other powers.

For the thrust toward a larger European polity does exist. There is a European consciousness, more inchoate than the national consciousness, that should not be ignored. There is, after all, rooted in history a Carolingian Europe that is no less valid than the Capetian or Merovingian tradition. Indeed, the stirrings toward a truncated European unity that came in the immediate postwar era did not derive so much from abstract, "objective" forces as from the communality that had already existed. De Gasperi, Adenauer, Schuman—these three men saw in Europe's heritage a Roman Europe with its legal traditions, its culture, its religion. This was the remembered unity of Europe, and upon this base was erected the various economic and technocratic bureaucracies.

It is between these two poles—the thrust toward a larger entity and the persistent viability of the nation-state—that the tension that is inherent in European politics exists. If Europe, however, is to transcend the nation-state, it is not likely to become transformed simply into a larger nation-state. A Rousseauistic general will of the European people does not exist nor is it seemingly hovering over the horizon. Moreover, functional institutions as embodied in the Common Market are unlikely to produce this end.[9]

The drive toward some form of European unity—what I have called elsewhere, a concert of Europe—is a persistent force, as nagging a virus as the notion of the nation-state. The thrust has been, at bottom, political, for only by forming a European entity can Europe define its place in a world of shifting coalitions and overlapping alliances. In the post-Gaullist era even European federalists have admitted that political will—not economics—would prove the motor force of a uniting Europe. The movement away from bipolarity has thus given Europe both more freedom of action and less stability. The moorings which, despite the Suez crisis of 1956, still bind Europe to America seem less and less solid in an era, if not of détente between America and Russia (for détente is a handy word for whatever purpose you wish it to serve), of ever-closer relations between the two superpowers. The frequent summit meetings between Russia and America, the continuing negotiations over limiting strategic weapons, even the near-clash over the Mideast appeared to most Europeans as a world in which the two superpowers would order things as they saw best, with Europe as a vassal to their behavior. Because of Europe's dependence for security on the United States and the resentment of such dependence, Kissinger could complain that getting Europe to realize our "common interests" was a greater problem than "regulating competition" with our enemies.[10]

Beyond the ever-present specter of a Russo-American entente has been the emergence of a world in which a neo-classical balance of power is likely to be ineffective, even were it to exist. What Nixon envisaged as a five-power world of China, Russia, America, Japan, and Europe, each balancing the other, proved to be a prelude to a world more chaotic, a world in which relatively small nations such as Iran and Saudi Arabia gained enormous wealth, and hence would be able to exert a significant measure of power over the behavior of the so-called Big Five. A populous but seemingly ungovernable state like India exploded a nuclear device which gave her a foot in the door of the nuclear club. In questions such as the regulation of the seabed, control over multinational corporations, the modification of global environmental forces, new coalitions have sprung up that no longer involve traditional alliances.

This very freedom of action and fear of the resulting vulnerability of the great powers paradoxically may provide a new impetus toward unity. For in such a world a collection of European states without some concerted monetary, trade, and defense policies would be likely to lose even more of its power to affect the international system than it previously had when it more or less accepted American leadership. In short, political Europe, if it were to emerge, may be a response to a world in which the demands on the nation-state are greater than ever but which the nation-state finds it harder and harder to fulfill.

Assuming then that a European entity is still possible, is what Fritz Stern has called the "community of fate" that exists between Europe and America such that Washington can bear with good grace the divergence of interests? Or, more strongly, might not the interests of the two still converge on European unity? Even if Europe through its own resources were to grow more powerful, more independent, could it truly threaten America? This is the nub of the question. In fact, the opposite is true.

V

While a unifying Europe would probably prove most truculent to U.S. policy in the short run, it is a fragmented Europe that represents the real threat to American foreign policy. Such a fragmented Europe could revive questions which have been settled as a result of the end of the great European civil war. The German question, for example, only recently resolved and thus still fragile, might be reopened; relations between Eastern and Western Europe which are beginning to result in new linkages, precisely because of the realization on both sides that the past cannot be undone, could be endangered.

In a fragmented Europe a special relationship might develop between West Germany and the United States. For the Federal Republic, more than Britain and France, would possess the economic power as well as the political motivation to play the junior partner in an American hegemonic system to dominate the continent. If a Deutsche mark zone emerges in a kind of North European-West German co-prosperity sphere and this is linked to the dollar in a mark-dollar axis, the political effects could be to fragment Europe in such a fashion as to make the prophecies of Americans who predict a Finlandization of Europe self-fulfilling. Those Americans urging that "Germany be the focus of [U.S.] economic policy toward Europe" because of the "confluence of U.S. and German interests on the most critical questions of international economics" are playing a dangerous game. One of the surest ways to undo the postwar settlement of Europe would be to wean away Germany from its ties with the other members of the Community.[11] For when it is urged that we make Germany our preferred partner, it is done without taking into account the full political implications of this move. What is stressed is that America and West Germany are the two largest trading nations in the world, that both espouse liberal trade policies and resist protectionist pressures, and that both prefer liberal rules to govern international investment flows rather than efforts, particularly by the British and the French, to create a "European industrial policy" that might discriminate against the United States.[12]

The world may indeed be moving toward a tripartite monetary system of the dollar, the yen, and the mark, with the last the basis for a European currency, particularly if the Europeans begin to align their economic policy in order to make such a monetary union possible. However, if a dollar-mark zone were to emerge, the scuttling of "Europe" would be well under way.

If America will come to believe that she has not created a Frankenstein monster, who, as the greatest trading bloc in the world, would undermine America's economic and financial security, then European unity might be seen as finally unthreatening to the United States. Indeed, one of the beneficial results of the Yom Kippur War and the subsequent use by the Arabs of the "oil weapon" has been to demonstrate the inherent economic power of the United States, thus freeing America from the fear of being overwhelmed by her erstwhile allies. There is no need for Washington to act in a manner designed to inhibit the rather elusive quest by the Europeans for their own identity. But even if America accepts that a fragmented Europe threatens her far more than a united one, still one ought not to expect too much from a "European Europe." And particularly one should not indulge in dreams of a grand design to link Europe and America as dual pillars in a neo-Atlantic community.

VI

But can or should the United States do more to encourage unity? If this means that America provide the rather overt support she gave in the 1950s, the answer is no, especially in an era of competing nationalisms. But, in a negative way, by certain acts of self-abnegation, America should avoid restraining the Europeans whenever they take whatever steps they prove capable of in creating a European political will—even if these steps contravene perceived U.S. interests. Moreover, what may have once seemed a vital national interest of the United States may turn out to be of far less import than U.S. policymakers, reacting to breaking situations, initially thought. Far better for Washington to have an ally with a sense of identity than a group of separate but alien states with the attendant resentment and disorderly conduct such a situation would imply. What is required, then, is for the United States to adopt a policy toward Europe that at the very least could be described as benign agnosticism.

Above all, the United States should be wary of the search for a new institutional system of world order which will "solve" its European dilemma. For Henry Kissinger to drag

Japan into a tripolar system as he did in his Atlantic Charter speech without spelling out how this could be done effectively is to do a disservice to America's allies on both sides of the globe. While Japan, Europe, and the United States will have to work in concert if there is to be a sensible reordering of the monetary system and a series of trading mechanisms which would benefit all the advanced industrial nations, it is a risky business to try to involve Japan in security arrangements with Europe when neither Japan nor Europe perceive their vital interests as jointly threatened in this area. If Europe has regional security interests, so, too, does Japan. And they are not necessarily congruent. That Europe, Japan, and the United States will find themselves together in numerous coalitions over issues affecting the common interest of all three entities is doubtless true; but in other issues, the three may find themselves at odds. This is not disastrous for the international system such as it is or as it is likely to remain in the near future. Moreover, an attempted institutionalization of the relationship may well prevent the solution of some of the problems discussed above in the U.S.-European context.

To expect America to shed the image she has had of herself throughout the postwar years, to ask her to act in a spirit of self-abnegation, surrendering that drive for hegemony that seems endemic in the rise of great powers, may, after all, be asking too much. It certainly runs against the grain of a traditional and, in my view, generally accurate Hobbesian view of the world in which "a general inclination of all mankind [is] a perpetual and restless desire of Power after power, that ceaseth only in death."

It may be also asking too much to expect the European conglomerate to attain a European consciousness, without which there can be no European will. Nor do I expect that if Europe were to find its vocation acting in concert, this would simply be a larger nation-state. The new European consciousness might produce a creature quite different from what we have known or imagined—neither a confederation nor a federation, neither an overblown nation-state nor a quarreling cacophony of powers held together merely by the gossamer of a customs union. However, even if Europe were to move toward unity rather than fragmentation and even if the United States were to move to blunt its thrust for hegemony, the international system would probably not change in any dramatic fashion.

Indeed, if Washington were to act with the better part of wisdom, then it should not anticipate an international order that will be anything other than quite messy for some time to come. Events have shown that questions posed in the schematic fashion of "what price Europe"—the very question Kissinger asked a decade ago—do not allow for the ambiguity of the European identity since the end of World War II. Nor do they allow for the reduced importance of the U.S.-European connection in the context of changing global power relationships. It is not merely that a Europe only partially achieved requires less than a full surrender of U.S. hegemony; it is also that U.S. hegemony over Europe means less and is thus easier to abdicate in a world in which many new rival centers of power have started to emerge. Neither a two-power nor a five-power world seems in the making, but a rather more anarchic system where Europe's role would prove only as effective as Europe wishes to make it. Nor does it appear possible, in this context, for America to restore the simpler pattern of international order that characterized the postwar era in which questions such as Henry Kissinger's seemed both natural and valid.

Certainly it would be quixotic if America tried to check the dangers of disorder by attempting a unilateral or superpower imposition of order upon others; moreover, to try to preserve the status quo would be no guard against disorder. On the contrary, the drive to maintain the status quo generally unleashes even greater forces of dislocation. If not the status quo, then a new structure of world order? But system-builders beware. Chaos is not easily "managed." Shifting coalitions, overlapping alliances, interdependencies—all render such "managements" of the international system even more difficult.

To live in a relatively anarchic world without fear and without searching for catchall superstructures may severely test the wisdom of mankind. The new rules of the game may be slow in coming. Perhaps the relatively modest efforts to change the nature of the European-American relationship would in themselves assist in the discovery of what the new rules are likely to be. If so, they may even help us to arrive at an answer to the question Camus posed: how to live in a world without justice and without grace.

NOTES

[1] *The Wall Street Journal*, November 16, 1973.

[2] *International Herald Tribune* (Paris), October 29, 1973.

[3] *Strategic Survey 1973*, published by the International Institute for Strategic Studies (London), 1974.

[4] See Theodore Draper, "Détente," *Commentary*, June 1974, pp. 25-47.

[5] Address by Henry A. Kissinger, London, December 12, 1973, *Department of State Bulletin*, No. 452.

[6] *The New York Times*, December 15, 1973.

[7] *Time*, March 25, 1974, p. 31.

[8] *The New York Times*, March 16, 1974.

[9] Stanley Hoffmann, *Decline or Renewal?* (New York, 1974), Chapter 12.

[10] *The New York Times*, March 12, 1974.

[11] For an analysis of the U.S.-German "special relationship," see C. Fred Bergsten, "U.S. Foreign Economic Policy and Europe: The Ascendance of Germany and the Stagnation of the Common Market," *Hearings on the Implications for the United States of the Enlargement of the European Community*, House Foreign Affairs Committee, 93rd Congress, November 18, 1973.

[12] Ibid.

Chapter 4
THE EUROPEAN CROSSROADS

Zbigniew Brzezinski

Europe is the crossroads for the central choices confronting modern society.* Europe is where the two principal alternative concepts of modern society most directly compete; Europe is where the American-Soviet rivalry is played for its highest stakes; Europe, finally, is the missing link in the needed global response to mankind's novel problems. All of this makes Europe the intersection point for some of the most fundamental dilemmas of our time:

(1) Doctrinal: European society remains the primary arena for the competitive clash between the two principal philosophical and political reactions of man to the onset of the industrial age.

(2) Regional: As an extension of that doctrinal clash, Europe is not only divided regionally but it remains the central focus for the wide-ranging competition between the United States and the Soviet Union, détente notwithstanding.

(3) Global: Europe is much less cohesive and politically purposeful than the other advanced industrial and democratic

---

* In speaking of "Europe" I have in mind primarily Western Europe, an entity of several sovereign states, linked by a process and a framework of economic cooperation, and infused with a sense of European identity which varies in intensity from nation to nation.

countries, on whose collective response the solution of the novel and global problems—especially those confronting the developing world—largely depends.

The first dilemma raises the fundamental question of the future of modern democracy; the second poses the question of Europe's future political orientation; the third signals some uncertainty concerning Europe's will and ability to cooperate effectively with other states in dealing with the wider global issues which are surfacing with alarming urgency. All three illustrate the vital importance to America of the American-European connection, for American interests depend on a positive and reassuring European response on each front.

A crisis of democracy in Europe would most likely be contagious. This is not to say that American democracy would falter as a consequence, but it is not unreasonable to postulate that the waning of the appeal of democracy abroad would further reinforce the tendency toward ultra-pessimism in the West as a whole, thereby also sapping the dynamism of what is the world's largest effective democracy. A significant reorientation of Europe in the East-West competition would similarly have a direct impact on America and it could perhaps tip decisively the scales of history to America's disadvantage. Finally, without a more active and politically more purposeful Europe, committed toward wider cooperation among the advanced countries of the world, a constructive reshaping of the existing and badly strained international system does not seem feasible.

II

A strong case can be made that Europe, especially its more advanced Western half, is today entering a crisis in many ways similar to that experienced during the preceding decade by America. During that decade the United States moved beyond the industrial age and began to enter a phase of historical development not previously demarcated by any other society. It was this plunge into uncharted historical terrain that produced in America the tensions and the dislocations which cumulatively resulted in a profound change in the cultural and social mores of this country, in a significant upheaval in generational and sexual relations, in a far-reaching and still ongoing adjustment in race relations, as well as in the appearance of a still-to-be-defined new relationship between private and public morality (of which the Watergate syndrome has been very much a symptom). All of these changes have been connected with, and perhaps have been prompted by, far-reaching shifts in American employment patterns, and they were doubtless exacerbated by the new social significance of mass communications and mass education.

Contemporary Western Europe is beginning to experience a similar historical transition. Many of the solutions and arrangements contrived during Europe's industrial revolution have all of a sudden become obsolescent. The Americanization of Western Europe's social habits has only in part provided a remedy to deep-seated social ills, and it, in any case, is not a sufficiently profound phenomenon to provide an effective response to the new difficulties which West European society is now confronting. The society is undergoing a sudden decline in political stability and an intensifying radicalization of its intelligentsia and its youth, including new class and ethnic cleavages (e.g., the millions of rootless foreign workers)—all in the context of an accelerating social change in many ways similar to that experienced by America in the preceding decade.

What makes the European experience more ominous, however, is that it is taking place within societies suffering from deeper cleavages between the two principal responses of man to the industrial revolution than has been the case with the United States. In many ways, the New Deal saved American democracy, as well as the American socio-economic system, by creatively adapting to, and fusing in the American context, Europe's liberalism and Europe's Marxism. Both liberalism and Marxism offered creative and optimistic responses to the early traumas of the industrial age, and their adaptation within America was facilitated by the relative absence of deep ideological cleavages in American society and by American pragmatism. The flexibility and mobility of American society diluted the extremes.

In contrast, in Europe liberalism and Marxism have been associated with profound and often antagonistic social cleavages. With American-type social flexibility and mobility lacking, and with doctrinal conflicts possessing a legacy and a history of their own, Marxism and liberalism in Europe to this day have remained highly competitive and still relatively antagonistic sources of loyalty for competing groups and social classes. Moreover, the European left has a deeper political and intellectual tradition than the American, and the surfacing of social tensions is likely to be exploited more effectively by the European left than was the case with its more naïve and less experienced American equivalent.

This is why Professor Kissinger was right—even though Secretary Kissinger was wrong to have said it publicly—when he asserted that many European governments lack underlying legitimacy. The fact is that in several European societies (particularly Portugal, Spain, France, and Italy) the extreme right and the extreme left nonliberal and nondemocratic forces still command a significant portion of the electorate's allegiance. To be sure, the extreme right has been discredited by the failures of Fascism and Nazism, but the extreme left remains a particularly potent force. In a setting of crisis, it can pose a grave danger to the liberal and democratic forces.

The effect is to make Europe, again, the key battleground on which the future of democracy might well be decided. More specifically, it is in Europe that modern democracy confronts head-on six fundamental dilemmas:

(1) Can modern democracy exist without philosophical moorings? Both in Western Europe and in America liberal

skepticism has emerged as the dominant outlook, becoming, in effect, democracy's new established orthodoxy. Yet, as such an orthodoxy, liberal skepticism reveals itself to many as empty; it offers little to believe in, and thus it cannot become the basis for sustained commitment and optimism in the future. It is the emptiness of liberal skepticism as an orthodoxy —in contrast to liberalism's positive role as a challenger to established orthodoxies of the past—that has much to do with the contemporary shift away from a spirit of optimism. The idea of progress has given way to the notion of decay, and with it has come a profound crisis of belief within the democratic context, a crisis naturally exploited by the forces of Manichaean fanaticism.

(2) Can a democracy exist without socio-economic growth? West European democratization has produced increasing social justice through the sharing of wealth, but that sharing was made tolerable for many because it was accomplished by steady economic growth. This growth made it possible for West European democratic systems to institute socially progressive measures without having at the same time to impose strict governmental controls on all aspects of life. A compulsory redistribution of wealth was thus avoided. Today, West European democracies confront the prospect of slower rates of growth—perhaps even zero rates of growth. This poses the danger that Western European democracies will find their social pie to be much smaller than expected, with the result that the search for social justice will be pursued through increased governmental control, including more arbitrary division of social wealth. The fact is that the linkage of the older concern with liberty to the newer preoccupation with equality was made possible by economic growth. The absence of growth is almost certain to intensify social conflicts, thereby threatening the spirit of civility and compromise on which a democracy rests.

(3) Can democracy endure prolonged inflation? The historical examples available to us are not encouraging. Weimar

Germany collapsed because its social and political institutions could not absorb sustained inflationary pressures. Uruguay, at one time a model democracy in Latin America, was similarly destroyed by sustained inflationary pressures. Since it appears that the contemporary Western democracies, including Japan, are likely to be subjected to prolonged inflationary pressures, the political lessons of Weimar or Uruguay deserve serious attention. Prolonged inflation is clearly not only an economic problem but a direct political threat. It poses the risk of eroding public confidence in democratic institutions and undermining the fundamental social compromise on which the workability of West European processes depends.

(4) Can a democracy coexist with a communications overload? It is a fact that modern society, specifically European and American, is becoming saturated with data and information. The problem is no longer what one needs to know, but how one can interpret the data with which one is continually being barraged. The effect is to increase the difficulty of generalizing about the longer range, and to intensify public preoccupation with the immediate, which results in reducing the public's attention span. There is a marked tendency today for the public and its leaders to shift their focus from crisis to crisis, with one crisis becoming fashionable one year (environment), another crisis another year (energy), and another crisis still another year (food), with none of these crises given adequate and serious consideration. This problem is perhaps more severe in America than in Europe, but European societies suffer to a greater extent from the other dilemmas already mentioned and the communication problem interacts with them.

(5) Can a democracy endure without a national base? The decline of the nation-state as the principal source of legitimacy and social community appears to be a widespread phenomenon within the advanced countries. To be sure, European nationalism has been the source of many evils, and progress toward a larger Europe requires some dilution of the narrower kinds of nationalism. Nevertheless, it is also true that the na-

tion-state has been in our time the central unit to which man could commit himself on behalf of something larger than himself. The nation thus provided a focus for loyalty, for social sacrifice, and for public constancy. The decline of the vitality of the nation-state which has been experienced by several West European democracies—the waning of patriotism, the rise of ethnic, class, and group conflicts—is a symptom of a profound illness, only thinly veiled by alleged global humanism to which the younger people are particularly said to respond. Europe as a larger entity does not yet command the same degree of loyalty as the individual nation did, and one can wonder what in the meantime can serve as the basis for social legitimacy and stability.

(6) Can European democracy survive without an effective international system? West European democratic systems have become more and more intertwined with the global economy, particularly that of the United States but increasingly also with Japan and other parts of the world. West Europe is the principal trading region of the world. There is also more of an interrelationship in social and economic affairs within Europe than ever before. These interactions require for their effective flow the continued existence of a stable international system. The system today, especially on its economic and monetary planes, is in grave difficulty. The effects of higher energy prices are just beginning to be felt on the political and social levels, but the longer range prospects contain the risk of increasing monetary strains and social dislocations. The survival of European democracy has thus become intertwined with the need for an effective and increasingly just international system.

III

The incipient crisis of democracy in Western Europe is closely related to the division of Europe and to the appearance in Eastern Europe of a competitive and alternative model of a modern industrial society. That model, imposed by the Soviet Union on 130 million Central Europeans, has for many years lacked any genuine appeal. Based on a high degree of coercion, exacting large social sacrifices, insisting on a high level of social and political regimentation, it seemed to offer little that could be relevant to Western Europe. Indeed, the West European Marxist parties, especially the more politically sophisticated French and Italian Communist parties, have repeatedly gone out of their way to emphasize that their concept of a Socialist society was not based to any large extent on the East European experience.

West Europe's current difficulties, however, have the potential for rendering somewhat more attractive one central aspect of the East European response to modernity: its planned development. The apparent absence of inflation and of economic cycles, and the presence of steady employment (achieved through the device of generalized underproductivity), could become sources of political appeal, especially given the sudden potential for tension and conflict within Western Europe.

This sudden attraction (the scope of which should not be exaggerated) could at some point interact with latent resentment among many West Europeans over the division of their continent into two dependent parts, each to some extent modeling itself on the social experience of its patron state. As a consequence, the notion of a neutral Europe which can somehow be divorced from the American-Soviet competition has gained ground, especially among some portions of the intelligentsia. By opting out of that competition, some hope, Europe might also eventually find itself and define itself in terms less dependent on American or Soviet power or social experience.

During the years of intense American-Soviet competition these sentiments tended to be submerged by the more dominant mood of insecurity. West Europeans, fearful of the Stalinist specter, felt strongly that their philosophical as well as personal survival depended on a close relationship with the United States. In the East, in a reverse pattern, the newly installed and more narrowly based Communist elites identified their future with close dependence on Soviet support.

In the context of the developing American-Soviet détente —a détente based on the legitimization and perpetuation of the division of Europe—close linkage with the patron states loses some of its utility and appeal. It does so especially whenever either of these two patron states, or both of them, convey the impression that they are content with the continued division of Europe or are, at the very least, more than prepared to tolerate that division. This is why American passivity in the East-West relationship, the absence of American initiatives designed to build closer East-West European links, has tended to reinforce European suspicions of an American-Soviet condominium designed to perpetuate the favorable position attained by these two powers as successors to the place previously occupied in world affairs by Europe.

The Atlanticist concept is especially vulnerable to this suspicion for two reasons. Despite protestations to the contrary, the Atlanticist idea was and remains inextricably linked with the cold war, and it gains in vitality whenever American-Soviet relations deteriorate. Efforts to infuse Atlanticism with a wider global vision have repeatedly faltered for the simple reason that the focus of the Atlanticists has been primarily on the East-West relationship, with lip service occasionally paid to other issues. Thus any effort to enlarge or refocus American-European cooperation, especially to include Japan in it, tends to be feared by the more traditional Atlanticists.

Moreover, it is possible that American interest in a united Europe has somewhat waned, given the changed global context. The appearance of new and urgent global issues and the seeming decline (though, I fear, also a somewhat deceptive decline) of American-Soviet rivalry have devalued in the United States the centrality of the American-European relationship. America continues to *need* American-European cooperation on the large new global issues, but it may now need a truly united Europe less. Paradoxically, because of the internal European problems stressed earlier, the Europeans may now need a united Europe more than ever.

In addition, those West Europeans committed to the notion of Atlantic cooperation have been alarmed by certain symptoms of an apparent disengagement from Europe, a disengagement made more ominous in their eyes by the apparent shift in Soviet favor in the American-Soviet balance of power. The Atlanticist Europeans thus have been concerned not only about the American-Soviet accommodation undertaken over their heads, but about the possibility that America could no longer be relied on to provide adequate defense and protection for Western Europe. With the continued possibility of tension and conflict in certain portions of Central Europe, especially in Yugoslavia and the Balkans, the Atlanticist Europeans have seen in American behavior portents of an extremely dangerous and unstable future.

These frustrations and uncertainties produced by the continued division of Europe, and inherent in the larger East-West relationship, interact with the surfacing crisis of West European democracy. Together they make it more difficult for Europe to respond purposefully to the third large dilemma, that of the need for broader global cooperative undertakings.

IV

The possibility of an internal crisis within Europe, as well as the uncertainty about Europe's external attitudes, is all the more grave because of the tensions which the existing international system is now undergoing. That system came into being after World War II, in the years 1945-49, to replace the earlier international system, gradually destroyed by the two world wars. That earlier system, in a nutshell, had been Europe-centered, Britain-balanced, and London-financed. The new system became instead Atlantic-centered, U.S.-protected, and New York-financed.

In broad terms the post-1945 system was based on four key and interrelated assumptions:

(1) It was believed that close Atlantic cooperation was both desirable and possible, that European unity was an essential ingredient of that cooperation, that there was no conflict between a more united Europe and close Atlantic cooperation, and that eventually even Japan might be co-opted into that framework.

(2) It was expected that a liberal and self-adjusting free-trade and monetary system would eventually emerge out of cooperative Atlanticist efforts, and that in that system the advanced countries would continue to enjoy steady access to relatively inexpensive raw materials, permitting them both domestic growth and socially progressive policies, thus buttressing their democratic institutions.

(3) It was postulated that the Communist world and particularly the Soviet Union would remain outside the new international system, and that occasional Soviet threats would act, in fact, as a source of unity for that system.

(4) It was expected that the less developed countries would remain for a long time to come both fragmented and politically dependent on the advanced countries, to which they would continue to export raw materials while importing more expensive finished manufactured goods.

It had become evident by the early 1970s that each of the foregoing assumptions was in jeopardy. One could no longer assume automatic progress between European unity and Atlantic cooperation, nor for that matter could one assume that progress toward European unity would continue to be as promising in the future as it had been in the recent past. Fitting Japan into the Atlantic framework also encountered strong European fears and suspicions.

The economic assumptions of the postwar system also became more doubtful. Progress toward a freer and self-adjusting international system now seems less probable. Increased government intervention, in part as a consequence of domestic pressures, has been prompting the politicization of international economics, and in that context deliberate synchronization of international economic policies has come to require major acts of political will. At the same time, the scramble for resources has been intensifying conflicts among the advanced countries, even as it exposed some of their economies to enormous strains. This condition has been interacting with the crisis of democracy discussed earlier, especially since the post-World War II democracies have become accustomed to a steady increase in public and personal consumption and to a decrease in civic commitment and social loyalty. The former leads to inflation and the latter prompts nongovernability. The interaction of the two makes for considerable instability.

In addition, one could no longer view the Communist countries , notably the Soviet Union, but even also China, as operating outside the international system. The Soviet Union could operate increasingly within the system, playing one advanced country off against another and attempting to extract tangible economic and less immediate tangible political benefits from such maneuvers. This may signal a condition of greater normality in international politics, but it also did mean that the Soviet Union was no longer performing the previous function of a "unifier" for Europe and America.

Finally, the less developed countries were now inclined to become more and more assertive, with an increasing tendency to adopt policies of confrontation rather than of cooperation. The success of the OPEC countries is inescapably tempting to others, and the competition for resources was bound to be reflected in an increasingly complex political relationship between advanced portions of the world and the developing countries. At the same time, some of the developing countries, because of the increased food/energy costs, were likely to be confronted by extraordinarily severe difficulties, to which the advanced countries were not in a good position to respond.

The consequence of all the foregoing has been an intensifying challenge to international stability. The emerging global community might well be moving into a phase of international politics characterized by sharpening tensions between the advanced and the developing countries, by major regional social disasters, by a growing temptation for some of the Communist states to exploit these circumstances, and by deepening strains within the advanced countries, especially Europe, in some cases even threatening their political processes.

All of this will be taking place in the context of increasingly complex global dilemmas (food, population, development, energy, the future of the oceans—to name just a few), posing before Europe and America choices of historic magnitude. Can our societies insist on continued high growth? Can we seek social justice only internally and can we do so effectively with lower growth rates? Can we preserve democracy and promote simultaneously both social stability and social change?

V

It is not the intention of this analysis to draw a picture of Europe as the world's sick man. Just as America has shown signs of steady recovery from its phase of troubles, despite the most gloomy predictions of even some of its friends, so European society has a potential for considerable growth, and its vital signs are still strong. Europe has already emerged as the principal factor in world trade and in aid to the less developed countries, and a European foreign policy of sorts is taking shape. European community decisions and acts, particularly in the field of international economics, are beginning to exercise great weight on world politics, and a European perspective on these issues is also developing.

Accordingly, American policymakers should focus more on practical matters which engage both Europe and America and should avoid theological discussions about Atlanticism versus Europeanism. Americans ought to be realistic in recognizing what Europe is and is not, and what Europe is likely to be and not to be. A leading European political analyst, François Duchêne, has advanced an apt definition of Europe as a "civilian power," and his definition contains an important truth about what Europe is not. Europe is not yet, nor is it likely to be, a major military force in world affairs. Hence, Europe is not likely to become a world power in a traditional sense, and a world order based on the notion of active European participation in the more traditional distribution of power is not to be attained. Europe today, and in the near future, is largely a loose framework, primarily economic, and a political process that may become more than that but, at least for quite some time, remains something less than a state. This is why the traditional concept of a balance among five big powers (the United States, Europe, the U.S.S.R., China, and Japan) offered by Messrs. Nixon and Kissinger is simply irrelevant.

However, Europe as a "civilian power" is coming into being, and it is with this Europe that America ought to pursue, with greater psychological subtlety, a cooperative relationship with regard to the larger global problems. That psychological subtlety requires U.S. tolerance for special concerns of Europe, such as in the Mediterranean. This is asking no more of Americans than Americans have come to expect from Europeans, who do "tolerate" American hemispheric links and American preeminence in the Western Hemisphere.

Moreover, the North-South problem is clearly one in which there is room for both American-European and Japanese collaboration as well as some differentiation. On the global scale, such issues as food, population, energy, development, oceans, call for at least consultations and some cooperation. But there are also regional dimensions to these questions, and there Europeans and Americans might well choose to define different paths and pursue different priorities. A common approach in all cases is hardly the answer to all problems.

This is a major difference from the first postwar years, when the Atlantic relationship was the most obvious framework for defining the nature of the American-European connection. But détente and the appearance of centrally important global problems have been rendering the Atlantic relationship less historically central. For one thing, the stability and effective organization of the global economy requires the active participation of Japan, similarly "a civilian power," together with Europe and America, in the definition of a new international system. The crisis in the world economy thus calls for an Atlantic-Pacific response, and the forging of more cooperative links on a trilateral basis among Europe, America, and Japan is the basic point of departure for such a response, including in it also novel joint arrangements particularly with the "nouveaux riches" of the world economy, the oil producers.

The three advanced regions happen to share also fundamentally similar democratic systems. The crisis of modern democracy thus affects all of them, irrespective of its precise timing and sequence. Political consultations, the deliberate exchange of political experience, the fostering of a sense of commonweal particularly focused on the desirability of preserving democratic institutions, is hence a further imperative of trilateral cooperation.

None of this calls for doctrinal or rhetorical exercises. Trilateral cooperation is not a doctrine nor an effort to expand the Atlantic concept to the Pacific. It does not seek to create a wider variant of the earlier notion of the Atlantic community. The notion of trilateralism accepts Europe for what it is— partially a community of economic cooperation and partially a flexible amalgam of sovereign states—and it seeks to engage that Europe and Japan in cooperative responses and *in a process of collaboration* on the major problems of the day which otherwise are likely to get out of hand. It is neither an alliance nor a club, but simply a rational recognition of the fact that a number of contemporary issues require a cooperative—rather than a competitive—effort.

Such cooperation, perhaps it needs to be said, is not an effort either to dilute or obstruct European unity. That unity can only be forced by the Europeans themselves and only they can set its pace. There are, however, problems which cannot wait for a single Europe to appear, and a wider cooperative response can hardly be objectionable to those Europeans who genuinely desire more European unity. Perhaps it is not accidental that the strongest objections to trilateral cooperation have come from those who in the past have most obstructed the progress toward European unity.

In the light of the above considerations, the need for the time being and probably also for the future is not so much for documents defining in greater precision the nature of American-European, nor for that matter Japanese-American-European, relations. The need, rather, is for a widening pattern of multilevel consultations on the central internal and external issues which these societies confront in common. This can take a variety of formal and informal shapes, either building on existing institutions or developing new ones. One approach might be to explore the possibility of extending the Davignon technique in some modified form to include Europe, America, and Japan. An important step toward such Atlantic-Pacific consultations was the agreement on an international energy program signed in Brussels in September 1974 by most of the European countries, the United States, and Japan. On more private levels, other arrangements could also be made and some have already been launched, as for example the encouraging experience of the Trilateral Commission.[1]

In brief, the three central dilemmas of our time call for a gradually increasing cooperation among the world's three most advanced democratic regions. The fact of the matter is that these regions—more than any other—have become in the course of the last quarter of a century part of an interdependent economy and polity. Their internal problems—be they inflation or social frustration—tend to be exported and insoluble, except through wider cooperation. Similarly, the division of Europe has become part of a wider fabric of issues, which ultimately can be resolved only through broad accommodation within a more cooperative global framework.

Rudimentary global political and economic planning is the required reponse—though obviously its effective implementation is still a long way off. But it can only be promoted if Europe, even in its present somewhat politically shapeless form, becomes increasingly engaged on a practical and many-faceted basis in an effort to solve cooperatively with America and Japan the doctrinal, regional, and global dilemmas, to which it alone, or just with America, cannot respond effectively. That is the challenge facing our statesmanship in the post-Atlanticist era.

NOTES

[1] In a report prepared for the Europe-America Conference held in Amsterdam in March 1973, I recommended more specifically that further efforts be made along the following lines:

"(1) To stimulate a greater degree of shared political perspective among the governmental bodies of the three units, to promote the practice of regular and increasingly formal political consultation, to develop common political interest, it will be desirable:

a. to adopt as a matter of regular practice the holding of annual trilateral cabinet meetings, somewhat on the model of U.S.-Japanese cabinet meetings. In the trilateral setting, this could involve the EEC Council of Ministers as well as the Japanese and the American sides;

b. to reinforce the above with a standing secretariat, particularly with a common policy planning and review staff, in part as backup for (a) above and in part as a stimulant to the emergence and crystallization of common perspectives and policies;

c. to promote consultations also in a larger framework, involving states outside the formal confines of the 'cooperating triangle,' it would also be useful to hold more frequent meetings of the OECD foreign ministers, so that common political problems can be frequently reviewed and also so that joint responses to the problems of development in the Third World can be further stimulated.

"(2) To promote on wider basis within the elites—political, economic, social and intellectual—of the three principal units a sense of common destiny and of shared responsibility in coping with the problems of political stability and social progress that beset the contemporary world, to develop within these elites more intimate personal contacts and franker exchanges of views, to overcome the cultural and linguistic barriers, which particularly inhibit Japanese participation in world affairs, it will be desirable:

a. to open up to Japanese participation some of the various informal Atlantic bodies, which have grown up over the last 25 years and which have contributed so much to the emergence of a mutual sense of trust and understanding. Political cooperation among democracies is impossible in the long run unless it is based on a solid foundation of open and sustained dialogue, reinforced by personal links among the respective elites. An example here might be the Bilderberg meetings; Japanese participation in them would be a forward step;

b. to create, in addition to the above, special trilateral bodies for the purpose of promoting common programs, studies and discussions. The very process of addressing a problem on a trilateral basis is an act of political significance;

c. to hold regular three-way meetings of the respective parliamentarians, on as wide a party basis as practicable."

For a comprehensive review of European-Japanese-American relations, see "The Crisis of International Cooperation," by François Duchêne, Kinhide Mushakoji, and Henry D. Owen, a report of the Trilateral Political Task Force to the Executive Committee of the Trilaterial Commission, *The Triangle Papers*, No. 2, 1974.

Chapter 5
A WORLD OF
MULTIPLE RELATIONSHIPS

Seyom Brown

North Atlantic relationships are losing their pivotal role in United States foreign policy. There are attempts in some quarters in Europe and the United States to re-energize the centripetal attraction of the North Atlantic coalition. But this is a retrogressive reponse to the forces of world politics likely to dominate the last quarter of the twentieth century. The new forces are centrifugal with respect to regional or ideological blocs, and potentially integrative on a global basis. A more realistic response to the disintegration of North Atlantica would be to decisively mount the centrifugal forces, recognizing that they are, in the main, historically progressive, and attempt to turn them to the benefit of the security, economic welfare, and other values of civil society whose protection inspired the North Atlantic concept in the first place.

Before suggesting outlines of a United States foreign policy constructively adaptive to today's disintegrative tendencies in U.S.-European relations, let us examine the various cross-pressures working against the magnetism of the North Atlantic core and inquire into their deeper sources.

II

The North Atlantic coalition has been subject to cross-pressures from the start. Each member has a unique combination of special international relationships which it has high incentives to maintain. These have always set limits on the attainable cohesion of the North Atlantic coalition. But the disintegrative effects of the centrifugal pulls have also been clearly limited until recently by a solid consensus in the coalition that a close concerting of policies toward the Soviet Union and the Warsaw Pact countries was vital to the security of all members. NATO was the most tangible expression of this consensus, and for most of twenty years it was generally accepted that if a member's indulgence of non-NATO relationships would seriously cut into its NATO obligations, the non-NATO relationships should give way.

The extent of the change that has overcome the North Atlantic coalition is seen in the growth in the importance of its members' non-NATO relationships relative to their relationships within NATO. This change in relative salience is partially a reflection of the reduced importance of what NATO membership can do for a country and partly a reflection of the increased importance of other relationships for one's security, economic well-being, and power.

The receding fear of direct military threats to Western Europe from the Soviet Union and its allies has reduced the grandeur of NATO and its primary peacetime function of maintaining the balance of power against the East. Even politically threatening Soviet/Warsaw Pact behavior, say, a resumption of harassment to Western transportation and communication to and from Berlin, is now deterred or countered less by military posturing than by Western suggestions that commercial relations with the Soviet Union and various ongoing negotiations may be complicated by Communist aggressiveness.

Insofar as a bipolar strategic balance remains an essential condition of this more benign diplomacy, it too is viewed increasingly out of the framework of mainline NATO assumptions. Weapons technology has progressed to the point where both the United States and the Soviet Union can destroy one another without the use of their forward bases in NATO or the Warsaw Pact. Concurrently the defensive military deployments in Western Europe and Eastern Europe have lost their ability to significantly screen the superpowers from destruction. Consequently, the United States and the Soviet Union must maintain flexibility to unilaterally deter or appease each other, unconstrained by their respective alliance systems. Meanwhile the codification of full U.S.-Soviet strategic parity in SALT and collateral superpower acknowledgments of mutual deterrence has given fresh impetus to old Gaullist suspicions that the central ribbing of the NATO strategic umbrella is weak and will not really open all the way even *in extremis*. Accordingly European interest has revived (and is being encouraged in some American circles) in further developing non-American strategic forces that would constitute credible minimum deterrents to the Soviet Union even if decoupled from the American strategic forces.

Increasingly, threats to the basic well-being of societies in the North Atlantic area are perceived to emanate from sources outside the Soviet sphere of control, against which NATO responses or actions taken under the NATO imprimatur are often inappropriate. The various NATO countries who refused to allow the United States to use their bases or to overfly their territories in order to transport military supplies to the confrontation zone in the 1973 Arab-Israeli war considered the Arab oil embargo a greater threat than the possibility that Russia would strengthen its foothold in the Middle East. The urgency of appeasing the Arabs prompted the West Europeans to disassociate their actions from NATO. Similarly, bilateral economic deals with Arabs and foot-dragging, most evident in the case of France, on efforts by the United States to form a countercartel of the industrialized oil-consuming countries reflected a fear in Europe that a confrontation of OPEC jointly by the NATO countries and Japan would play into the hands of militant polarizers and ideologies in the Arab world.

The whipsaw of the inflation-recession cycle and the pervasive loss of confidence in the ability of existing governments to manage the crises of "postindustrialism" are rightly seen in most countries as more threatening to parliamentary democracy than any coordinated strategy of subversion by international communism. Though undoubtedly the Soviets would hope somehow to benefit from the troubles of the Western countries, it is not at all clear that they are capable of effectively exploiting domestic instability in the West; indeed local Communist parties are often left to fend for themselves in their bids for power as the Kremlin practices détente diplomacy with the incumbent centrist or rightist regimes. Under the circumstances, left-of-center moderates are especially resentful of hints from the United States government that it might look with disfavor on electoral or governmental coalitions with the Communists. Such suggestions, most blatantly of late toward Italians, are at best regarded as gratuitous and at worse the most foolsih kind of intervention —strengthening rather than weakening the popularity of the Communists. The fact that a European government in which Communist party members held important portfolios might not be a welcome participant in all NATO deliberations is true enough; but it is a fact of life that may have to be adapted to by a modification of NATO, instead of through vain attempts by outsiders to manipulate domestic political situations that are a product of profound socio-economic forces.

Meanwhile opportunities for countries in NATO to further their political and economic interests through bilateral and multilateral cooperation with countries outside of the alliance have been growing. Such bypassing of the alliance on matters where at least consultation used to take place under its aegis has been particularly evident in the diplomacy of East-West commerce. Here the West Europeans broke away from the NATO harness earlier than the Americans, to develop their own trade deals with the Comecon countries, with China, North Korea, North Vietnam, and Cuba. In these various commercial negotiations, close coordination with the United States would have been a political encumbrance; moreover, in East-West trade, the West Europeans are natural competitors with the Americans. For similar reasons the United States, in dramatically expanding its own commercial and technological diplomacy with the Soviet Union, Eastern Europe, and China in the early 1970s, preferred to keep the negotiating tracks strictly bilateral—even where (or perhaps especially where) the United States practiced its "linkage" strategy of suggesting that progress in resolving outstanding international security issues (Vietnam, SALT, the Middle East) was a condition of progress on the more mundane issues.

Special relationships beyond the North Atlantic alliance radiate outward, not from a single core, but from many centers: Washington, Ottowa, London, Paris, Brussels, Bonn, Oslo, Rome, etc. Each center is part of a number of unique webs of commercial, cultural, and political intercourse, with its own cross-pressures and its own tensions. The webs overlap one another and compete for the loyalty of various populations. The West European countries lay special claim to economic relationships with the countries along the Mediterranean littoral, and southward, building on past colonial relationships, into sub-Sahara Africa. Through the Maghreb annex to the Rome Treaty, specific instruments of "association" (notably with Greece, Turkey, Tunisia, and Morocco), multilateral instruments of economic cooperation (the Yaoundé and Lomé Conventions with nineteen African states, and other former colonies in the Pacific and Indian Oceans and the Caribbean), and criss-crossing networks of special trade agreements (such as those with Israel and Spain), the EEC countries have been attempting to develop their own "co-prosperity sphere" within which they have privileged

access, as compared with the United States, Canada, and
Japan. Partly in reaction to these expansive tendencies of the
EEC, the United States has been attempting to revive the
motion of a "Western Hemisphere Community" (Kissinger at
Mexico City, February 1974), after a temporary retraction by
the Nixon Administation of the heavy-handed pan-Ameri-
canism of the Alliance for Progress. Both the Latin Americans
and the Canadians are more that ever determined to avoid
being drawn once again into a U.S. hemisphere of influence,
and have themselves been vigorously active in cultivating ex-
trahemispheric commercial relationships with Japan, with the
EEC countries, and throughout the Third World.

   Given the persistence of these trends, efforts by any member
of the North Atlantic grouping to gain community-wide en-
dorsement of its policies toward a country or bloc outside the
area will become more difficult in the years ahead. If a NATO
member wants the imprimatur of the Treaty Organization on
its actions in bilateral conflicts—say, Norway against the Soviet
Union over control of the Arctic continental shelf, Italy
against Yugoslavia over Trieste, West Germany against East
Germany on *Autobahn* transit rights, or the United States
against further expansion by Communist Vietnam in Indochina—it will have to pay a higher price to its comembers of
NATO than previously. This change in the price of obtaining
community-wide backing, itself reinforces the centrifugal tendencies described above, for it gives each member an incentive
to further develop its own extraregional diplomatic obligations that can be played off against the external relationships
of its colleagues.

                                III

   For each member of the North Atlantic coalition, the
widening of the circle of countries with whom cooperation is
important is produced by underlying technological and
socio-economic developments pervading the entire inter-

national system. These global, and long-term, trends are usually referred to by the catchall word "interdependence." Actually, the underlying developments are better understood as expressions of two kinds of interdependence: *intersectoral* and *interstate*. Each has its own dynamics and yet reinforces the other in many fields. Together they compound the difficulty of keeping NATO the centerpiece of U.S.-European relations.

The deepening intersectoral interdependence is a function of the full maturing of the industrial revolution. More and more, the inputs and outputs in one economic sector depend on and directly affect resources in other sectors of society. The production and distribution of energy, being central to the functioning of advanced industrial society, most dramatically reveals the extent of the intersectoral linkages. Shortages or increases in the price of petroleum, in addition to increasing the price of most manufactured goods (or slowing down their production and causing unemployment), produce shortages or price increases in nitrogen-based fertilizer, which affect the supply of food and the rate of inflation. The massive transfer of financial assets to the oil producers affects the functioning of international money markets, the flows of investment capital, and the exchange rates of currencies, all of which in turn feed back on domestic monetary and fiscal policies and thereby further affect the patterns of inflation and recession and the strength or weakness of various industrial sectors.

Perturb the industrialized economy in any of its sectors, and reverberations will be felt in many of its other sectors, often with unpredictable impact. This is no less true outside of the energy field. Change the price of money, and the pattern of urbanization, depending as it does on the availability of construction loans, will be altered. Invent a cheap synthetic for one of the mineral components of steel, or reduce the demand for steel itself, and large communities may be compelled to make major economic readjustments. This is hardly a new phenomenon (witness the impact of the invention of the cotton gin on the economy of the southeastern United States in the nineteenth century, or the displacements in England and the continent caused by the introduction of power looms). But the proliferation of connections and sensitivities between sectors has become so dense that rapidly spreading impact across sectors now is a premise of most national planning—especially where the democratic political process compels the government to provide compensatory adjustments to adversely affected regional or occupational groups.

For advanced industrial countries, managing the domestic political economy with its deep intersectoral interdependencies has become a complicated art, requiring such fine tuning that there is an understandable reluctance to subject economic policies to international decision processes. Although foreign affairs officials of some of the most advantaged countries—the United States and the Federal Republic of Germany, in particular—talk a good game of internationalism, they in fact are constrained to keep as much flexibility for national unilateral action as possible. The governments of weaker national economies are even more hamstrung by domestic protectionist pressures. Most governments appear to be conducting their foreign economic policies according to the rule of thumb: what's mine is mine, what's yours is international.

The national protectionist response to the deepening intersectoral interdependencies will be ultimately futile, however, since the geographic scope of the intersectoral links defies existing political jurisdictions. Many of these links are transnational or global, cutting across alliances and blocs as well as national boundaries. Frequently, essential components of an industrial process are produced in a part of the world far removed from the place the end-product is manufactured. This *interstate* interdependence is a consequence of the contemporary revolution in technologies for moving goods, people, money, and ideas rapidly around the globe. In the larger scheme of human evolution, such interdependence is irreversible (though this does not rule out anachronistic attempts to restore local economic sovereignty). More and more, buyers and sellers participate in the global market as investors, tourists, or as consumers of foreign-produced commodities. In the process they develop preferred foreign products and marketing outlets, which would be more or less costly to give up, and thus constitute degrees of foreign dependency.

Few foreign relationships are absolute. Most *can* be severed. But even those who are less dependent on the perpetuation of the relationship are rarely indifferent to the prospects of severence. Thus, although the Federal Republic of Germany may not *need* to sell a portion of its industrial product to the countries of Eastern Europe, sectors of the Germany economy would be injured by a sudden retraction of their East European markets, and such groups are likely to constitute an active lobby against foreign policies that would bring back the more restrictive policies of the cold war. Similarly, it was hardly surprising that the most vigorous lobbying in the United States against efforts to tie most-favored-nation trade privileges and export credits for the Soviet Union to the Jewish emigration issue came from the most advanced and internationally mobile elements of the American economy.

An intermingling of intersectoral and interstate independencies is also at the center of the growing political controversies over the use of the earth's nonterrestrial realms: the ocean waters and the seabed, the air and the weather system, and outer space. Previous assumptions that these realms were so vast and abundant as to allow all users open access and free use are no longer tenable. Technology has produced congestion in particular locations and heightened competition to exploit their resources. Their efficient and peaceful use, it is now generally recognized, requires substantial coordination among various types of users, and sometimes joint international management of commonly used areas.

IV

The growing global diversification and interweaving of international relationships must transform our vision of the kind of North Atlantic community that will be both politically realistic and historically progressive. The vision will need to be considerably more pluralistic than that which has animated the dreams of Atlanticists such as Jean Monnet and George Ball.

In the webs of intersectoral and interstate interdependence now being woven, cooperative groupings formed around a set of interdependencies in one field, say petroleum production and consumption, will often be incongruent with transnational commitments in other fields, say, those based on culture or ideology. Coalitions to secure these different interests against hostile threats will involve varying sets of countries. A partner in one set may be an adversary in another set. Moreover, each national government will itself be subject to cross-pressures by domestic constituencies favoring particular external coalitions in opposition to others.

Assuming a long-term increase in such external and internal cross-pressures, governments of the advanced industrialized countries are especially likely to find it difficult to sustain or construct permanent multipurpose alliances premised on pervasive antagonism between particular nations or blocs. The implications of these trends reach deep into the foundations of NATO, constructed as it was on the assumption of a two-camp power competition (at least in the Northern Hemisphere) with stable memberships in each camp across a wide variety of issues.

How the North Atlantic coalition adapts, in fact, to the stresses and strains of the new pluralism will depend largely on the concepts that animate the statesmanship of its major members, particularly the United States, and the skillfullness of the diplomacy by which these concepts are implemented. We need not dwell here on the maladaptive response, which would be an attempt to resurrect the conditions of the cold war that led to the formation of NATO and its function as the energizing nucleus of the community. I am assuming, of course, that the Soviet Union does not revive the gross anti-Western aggressiveness of its cold war policies, the correlative of which would be a return to a rigid bloc-to-bloc diplomacy especially in Europe. Realistic U.S. policy responses to a continuation and maturation of the new pluralism appear to me as either (1) a relatively passive accommodation to the emerging pattern of sub-community and extra-community relationships of the North Atlantic countries or (2) an active policy of relating U.S. interests to the dominant currents in an effort to influence the shape of the emerging international system.

The alternative of passive accommodation contemplates a U.S. posture of detachment toward the degree of integration achieved by the Europeans, and a willingness to expand special relationships with particular members of the European Community where there are solid transatlantic interdependencies. The United States would not become as exercised as it has in recent years over the procedures the Europeans develop for consulting as a group with the United States; but neither would the United States feel impelled to put all of its European relationships on an equal plane; and, depending on the matters under discussion, the U.S. government would feel free to consult bilaterally with one or another of the European governments outside the Community framework.

On East-West security matters, the United States would not insist upon NATO-wide consensus or cooperation, but would go along with the transformation of NATO into an umbrella organization for bilateral and special multilateral defense arrangements, varying in membership and mutual obligation according to the unique configurations of defense needs of the different sets of countries. Thus the mutual security arrangements for countering possible Warsaw Pact threats to maritime transit between the North Sea and the Baltic could involve as primary members West Germany, Denmark, Norway, and neutralist Sweden, with the United States perhaps pledging a residual strategic guarantee; but there would be no need to involve southern NATO countries—Portugal, Italy, Greece and Turkey—in either the planning or commitments. Not incidentally, such particularistic defense arrangements would provide a less embarrassing basis for coping with an Italian government that included the Communists, or a Portuguese government whose political complexion cast doubt on its reliability as a NATO-wide security partner, than simply reading them out of the regional coalition. Key arrangements for the conventional defense of the European central front could be essentially between the United States and West Germany, if France, Britain, and Canada were reluctant to share the defense burden in sufficient measure; alternatively, if France and Britain were to join West Germany as the core powers in a revived European defense community, including joint planning and management of European nuclear forces, the United States could move toward a more residual European defense role. Existing arrangements and plans for NATO-wide integration of forces, e.g., in air defense, might have to be kept restricted to narrowly defined tasks. Since multilateral command and control systems are likely to be politically cumbersome in many of the plausible contingencies that would require the commitment to battle of air defense forces, it would be better in any case if the integration of forces was not very pervasive. Likewise, the United States might maintain flexibility for projecting its power into the Middle East through bilateral arrangements with countries on the Mediterranean littoral, independent of formal NATO involvement. In moving toward these kinds of limited-member security arrangements, the possible reduction in numbers of weapons and troops committed to respond initially to an attack would be more than compensated for in the enhanced credibility of the mutual commitments.

A more active U.S. response—the policy I would propose— to the centrifugal forces acting upon the North Atlantic coalition would incorporate the adaptations just outlined, but it would pursue these policies as part of a consistent strategy of transforming the international order from a system of blocs into a globally pluralistic system in which coalitions and adversary relationships form around particular issues. The tendency to define whole countries as either friends or opponents would be abandoned; but transnational coalition between various sectors of national societies would be expected to form congruent with the lines of contemporary interdependence. (This would not preclude the European Community from acting as a unit on many international economic issues.) Rather than opposing "nonalignment" as a norm for interstate relations, the United States would positively endorse it as an essential element of the new legitimacy, and would join the West European countries in an approach to the Soviet Union and the Warsaw Pact countries to follow suit so as to dissolve the division of Europe. The Soviet Union has until now been allowed to preempt the high ground in urging a dissolution of NATO and the Warsaw Pact. The démarche I am urging would reverse these positions, allowing the United States to champion a vision of international relations which is more in line with our national values and diplomatic traditions and— were it to be accepted—would involve more painful readjustments for the Warsaw Pact than for NATO.

This approach would seriously revive the idea of a virtually complete removal of U.S. land-based forces from continental Europe contingent upon a withdrawal of all Soviet forces in Eastern Europe to behind the Soviet border. By itself such a wholesale military disengagement by the superpowers might appear to dangerously destabilize the East-West balance of power in Europe, since the Soviet forces would remain only 400 miles from Berlin while the U.S. forces would need to be transported 3,000 miles across the ocean to reach Western Europe. Indeed, it is precisely this asymmetry in deployment distances that has complicated all attempts to establish an agreed basis for determining "essential equivalence" of the superpower forces in Europe, and thus also for reducing them—either marginally or comprehensively. The coupling of military disengagement with alliance dissolution, however, is designed to redress the disadvantage to the West of this military asymmetry by making it very difficult politically for the Soviets to redeploy their forces into Eastern Europe.

Under the present system the U.S.S.R. can augment and rearrange Soviet forces in Eastern Europe under the cover of basic Warsaw Pact agreements, without the need to engage in major negotiations with each of the governments. Moreover, such increases in Soviet capabilities in Eastern Europe can be made incrementally and therefore somewhat ambiguously at each step with respect to their meaning for the East-West balance of power, with the result that the Western democracies might not be able to react decisively to a disadvantageous gross change in the balance until well after the fact. Under the system I am proposing, any redeployment of Soviet forces into Eastern Europe would constitute the crossing of an unambiguous and internationally recognized threshold. The U.S.S.R. would be expected to negotiate any such change with the affected countries, who would be politically strengthened by the new nonalignment norms for objecting to Soviet demands. A violation of these norms by the Soviet Union would by itself be a major political warning to others in the system that a new, and perhaps stronger-then-ever, anti-Soviet coalition was required. In short, the political deterrence placed by a truly pluralistic all-European system against Soviet hegemonic temptations would more than compensate for the tactical military-deployment asymmetries that might flow from the contemplated superpower withdrawals—military asymmetries which are evident only in the imaginary scenarios by which the military planners size their forces, and which in any event would be rapidly set right by the West during the period of political confrontation that would precede any real war for the control of Europe.

The main virtue of the post cold war system I am proposing, however, is that it would remove the military factors into the wings in the play of power relationships in Europe and would bring the political and economic factors of power on to the center stage. With economic interdependecies especially allowed to develop more freely and dynamically, the notion of "Finlandization" could finally be discarded. Rather, the United States and the West European countries would form the core of attraction for drawing other countries into the new pluralistic international order based on nonalignment and multiple associations. The animating concept would be a world society analogous to the most advanced domestic societies, where a dense interlinking of interdependent groups makes most groups unwilling to escalate specific conflicts of interests into life-and-death causes and renders the society as a whole resistant to polarizing pressures that could lead to civil war.

Such an inclusive strategy would not wait for the new international system to mature first on a North Atlantic or OECD basis before extending it outward (particularly in the form of commercial arrangements) to embrace the more "difficult" elements of world society—the Communist countries and the developing countries. A policy of excluding the difficult cases would leave them relatively free of the constraints of the multiple-relationship world, while the non-Communist industrialized countries became increasingly preoccupied with managing their own interdependencies. As long as the Communist countries and the alienated Third World have less to lose than do the OECD countries by policies of immoderation and confrontation, then the threat to escalate East-West and North-South issues can be exploited to the disadvantage of the

OECD countries; and there will be more opportunities for the Soviet Union and China to pose as leaders of the "anti-imperialist" forces.

In sum, reorientation of North Atlantic relationships I am suggesting—whether in the passive or active mode—views the centrifugal pulls on members of the North Atlantic coalition as a positive basis for a more broadly based integration of global society. It views the loosening of U.S.-European relations as a healthy part of the process, particularly as this indicates a proliferation of relationships eastward and southward. This transformation of the international system is bound to be lamented by Atlanticists on both sides of the ocean; but its time has come.

Chapter 6
AMERICA, EUROPE AND THE OIL CRISIS: HEGEMONY REAFFIRMED?

David P. Calleo

Styles change in international relations as they do in all fashionable arts. Only a few years ago, many experts, even those drawing up the President's foreign policy reports, were predicting a new era of international pluralism. America, it was thought, would consolidate and devolve much of its postwar hegemonic responsibility. A new "pentagonal" world system was emerging. In particular, the economic and political recovery of the European states, their impressive capacity for regional cooperation, and their growing dissatisfaction with the status quo prompted several writers, like myself, to believe American devolution particularly appropriate in Western Europe. We should devolve our primary responsibility for European defense to a coalition of European states, I argued, and our monetary hegemony to a genuinely multilateral system.[1]

In recent months, opinion has shifted strongly, at least about Europe. The oil producers, by challenging the American-built postwar system in the Third World, have, whatever the other consequences, appeared to reinforce strongly American dominance over the "Atlantic" world. Many observers now believe American hegemony over Europe not only firmly re-established, but inescapable for the foreseeable future.

The apparent reversal in Europe's fortunes is ascribed to diplomatic design as well as economic accident. The Nixon-Kissinger foreign policy, it is thought, coldly and skillfully contained European revisionist ambitions. America's détente with both Russia and China, among other uses, has preempted European attempts to exploit Soviet-American-Chinese differences. In particular, American collaboration with a conservative Russia, encouraged to become increasingly dependent on our trade and technology, has effectively reinforced the European status quo. Russia continues its control over the East; the United States continues its hegemony over the West. Neither superpower has any interest in withdrawing from Europe. And neither has let itself be used to undermine the other. In short, American policy has deliberately chosen to uphold the European status quo rather than promote either transatlantic or pan-European reform.[2]

Mr. Kissinger's Metternichean or Bismarckian triumphs notwithstanding, the oil crisis of 1973 has seemed the principal cause for America's apparently rejuvenated hegemony and Europe's corresponding decline. For many observers, the energy crisis blew away any illusions about Europe's economic power, and exposed the insubstantial foundation of its political coalition. And as the world grows more straitened economically, many suspect that Europe's dependence, even if inevitable, will grow less comfortable.[3]

How can we judge this new skepticism about Europe? Have recent events decisively reaffirmed American hegemony? Or is the present flux only the troubled beginning of that more plural world which analysts have long been expecting?

Obviously, no one standing in the midst of these events can speak with great assurance about the future. As hegemony, like beauty, exists primarily in the eyes of its beholders, superpowers may see themselves running the world, even if events often look different from other perspectives. And in the absence of decisive military contests, contradictory views of reality can often coexist without undue mutual disturbance.

We can perhaps most profitably begin our analysis by clarifying what is meant by hegemony. Hegemony I take to mean leadership or predominance within a common system. It thus requires both that there be an integrated "system," and that someone be predominant within it. The American role in Western Europe has been hegemonic because we have been the predominant power within an integrated system of "Atlantic" states. That Atlantic hegemony can be illustrated concretely in military, economic, and diplomatic spheres. Militarily, American hegemony has meant not only that Europe depends on an American nuclear guarantee for effective deterrence, but also that the United States leads Europe's conventional defense. Economically, hegemony has meant a dollar standard with the United States exempted from the balance-of-payments restraints common to other countries in the system. Diplomatically, hegemony has assigned the United States the primary initiative in major diplomatic efforts, and an effective veto over serious secondary efforts by others.

Hegemony, it must be said, is not a synonym for exploitation. The dominance of one may be exercised in the interest of all, and may be accepted more or less freely. Certainly America's postwar Atlantic hegemony has brought many benefits to Europe and been widely supported there. American hegemony, of course, has also often met European resistance, and not always been successfully exercised. On certain occasions, European states have challenged American predominance; more often they have sought to withdraw themselves, at least selectively, from the system within which our hegemony prevails.

The possibility that the hegemonic Atlantic system would not persist indefinitely, at least in its present form, has led to widespread speculation about how it might evolve. Four broad alternatives have seemed to present themselves.

One is a perpetuation and extension of American hegemony

into a progressively integrated Atlantic system, with economic life probably increasingly dominated by multinational corporations, most of them American.

A second alternative foresees the progressive integration of European states into a cohesive European bloc, which tends not only to separate itself from American hegemony in all spheres, but to withdraw from any closely integrated Atlantic system.

A third sees an integrated Atlantic system preserved and extended, but perhaps with a closely integrated Europe as one of its elements and, in any event, with governance which is increasingly multilateral rather than hegemonic. In other words, American unilateral management of the integrated system is to be replaced progressively by international organizations or some sort of plural directorate.

A fourth foresees a gradual disintegration of both the existing transatlantic and European systems, with nation-states, as in the 1930s, increasingly isolating themselves by protectionist and nationalist policies.

We might, therefore, rephrase our original question thus: how has the oil crisis altered the prospects among these alternatives? Has it, as so many believe, greatly strengthened the perpetuation and extension of American hegemony?

Before we may start to answer, however, we must, as the oil crisis forcefully suggests, put the "Atlantic" system itself into its broader world context. For the postwar international order has encompassed not merely the pan-Atlantic system of intimate European and Japanese dependence on the United States, but also a broader world system of American hegemony over most of the non-Communist Third World. This is the "world" as distinguished from the "Atlantic" system. After the disintegration of the old European empires, much of the old colonial world has become a sort of Latin America, a new Pan-American union—from which, of course, Russia snatched Eastern Europe, and China radically divorced herself. In historical perspective, this postwar world system corresponds to the mid-nineteenth-century British model of a "liberal" empire. In such a model, a unique "world power" is able to maintain an easy access to raw materials and markets, generally with only indirect political intervention. This liberal phase of British imperialism, faced with rising German and American power, gradually gave way to the direct control characteristic of the "new imperialism" of the later nineteenth and early twentieth centuries. Paradoxically, colonialism, defined as direct control, resulted from a more plural world order.

After World War I, Britain, despite her victory, was unable to reassert her old hegemony. After World War II, the United States took Britain's role, as had long been anticipated, and re-established a liberal world system. Many saw the Vietnam war as a decisive struggle to maintain that open order. The oil crisis, following a few years later, suggests that America's liberal empire is now much enfeebled. Hence, easy access to supplies and markets can no longer be taken for granted and the world begins to look to blocs.

Europe's postwar Atlantic dependence has to be seen within the context of this larger American world system. If, after their defeat at Suez, the European powers progressively retreated from their own political and military extensions into the Third World, they nevertheless benefited from a general order sustained by the United States. Europe enjoyed many of the fruits of imperialism without having to sustain its costs.

Significantly, many who urged greater European independence within the Atlantic context were also most skeptical of America's capacity to sustain the postwar world system. De Gaulle, for example, in pressing Europe to throw off America's Atlantic hegemony, constantly warned of the dangers which a disarmed and complacent Europe would face in the more intensely competitive world, bound to resume, he believed, after the postwar interlude. Hence, not only his efforts to refashion and sustain France's African connections, but also his assiduous courting of nationalist regimes in the Middle

East, Asia, and even Latin America. Similarly, it is difficult
not to infer similar views behind the persistent association
policy of the European Economic Community in Africa and
the Middle East, despite increasingly vigorous American
opposition.

If we consider the Atlantic relationship in its world context,
we may say that the United States today faces a double challenge. The first lies in a growing tendency of the European
states to separate themselves from American hegemony within
the Atlantic system. The second lies in the gradual disintegration of the American "informal empire" over the Third
World—a development made striking through the oil crisis.
To rephrase our question once more: how has the simultaneous disintegration of the world system affected the disintegration of the Atlantic system? Can we accept the popular
view that America's declining hegemony over the world system strongly reinforces its hegemony within the Atlantic system? Are Europeans, in danger of losing the fruits of the
American world order, all the more dependent on the United
States?

Succeeding sections explore various aspects of a broader
answer. For a start, we should discuss the general evolution of
the transatlantic system in the years before the energy crisis
and, in particular, the origin of the European challenge to
American hegemony.

Europe's Postwar Challenge to American Hegemony

Europe's challenge to American economic hegemony has
long been obvious. American predominance was, of course,
never firmly established in the economic, as opposed to the
military, sphere. Immediately after the war, those liberal policies so assiduously fostered by Cordell Hull sought to create a
closely integrated Atlantic economy, within which, under the
prevailing circumstances, the United States would inevitably

occupy a hegemonic position. Europeans, the British in particular, regarded these policies as both politically imperialist and economically disastrous. As the cold war progressed, the United States, fearful of Communist influence over a devastated Europe, abandoned its liberal economic dogmas for the sake of quick European recovery. As a result, a protectionist European bloc grew up under American patronage. In effect, a transatlantic compromise reconciled American and European aspirations. Whereas the military sphere was organized along hegemonic "Atlantic" lines in NATO, Europe developed its own "European" economic system, institutionalized ultimately in the Common Market.

In the late 1950s, however, the United States began to return to its earlier economic Atlanticism; in other words, American policy shifted back toward building an integrated economic system, within which the United States would perforce be the dominant power. Hegemonic policy revived forcefully with the "Grand Design" of the Kennedy Administration. Policies to reinforce American military hegemony were paired with new economic and political policies to absorb the European bloc into Atlantic partnership. At the same time, Gaullist France was beginning to condemn American hegemony not only in economic but also in military and diplomatic relations. In short, both sides were abandoning the postwar compromise.

The sharpest conflict developed over the monetary system. In the 1950s the Europeans had been allowed to build a discriminatory monetary bloc of their own, organized around the European Payments Union. By 1958, convertibility was restored and a universalist "Bretton Woods system," a monument to the early liberal phase of postwar American policy, began to operate. The hegemonic nature of the Atlantic monetary system gradually became apparent. By the early 1960s the United States had clearly developed a structural balance of payments deficit. A persisting American deficit, given the postwar practice of holding dollars as official and

private reserves, meant ever-increasing dollar balances abroad,
as well as a mounting nervousness among their holders.
American financial ingenuity turned to a series of *ad hoc*
measures to increase "world liquidity," which could be trans-
lated to mean credit for dollar deficits. None of the American
measures, however, offered any permanent solution for the
dollar's steadily deteriorating position.

In 1965 the French turned the monetary question into a
major political issue between Europe and the United States.[4]
De Gaulle asserted with vigor France's long-standing disapproval of the dollar-exchange standard, a system regarded both
as politically imperialist and economically unsound. In the
official French view, an imperial monetary system, based on
the dollar, was being used to finance America's swollen military presence throughout the world, as well as an increasing
penetration of Europe's economies through direct investments. Above all, American deficits fueled an inflation in
other countries which would, if unchecked, gravely undermine
the economic and social stability of the Western world. In
1965, de Gaulle demanded a return to his preferred version of
a multilateral liberal order—a gold standard, without reserve
currencies, which required all countries to maintain equilibrium.

In subsequent years, the Vietnam war, by prompting an
inflationary spiral in the United States, deteriorated the
American trade surplus, a development which further eroded
the confidence of foreign dollar holders. By the late 1960s,
American payments deficits, swollen by speculation, began to
reach an hitherto unimaginable scale; the United States was
gradually forced to abandon convertibility.[5]

The United States, nevertheless, rejected direct steps to cut
the dollar outflow by limiting tourism, investment, or military
expenditures. Instead, American policy turned to floating exchange rates. If foreign countries were unwilling either to
accumulate further or to spend their surplus dollars, we argued, their currencies and trade would have to bear the con-

quences. Their money would either appreciate, or the dollar devalue, until the consequent trade effects brought equilibrium to the American balance of payments. In other words, insofar as Europeans refused to hold our surplus dollars, the trade benefits of the dollar's consequent depreciation would cover the American deficit.[6]

For Europe, the implications of the strategy seemed highly unfavorable. Greatly dependent, as they were, on trade, European countries were not eager to sacrifice their export surpluses, particularly in the high technology and armaments sectors where they were struggling, against considerable odds, to compete with the Americans.[7] At the same time, alarming domestic inflation everywhere seemed to compel increasing resistance to further dollar accumulation. But against an American policy which refused either to stem outflow or to defend the currency, what could the Europeans do?

Through the usual welter of conflicting short-term aims and perspectives, European governments groped for a long-range solution. Increasingly, that solution was seen in a European Monetary Union. Actual motives for supporting the union varied widely, but the historical logic is relatively clear. A monetary union could develop the machinery needed to disengage Europe's economic union from American monetary hegemony. European economies would no longer be at the mercy of erratic American domestic monetary policy. Otherwise, Europe risked reversing its own general economic integration. A successful union to govern intra-European monetary relations could, moreover, hope to force the United States to accept a multilateral, nonhegemonic discipline, and thus establish a genuinely liberal international order.

Whatever their hopes, Europeans had not got very far toward a monetary union before the oil crisis of 1973. After formal devaluation in 1971, the dollar's position had continued to deteriorate. While fear of trade diversion and inflation fed commitment to the monetary union, the inherent complexity of the enterprise, as well as the differences among short-range national economic policies, interests, and vulnerabilities, all discouraged rapid progress. To many observers, the European states seemed capable neither of forcing the United States to accept the discipline of a nonhegemonic monetary system, nor of sustaining their own economic integration. The end result of rejecting American monetary hegemony, instead of a multilateral system, or even a world of well-defined regional blocs, looked to be a monetary order disintegrated into nationalist fragments, as had happened in the 1930s. Perhaps, as the effects of monetary disorder had become sufficiently intense, Europeans would have been driven to build the collective monetary machinery to preserve their economic union. But they were already in serious disarray before the oil crisis fell upon them in 1973.

The Oil Crisis and Its Lessons

The new oil prices weighed heavily, but unevenly, on most European currencies. European governments, needing short-term capital to finance basic deficits, began to borrow heavily on the Eurodollar Market.[8] Domestic deflation seemed urgently necessary to counteract inflation and payments deficits. But the drain of money from Europe to the oil producers threatened European governments and businesses with a dangerous liquidity crisis and the prospect of a major recession to follow.

In short, with stunning swiftness, Europe's financial and economic strength appeared to have collapsed, and with it, any European challenge to American economic hegemony. By contrast with the vulnerability of European currencies, the dollar's position seemed to have improved sharply. Relative invulnerability, along with military and diplomatic power, seemed to give the United States great advantages in establishing satisfactory new arrangements with the oil producers.

The American strategy for dealing with the crisis, moreover, not only made the most of the country's natural advantages, but also appeared designed to reinforce America's faltering hegemony over Europe. As its immediate reaction to the oil crisis, Washington promoted a collective user's bloc. A solid Western bloc, we hoped, would break the newly founded producers' bloc and return prices, and the general situation, to the old status quo. Most European governments, far more dependent on Middle Eastern oil than the United States, were skeptical of the whole approach. Moreover, a users' bloc, as the French saw it, would tend to give the United States the initiative in negotiation with the producers and inhibit separate European approaches. Indeed, the users' association seemed merely another expression of Washington's renewed "global" approach to the world's problems, an approach, as Secretary Kissinger's Pilgrim's Speech strongly suggested, which left little room for separate European policies or initiatives.

Globalism, of course, like interdependence, can easily be seen as a euphemism for hegemony. After bilateral consultations, the United States defines the common position on the common problem. Europeans are not to develop a separate anterior position of their own. For in a world whose problems can only be resolved "globally," Europe has no separate interests from the United States. Whatever the substantive merits of American proposals for oil, finance, or food, the pattern seems transparently hegemonic.

Hegemony, as noted earlier, need not be exploitative, and is easier to bear when comfortable and when the hegemonic power is sufficiently secure to be generous. But as the deterioration of the international system makes the world more straitened for the industrial countries, the United States naturally grows increasingly preoccupied with protecting its own national interests. Thus, in the oil crisis, while preaching a collective approach to the Europeans, the American government conducted a series of bilateral negotiations designed to seize the high ground in the greatly expanded Middle Eastern markets for arms, industrial equipment, and technology. The principal result of these American efforts was the giant eco nomic agreement between the United States and Saud Arabia. At the same time, American policy sought to build channels to entice to the American market those huge liquid funds starting to flow to the Middle East, mainly from Eu rope. Similarly, we did our best, many believed, to sustain the international oil companies, mostly American controlled, as intermediaries between the producers and the European and Japanese markets.

American economic strategy derived powerful support from our general diplomatic and military position in the Arab-Is raeli conflict, where we had assumed a complex and precariou mediating role. Our supposed military leverage over Israe could be used to encourage American economic aims among the Arabs. A general understanding with the Soviets rein forced our commanding position. Needless to say, any Eu ropean interference in the sensitive diplomatic negotiation was unwelcome. In such delicate matters involving super powers, America was to be Europe's trustee.

Whatever its merits, the American strategy, if successful would leave Europe's economies even more heavily depend ent on American goodwill. American oil companies would continue to monopolize access to the producers. American industries would be the chief beneficiaries of increased trade The American capital market would be the primary recipien of surplus capital. In short, the greatly increased wealth of the oil producers, drawn in large part from the Europeans, would be channeled principally to the United States. European could hope to finance their deficits from the American capita market.

A moment's reflection of Europe's interest reveals th depth of the transatlantic conflict brought out by the oi crisis. In the short term, Europe needed to borrow heavily hence was vitally interested in "recycling" arrangements. Fo Europe, however, borrowing money from the Arabs or th

Americans could not be a long-range solution. To return to financial equilibrium, the European countries needed to restore their trade balances. This they hoped to do, in part at least, by long-range agreements with the Middle Eastern countries. Since the Europeans were the Middle East's largest customers, had traditional ties with its peoples, were geographically proximate, and the world's largest market for imports, a long-range partnership seemed logical. The Europeans believed they had a good deal to offer. For the long run, the industrial development of the Middle East would require not only a major importation of machinery and technological advice, but access to foreign markets. Certainly, the European states, so dependent on foreign oil, and so unlikely to undertake a military intervention, seemed a safer place for Arab investments than the United States. The more heavily invested the oil-producing states became in Europe, of course, the more linked they would become to Europe's economic fate, and the less able to hold European economies hostage to American good behavior. To be sure, for Europe to establish such an economic bloc with the Middle East could be expected to involve a painful transfer of real resources. Nevertheless, it was difficult to foresee how Europe could otherwise avoid a precipitous economic decline. This view, with several variations, has generally prevailed in Europe. Hence the European states quickly detached themselves from American diplomatic hegemony and began an intensive Middle Eastern campaign of their own.

It will doubtless take several years before the success of Europe's initiatives can be measured. At this point, some impressive long-term agreements have been signed.[9] Even with Arab cooperation, however, European economies face not only intense short-term financial disruptions, transmitted through an already disordered monetary structure, but also profoundly difficult long-range problems, some of which will be taken up below. As Arabs and Iranians never tire of saying, prosperous Europe has grown habituated to unnaturally cheap energy costs. With fuel costs now catching up with other prices, European economies need to cut domestic consumption in order to generate sufficient new exports. To transfer real resources abroad on such a scale may prove to be a task beyond the economic or political skill of European governments, particularly in a period of exploding inflationary expectations.

These great difficulties come at a time when European governments already face, it is said, a deep crisis of "legitimacy." Years of rapid growth have created new expectations without eliminating old inequalities. Political consensus is precarious and governments have little margin for maneuver.

In addition to their domestic difficulties, European states still seem deeply divided among themselves. Indeed, for many observers, the oil crisis itself appeared to reveal the great extent to which *sauve qui peut* remains the policy of the European states. The European Community is widely seen as only a fair-weather construction, which will collapse in a major storm. In a world which grows more straitened and dangerous, Europe's weak and disunited states are seen as increasingly unlikely ever to reach a sufficient degree of cohesive strength to dispense with American hegemony, benevolent or otherwise. For this era, the European challenge is over.

The judgment may be correct, but seems premature.

Future Prospects of the European Bloc: Major Problems

Europe's union today faces three major difficulties: the energy crisis, the grave weakness of two of its principal members, and a continuing military weakness toward the superpowers. Success in resolving these problems collectively can hardly be taken for granted. But while Europe's weaknesses are obvious, its strengths are not always well perceived. Europe's present coalition must always disappoint those who expect from it a supranational federation which acts like the United States.

How well can it be expected to cope with its difficulties?

In the oil crisis the tactics followed by the European states appear to have worked tolerably well. Europe's best strategy, it was decided, lay not in trying to break the cartel to get a lower price, but rather in gradually placing the whole European-Middle Eastern relationship on a more comprehensive and long-range basis. A period of bilateral discussions and arrangements has given a more stable structure to European-Arab interdependence and may eventually be followed by a general European-Middle Eastern economic accord, with some intergovernmental machinery, to consolidate and organize general relations.[10]

Similarly, intra-European relations during the crisis, while they indicated the distinctive positions and perspectives of the European states, also revealed a considerable degree of enlightened cooperation. If European states competed with each other, mutual dependence does appear to have put a term on that competition. If each country sought to look after its own oil supply through bilateral negotiations, no one was, in fact, left dangerously short, a situation which would soon have become intolerable in a group of closely interdependent states.[11]

The Germans, who alone among the major European countries still had a comfortable payments surplus, apparently seeing their own prosperity inevitably linked to that of their neighbors, offered to help with their partners' deficits in return for rather obvious measures of domestic restraint. German and French domestic economic policy now appear increasingly coordinated.[12]

In summary, while the oil crisis has unquestionably faced the Europeans with extremely difficult economic and political problems, the sudden precariousness of their prosperity has both suggested the limits of American goodwill, and jolted Europe into attempting an ambitious set of coordinated policies. To preserve their own union and prosperity, European states have been forced both into more intensive collaboration at home, and into ambitious schemes in external diplomacy. Obviously, no one can say how well they will succeed. But the widespread belief that they must fail seems premature.

Optimism about a reinforcement of European integration, and in particular of its Franco-German axis, can easily be offset, however, by the corresponding attenuation of Italy and Britain. For both countries, the oil crisis has come on top of a long-standing national crisis which reaches to the very foundations of their economic and political systems.

The British and Italian cases reveal a fundamental characteristic of European integration. Contrary to the theories which attended its birth, the European Community has not advanced toward supranational federation. Even if closely interdependent economically, increasingly conscious of mutual interests, and progressively skillful in coordinating national policies, the Community remains a coalition of national states. Each state cleaves to its partners in hopes of increasing rather than giving up its effective sovereignty. Each expects greater mastery over its national economic environment from organized cooperation with its neighbors than from isolation. Such a coalition, however, is suitable only for countries strong enough to hold their own in competition with energetic neighbors. Hence, joining the Community as the cure for national weakness is a policy likely to lead to grave disappointment. For the weak, participation in an open economic system risks disaster.

Up to a point, of course, the strong can carry the weak, and are more or less constrained to do so by the union's confederal nature. In a confederation, as within a single nation-state, all parts can hardly be expected to be developed equally and within the same cyclical phase. In a confederal community, however, the weak have their strong political leverage and must be accommodated if the association is to progress. But there are limits to the patience of the strong. An apparently temporary and remediable weakness is more easily tolerated than a congenital incapacity to compete.

Italy, for example, has always posed special problems for the Community which could nevertheless be seen as the temporary difficulties of a late-developing country. But the Italian political system's prolonged inability to cope with the administrative and social problems of modernization makes the viability of Italy's membership increasingly questionable. The fundamentally unsound nature of Italian budgetary and financial practices makes Italy an unlikely partner in reforming the international monetary order.

The British pose the Italian problem magnified by several degrees. Not surprisingly, joining the Community has not cured the long-standing weakness of the British economy. Indeed, should Britain ever be constrained to live up to the normal conditions of membership, her economic situation would probably worsen even further. The country's political commitment to a European future appears highly volatile. A lingering affinity for Atlantic hegemony magnifies the natural tendency of a weak Britain to play off European against American ambitions. The City of London's stake in the present monetary disorder, the Eurodollar Market in particular, makes Britain a shaky partner for European efforts at monetary reform.

Both the Italian and British situations are long-standing, but seem to be growing worse. The Italians move closer to a political collapse which may estrange them, at least temporarily, from their partners. A divided British government now faces a relentlessly accelerating economic crisis. In short, both Britain and Italy may cease to participate in the Community. In any event, a successful resolution of their national problems can hardly be taken for granted.

Their formal dissociation, however, might not prove as disastrous for Europe as might at first be imagined. As long as the Franco-German core holds, with the Benelux countries inevitably drawn in, the European Community may well be more effective, both internally and externally, without the formal membership of Britain and Italy. A coalition is not necessarily stronger because it has more rather than fewer members, particularly if its reluctant additions bring in a discouraging diversity of problems and interests. Even if officially out of the Community, both Britain and Italy would also necessarily be drawn into some form of negotiated association. While England and Italy obviously belong within the European construction, progress might be easier if they remained outside the framework of full membership during a difficult transitional period.

A third fundamental problem facing the European coalition is its military weakness. While the European states have formed an increasingly independent bloc in economic and political spheres, they nevertheless have remained highly dependent militarily on the United States. As argued above, the division between military and economic spheres, with a separate pattern of relations for each, constituted the political compromise on which the postwar Atlantic system was built.

While the European states would generally be content to remain American nuclear protectorates, if their dependency did not impinge too heavily on their economic and diplomatic interests, the rather unnatural distinction between military and economic hegemony has been breaking down; the economic costs for Europe's protection have been growing. In particular, the threat that European disengagement in the economic sphere would provoke an American disengagement in the military sphere has been a powerful limit on collective European efforts. Hence, as economic and diplomatic tensions rise, Europeans must look more seriously at their military options. What are they?

The Europeans, of course, could turn to a disarmed neutralism, a position which would risk exchanging American hegemony for Russian—not an attractive option for governments seeking greater national independence. A more likely alternative lies in supplementing or even replacing the American deterrent with the British and especially the French national deterrents. Both countries have somewhat detached themselves from American military hegemony. For Britain, which has accepted American nuclear help and control, the attempt at autonomy may be more apparent than real. But the French have built an independent force without American help. After considerable harassment and ridicule, their deterrent is beginning to be taken seriously. With greater resources, its apparently sound technological base might provide the foundation for a larger "European" force. With such a force at their disposal, Europeans, even if still within an Atlantic alliance, would be far less dependent on the United States. A European coalition, with a serious nuclear deterrent, could cut loose from an American-run security system or, more probably, demand a multilateral Atlantic system, with European and American deterrents coordinating. In any event, America's military power could not so easily be used as a sort of ultimate deterrent against Europe's economic independence. What are the present prospects for a European nuclear coalition?

While it has long been possible to imagine the British and French collaborating on some form of collective deterrent, it has been difficult to see how the Germans might be fitted in, or induced to join the effort.

In theory, of course, the Germans might reject American hegemony in any of three ways: by a policy of neutralism and disarmament, by joining some European construction, or by building a national force of their own. Any of these alternatives has seemed highly improbable. In the cold war era, Germany's fear of Russia, Europe's general suspicion of Germany, plus the weakness of any conceivable European deterrent, all bound the Germans tightly to Atlantic defense. Even if various German politicians have occasionally shown interest in a collective European deterrent, Germany would be likely to participate in such an enterprise only with the blessing of the United States, particularly as long as *Ostpolitik* was foremost in German diplomacy. The American government, however, has evinced as little enthusiasm for European nuclear forces as has the Russian. Indeed, American governments have shown themselves even unwilling to reduce their leading role in Europe's conventional defense. Today, after years spent launching the ponderous negotiating machinery of Mutual Force Reductions, the Americans appear to have set terms which still seem unlikely to be negotiable.[13]

American determination to preserve the military status quo is, of course, more than matched by the Russians. The Soviets show no sign of relinquishing their heavy-handed control over Eastern Europe, and the uncontested military hegemony which that control presumably requires. Russia greatly fears a potentially revisionist Germany with nuclear arms. Hence, Soviet enthusiasm for the Nuclear Nonproliferation Treaty, and strong opposition to any joint European nuclear force.

So far, at least, this mutual displeasure of the superpowers has been more than enough to discourage the Federal Republic. Nor have the French been particularly eager. Throughout much of the 1960s they, too, were assiduously cultivating good relations with Russia and Eastern Europe.

Today, however, general European expectations from an opening to the East seem much reduced. Russian conservatism, both at home and in Eastern Europe, dampens hope for any gradual and peaceful abdication of Russian control of its "satellites." At the same time, the mounting friction with the United States over economic matters and the obvious advantages which military hegemony gives in economic negotiations will doubtless encourage a renewed European interest in withdrawing from American military as well as economic hegemony. Thus the developing French nuclear force suggests a potential option for Europe which may well grow more attractive. American nuclear hegemony over Europe may prove a diminishing asset, less and less able by itself to command a corresponding hegemony in the economic and political fields.

While the preceding analysis of the oil crisis, the British and Italian predicament, and Europe's military prospects hardly constitutes a comprehensive view of the problems and prospects of a European coalition, it does suggest that the obstacles, while formidable, are not insurmountable. In other words, nothing in the present situation would seem to make it inevitable that Europe's collective efforts in the oil crisis must break down from the weight of their own internal contradictions. The coalition may well break down, but it need not. European states are obviously facing greater difficulties than at any time since the immediate postwar era. But the prospect of acute discomfort may provide the inspiration which has so far been lacking for the European states to establish a more autonomous control of their environment.

The Alternatives Reconsidered

How do such major trends, as we describe them, affect the prospects of those alternatives for the Atlantic system discussed at the outset?

(1) The first alternative was an indefinite continuation of American hegemony over an Atlantic system. If no urgent incentive yet exists to challenge that hegemony in the military sphere, it is much shaken in the economic, and especially the monetary, sphere. While the United States may well draw back from the blatant nationalism typical of the early days of the energy crisis, and European states will hope to avoid open confrontations, serious tension between European and American vital aims and interests will remain, and is likely to become intense if the general economic crisis worsens, or the Middle East truce breaks down. In other words, American predominance is likely to be accepted less and less willingly by Europe. While it can be argued that Europe's position is so desperate that American hegemony will prevail in any event, continuing deterioration for Europe would be likely to result in radical governments, less attached to the waning comforts of the status quo than present regimes, and thus prepared to take more extreme measures to restore domestic equilibrium.

The possibility remains, of course, that the United States may succeed in breaking the oil cartel and thus appear to restore something like its old hegemonic position in the world political economy generally. But while events in the Middle East and the Third World generally will doubtless continue to be tortuous and filled with adventures, a reversal of the trend toward a more plural world system seems unlikely. And in such a plural world, to repeat, Europe as a whole is unlikely to remain under American hegemony.

(2) If the European states do reject American hegemony in monetary and diplomatic affairs, their own coalition, a multilateral European bloc built around the Community, would seem an obviously desirable alternative.

Such a European system, to achieve a degree of self-sufficiency adequate to replace American hegemony, would seem to require, in addition to an effective consensus on internal economic policy, a strong collective diplomatic policy toward the world outside—in particular toward the United States, the Soviet Union, and the oil- and other raw-material-producing states in Africa and the Middle East. Moreover, as argued above, such a bloc is also likely to demand a more intensive European military collaboration.

The success of the European enterprise would appear to depend, at a minimum, on France and Germany's capacity to sustain their close collaboration through the inevitable stresses of building a European alternative to American hegemony. In addition, the two core states must ultimately be able to attract and hold the weaker and more peripheral members, without having to compromise away their ambitions in order to do so.

The military question is very likely to prove the most difficult. Europeans, as we note, still appear to have little enthusiasm for a military coalition, even if support for it may grow in consequence of economic and diplomatic frictions, as well as greater technological possibilities. But the Germans will continue to be torn, and both American and Soviet reactions are likely to be strongly negative.

German indecision, moreover, is sustained by a persistent American tendency to court Germany and perhaps Japan into a "trilateral" partnership. While such a policy for re-establishing a renewed pan-Atlantic hegemony is likely to founder upon Germany's close identity and interdependence with Europe, it may work well enough to frustrate Europe's own progress toward cohesion.

Under the circumstances, the nascent European and the deteriorating Atlantic coalitions may continue to frustrate each other indefinitely. Like Britain and France in the interwar period, America and Europe may end up defeating each other, to their mutual loss.

(3) America's hegemony could, of course, be replaced not so much by a separate European bloc as by a more genuinely multilateral Atlantic system. In other words, both Europe and the United States could remain within a common and integrated system, but with American predominance replaced by a plural directorate. In view of the relative strength and invulnerability of the United States, however, such an evolution would seem to require a reasonably coherent European bloc as its precondition. Multilateral systems are unlikely to be other than hegemonic if the members are not sufficiently equal, independent, and assertive. As events in the oil crisis strongly suggest, should the larger international order break down, the United States and Europe will be less likely to see their interests as identical. Nor is it realistic to assume that more adequate machinery for consultation will somehow charm American leaders into greater concern for European interests, unless the Europeans have also the power, within a common system, to compel accommodation. In short, without a strong European bloc, the Atlantic system is unlikely to reform itself away from hegemony.

(4) A final alternative would foresee Europe's disengagement from an American-dominated Atlantic system, but without any coherently integrated European system forming in consequence. Given the inherent difficulties of forming a

viable European coalition, and the probable effects of American and Soviet hostility to such a bloc, disintegration of the Atlantic system will be accompanied by disintegration of the European. Both Atlantic and European systems, having defeated each other, will fall to pieces. The collapse will most probably manifest itself in a rebirth of economic nationalism. A breakdown of the current international monetary and banking system, for example, could easily lead to the protectionism typical of the 1930s. In the face of an unworkable international order, national states can be expected to shelter their economies as best they can from an unfriendly and unpredictable world order.

Crash as Cure?

In the life of modern states, catastrophes are seldom fatal. Sometimes crises have their benefits. For example, in the United States, the breakdown of the economic system in the 1930s brought a more enlightened and stable domestic order.

The postwar international system built on American hegemony doubtless needs fundamental changes. Long-standing systems, with their tangle of interests dedicated to preserving the status quo, are naturally averse to reform. This conservatism receives additional reinforcement from our growing skill in patching up essentially unsound arrangements. That has been the story of America's European policy over the past fifteen years.

Economic collapse might be the necessary prelude to building a new international order, if the damage could be sufficiently limited; in particular, if it did not violently alter the political or social systems of Western countries. National systems, having regained their internal equilibrium through protectionism, might negotiate a series of limited regional arrangements which could gradually widen into a plural and open world system. Conceivably, a European bloc would eventually reconstitute itself and, in due course, negotiate a return to more intimate transatlantic relations. A crash, in short, might prove the only way to purge the Atlantic system of that overextension of American economic and political ambition, and corresponding European dependence, which has become mutually insupportable. At the same time, a crash might prove to be the only way to break the spiral of debt and inflationary expectations which so completely distorts national economic and social systems.

Such a cure would be less pleasant than the disease. The prospects for democracy would be shaky in more than one Western country. International disorder, moreover, could always spread from economic to military realms. Indeed, a common if not universal view believes a war was needed to resolve the last major international economic breakdown. Since the madness of nuclear war is now sufficiently obvious, however, we may hope that a major international crisis would stop short of the military sphere.

But what may happen to our Western societies without a war to resolve their problems? Will they turn to revolution instead? Will violence, repressed abroad, have to find its outlet at home? These are the sorts of questions which have almost been forgotten in the burgeoning prosperity of the postwar imperial system. Now they have forcefully returned with the reappearance of scarcity and depression in the capitalist world. Perhaps, unlike in the interwar period, prosperity can be re-established on the old "global" pattern; or perhaps a more manageable partition of the system can be achieved between Europe and America. As the interwar experience suggests, however, the old system may well break up in convulsions and states may find shelter in nationalist blocs. But this time, if a war is unlikely to re-establish hegemony, perhaps a new dual system may be built after a prolonged time of troubles.

No one can pretend to see clearly what will emerge from the adventures of the next few years. Will anything reverse the gradual erosion of American imperial power and the rise of new power in the Third World? Nothing, I suspect, short of war itself. But if the world is to be more plural, we may also see a more independent role for Europe.[14]

NOTES

[1] For my earlier views, see Robert Osgood et al., *Retreat From Empire?* (Baltimore, 1973). See also *The Atlantic Fantasy*, (Baltimore, 1970), and *America and the World Political Economy*, with B. M. Rowland (Bloomington, Ind., 1973).

[2] Motives for East-West cooperation are, of course, more complex than the bald statement in the text. Europeans have sought to encourage détente in the hopes of gradually breaking down the barriers between Western and non-Russian Eastern Europe. After Czechoslovakia, it was clear that success required incorporating Russia as well, which meant ostensibly recognizing the status quo while setting in train forces which would undermine it. These European policies would seem essentially at cross-purposes with those of the Americans, which have been concerned with stabilizing the European situation and thus eliminating an obstacle to closer American-Russian cooperation.

[3] For a distinguished and pessimistic view of Europe's present position, see Fritz Stern, "The End of the Postwar Era," *Commentary*, April 1974, pp. 27-35. Also see Walter Laqueur, "After Appeasement of the Sheiks—The Idea of Europe Runs out of Gas," *The New York Times Magazine*, January 20, 1974, part IV, pp. 13-46.

[4] Charles de Gaulle, *Press Conference*, February 4, 1965. For the theoretical foundation, see Jacques Rueff, *The Age of Inflation* (Chicago, 1964); also Rueff's *Balance of Payments* (New York, 1967).

[5] Establishing the two-tier gold system, as Jacques Rueff observed, effectively ended dollar convertibility into gold. By agreeing not to buy or sell on the private gold market, central bankers could only convert their dollars through the United States government, increasing its ability to exert pressure. Rueff argues the dollar became effectively inconvertible for any country under United States mili-

tary protection. See Rueff, *Monetary Sin of the West*, (New York, 1972), pp. 184-189. For an excellent analysis of the last phases of the dollar standard, see Harold van Buren Cleveland, "How the Dollar Standard Died," *Foreign Policy* 5 (Winter 1971-72): 44-51.

[6] See Gottfried Haberler, *Money in the International Economy: A Study in the Balance-of-Payments Adjustment, International Liquidity, and Exchange Rates* (Cambridge, Mass., 1965), particularly pp. 26-31. Also see Lawrence Krause, "A Passive Balance of Payments Strategy for the U.S.," *Brookings Papers on Economic Activity*, No. 3, 1970.

[7] See Hans O. Schmitt, "Capital Markets and the Unification of Europe," *World Politics* 20, No. 2 (January 1968): 228-244.

[8] The OECD forecast the following current account balances for the first two quarters of 1974 as compared with the same period in 1972 and 1973:

	1972	1973	1974
France	284	200	–800
Germany	379	3,850	1,000
Italy	2,549	–1,750	–1,350
United Kingdom	219	–2,800	–3,000

(all prices in SDR units)

For additional figures, see OECD *Outlook*, No. 14, July 1974.

European enthusiasm for a system based on rapid adjustment was understandably in suspense. The European Monetary Union itself, already faced by significant technical and political problems before the Arab-Israeli war of 1973, was shattered as France joined Britain and Italy outside the "snake." But Giscard d'Estaing,then Minister of Finance, called the French float only a "parenthesis" (in progress toward a common monetary policy). *Le Monde*, January 22, 1974, p. 2. By the summer of 1975, France with Giscard as her President had, in fact, returned to the "snake."

[9] Throughout 1974 there were at least a dozen major bilateral agreements, including the French-Iranian agreement of February 19, the French-Libyan agreement of February 19, the German-Iranian agreement of February 23, the Italian-Iranian agreement of March 11, and the French-Saudi arms deal for $800

million on December 4, 1974. In addition, there have been a large number of quasi-governmental and private arrangements for cooperation and long-term assistance. For a week-by-week breakdown of the agreements, see *The Petroleum Economist*, Ludgate Hill, London. There has also been a certain amount of direct investment by the Arabs. The Iranians purchased 25.04 percent of Krupp Steel (see *The Financial Times*, July 19, 1974); the Kuwaitis bought controlling interest in St. Martin's, a large London property firm (*The Financial Times*, September 25, 1974), as well as 15 percent of Daimler-Benz at the end of November (*The Financial Times*, December 2, 1974).

10 For the early problems of initiating general discussions on energy see *The Economist*, July 27, 1974, p. 52. The most comprehensive general accord with a bloc of non-European countries has so far been the ACP-EEC Convention of Lomé, signed on February 28, 1975, with forty-six countries in Africa, the Caribbean, and the Pacific. It allows nonreciprocal access to European markets for nonagricultural products, tries to stabilize various agricultural prices, and gives substantial financial and technological aid. Multilateral machinery oversees implementation and promotes some joint planning. The same formula, suitably adapted, is being attempted in current negotiations (August 1975) with the Maghreb and Mashraq states.

11 Although the Dutch started to ration gasoline domestically on January 12, 1974, in response to the Arab oil embargo, there was apparently little need to do so. Supplies from Iran and Nigeria increased to provide for any shortfalls; the huge Rotterdam oil tanks remained full. The Dutch motorist could and was encouraged officially by his government to avoid rationing altogether by driving across the border to other European countries (*The New York Times*, January 13, p. 13). At the time, according to a Foreign Ministry spokesman, deliveries of oil for the first week in January (after the embargo) were greater than deliveries in the first week in December (pre-embargo) (*The New York Times*, January 13, p. 13). Rationing in Holland lasted only twenty-two days (*The New York Times*, January 24, 1974).

12 For illustration and analysis of heightened Franco-German policy coordination, see *The Economist*, July 13, 1974, and September 14, 1974.

13 Both the Russians and the United States seem to have extreme

positions on MFR. See Christoph Bertram, "Mutual Force Reductions in Europe: The Military Aspect," *Adelphi Papers* 84 (January 1972): 19.

[14] This paper has been much influenced by the comments of colleagues at the October 1974 conference at Bellagio, the John Hopkins Washington Center of Foreign Policy Research, and the Lehrman Institute. In particular, I wish to thank Wolfgang Hager, Benjamin Rowland, and Robert W. Tucker.

Chapter 7
THE ATLANTIC ECONOMY IN CRISIS

Edward L. Morse

The industrialized societies of the non-Communist world are currently confronting the most acute crisis in their relationships since World War II. Whether or not they successfully surmount this crisis, the pattern of their interactions will be different from what it has been in the past. The symptoms and the roots of this crisis are strikingly obvious and easy to identify. The options facing the governments involved are more obscure and less readily identified. This seems to be the case primarily because of the unprecedented nature of the current crisis, and the existence of apparently insurmountable political and theoretical obstacles to any immediate and satisfactory resolution.

It has become fashionable to argue that the major source of the current crisis is the challenge posed to the industrialized societies by the outbreak of the war in the Middle East in October 1973 and the imposition of a selective embargo by Arab oil exporters on Israel's sympathizers, together with the subsequent quadrupling of world oil prices through the successful organization of a cartel of world oil producers.[1] It was the perceived need of the majority of governments in oil-consuming nations to secure adequate and continuing supplies of energy raw materials that appeared responsible for the failure

149

of the partners of the Netherlands overtly to aid a fellow member of the European Community under the acute duress of boycott, which was also the first episode in the accelerated fragmentation of the Community in the winter of 1973-74. The collapse of the traditional year-end bargaining in Brussels, followed by the breakdown in the remnants of the European Monetary Union and the split within the EEC between France and the others on the formation of the International Energy Agency also lend credence to this view. So does the rapid turn-around in growth in all the Western industrialized economies and the subsequent reformulation of balance of payments forecasts for OECD countries from a modest surplus for 1974 of about $10 billion to an unprecedented collective deficit of over $40 billion.

It may also be argued, however, that the dramatic increase in oil prices is far less responsible for the crisis than is apparent. The energy crisis was responsible more for accelerating tendencies that had been surfacing for some time, for magnifying the mutual fears and suspicions that had been brewing across both the Atlantic and Pacific divides between these societies, and for telescoping a set of problems in both domestic and international governance that the major industrial powers had been attempting to postpone through *ad hoc* patchwork since the late 1960s. Thus a simple focus upon the immediate problems which appeared after the Middle East war is bound to divert attention both from an analysis of the nature of the current crisis and from review of the options now available to governments.

The second interpretation of the current crisis seems far more compelling than the first. The acceleration of world oil prices seems to have been in progress for several years preceding the Yom Kippur War, as the OPEC cartel grew in organizational solidarity and boldness. Certainly, debate in the United States about whether an upcoming energy crisis would be the result of shortages of supply or of market interference was common in both academic and governmental circles. The challenge that the bloc of oil exporters posed for the liberal institutions created after World War II was also by no means the first example of fragmentation in the economic system. The growing gap between developed and underdeveloped societies and the divergent trade policies pursued in Europe, North America, and Japan since the early 1960s had also represented a growing trend away from multilateralism and universalism. Nor did the inflation in all industrialized societies, which reached two-digit levels almost everywhere in 1974, have its origins only in the rapid increase in petroleum prices. Rather, the growth in inflation rates, the crisis in the supply of an array of new materials, and the emergence of problems of security of supplies antedated the winter of 1973-74.

If this interpretation is correct, what are the elements of change and crisis that underlie dissension within Europe, between Europe and the United States, and between them and the other industrial societies as well?

The *first* element in the crisis has to do with the recognition that systems of relationships established after World War II have undergone a fundamental transition. This recognition has involved an incredible flux in governmental policy since the late 1960s, as the various governments have attempted to cope with change, without being able to articulate either how they wish their own societies to evolve or what sort of international system they would prefer.

There was a time when the loosening of international structures seemed to point in an obvious direction. The monetary crises of the late 1960s and early 1970s, the establishment of policies of accommodation with the Soviet Union and the Eastern bloc, and the development of new trade relationships with the less developed countries represented an apparent trend. In the aftermath of the Vietnam war, the United States seemed to be in the midst of a steady decline in its relative international position, which the Nixon Doctrine and intimations of five-power diplomacy seemed to recognize.[2] To be sure, many informed Europeans and Japanese felt that in adapting to this decline, the United States government was acting far more imperialistically than it had in the heyday of American predominance and putative hegemony. Nixon shocks in Japan associated with the unannounced trip of Henry Kissinger to China in 1971 and the diplomacy of John Connally during the aftermath of the August monetary crisis were taken by the Japanese government to symbolize an incontrovertible set of facts: no Japanese government could any longer rely on the American connection as a means of bolstering its own domestic authority or as a means of freeing it from the necessity of developing an independent foreign policy toward the Soviet Union and China for Japanese territorial security, or toward the Pacific Basin or Europe for economic security.[3] Similarly, many Europeans felt that American diplomacy would enable them to accelerate the trend toward European unification, with the United States serving as an external enemy or federator against which they could react in unity, just as formerly they had reacted against the Soviet Union. Thus American diplomacy seemed to reinforce the decisions taken at The Hague summit of December 1969 to form a European monetary and economic union, to expand the Community to Britain and other members of EFTA (European Free Trade Association), and to develop plans for the coordination of foreign policies.

In short, the first reflex reaction to the apparent loosening of structures in the international system was the articulation of policies that pointed in the direction of a more pluralistic world, where governments or regions would be able to increase their own domestic and international autonomy and mutually to adjust their increasingly incompatible interests and objectives. This was welcomed in the United States, where the government seemed to have grown tired of running Western institutions and providing leadership for their evolution. And it was viewed as the first major opportunity for the Europeans to strike an independent course that would free them from the shackles of American hegemony. Only, perhaps, in Japan was this apparent international transition viewed with doubt and suspicion. For only in Japan did there remain an interest in the continued institutionalization of multilateral and global economic institutions, and the growth of an integrated world economy, on which Japanese welfare and economic security have depended for thirty years.

In spite of the apparently inexorable nature of the trend toward pluralism in the international system and the welcome it received across the Atlantic, there was always something problematic about it. There was a trade-off in this evolution between the inconsistencies of the old status quo and the unknowns of the future system. The system undergoing evolution was one in which American predominance bore political costs in Europe and Japan. Independence from America was inevitably welcomed. It had previously been a system in which American predominance meant that the Japanese and Europeans had lost a good deal of control over their domestic economic management, given existing asymmetries. In an open world, living with big brother across the Atlantic and Pacific had meant that domestic monetary policy had seriously to take into account the domestic credit policy practiced by the Federal Reserve System in the United States.[4] Independence from America, therefore, also meant greater control over domestic economic management in Europe and Japan, which was all the more important insofar as governmental authority depends in large measure on the efficacy of governmental policy in providing sustained economic growth as well as in a fair distribution of domestic wealth to all social groups.

Predominance, however, also carried visible and tangible benefits. It represented a clear security guarantee, and still does, in spite of the deterioration of the American military capacity and the incompatibility between American and European security interests vis-à-vis the Soviet Union. It also freed European resources for domestic economic growth rather than defense. American economic predominance was, furthermore, correlated with a set of economic institutions and relationships under which both Europe and Japan enjoyed unprecedented prosperity and uninterrupted growth in trade. While a pluralistic world carries the benefits associated with enhanced domestic and international autonomy, it has a major cost: no one can be certain that it can work as efficiently as the system of American predominance in providing both military security and a framework of economic prosperity. Monetary institutions have been particularly problematic. A world of relatively equal currency blocs would be one in which the dollar would no longer provide new liquidity, would no longer be a unique transaction or interventionary currency, and the American central bank could no longer be relied on as a sort of lender of last resort. While a pluralistic world may be politically desirable, it has never been clear that the Europeans or Japanese really want to try it.

What has been most problematic in the apparent tendency toward a global pluralism, however, is the reversal after the winter of 1973-74. The exorbitant costs of high-priced oil include the return of the dollar as the centerpiece of the world's monetary system, at least for the time being; the indefinite postponement of European plans for a monetary union; and the continued dependence of all industrialized societies on Third World countries for sources of supply of requisite materials.

The loosening of international structures at the end of the 1960s has not, therefore, brought an end to an era of American predominance. It has, however, represented fundamental changes in the international economy, which require urgent action. Among these are the growth in world inflation rates and the need to deal with its causes rather than to attack it with medicine that merely tempers its symptomatic effects;[5] the efforts of the Third World countries to join in collective actions to redistribute global income, which necessitates a new approach by industrialized societies in their relationships with the less developed countries;[6] and the exigency of creating international commercial rules to deal with security of supplies and export controls, which would balance symmetrically the existing rules and their emphasis on access to markets.[7]

A *second* element underlying the crisis is the rather dramatic paralysis of governments in the industrialized world and their inability to achieve domestic goals as a result of an undermining of the structures and institutions of political authority. Indeed, as Pierre Hassner has argued:

> The most general and basic conflict . . . can be defined as a crisis of authority or of legitimacy: existing authorities and structures keep their formal status and the physical means of power but are unable to satisfy either the political and psychological demands for participation and self-expression or the technological and economic demands for efficiency, which emanate from their followers or subjects.[8]

It is not clear what has been responsible for this new crisis in legitimacy in Western societies, although it does seem that there is a "persistence of power structures with a declining ability to perform their practical tasks and to attract loyalty and enthusiasm." [9]

Examples abound throughout the industrialized world. In the United States, for example, the loss of governmental authority has revolved about Watergate, wiretapping, and a series of misleading and disingenuous governmental statements, which began long before the Nixon Administration came to office. In France it is associated with the failure of government to handle gross inequalities in the distribution of wealth and the fear of small businessmen and others that their major position in French social and political life will be terminated by massive capital investments, rapid modernization, and the restructuring of society. The crisis in Japan smacks of the failure of the apparently unique Japanese system of consensus-building within government and among major interest groups to meet the current and manifold challenges. It is also associated with the inability of the current Japanese leadership to circumvent traditional intermediary political groups and to establish a direct relationship between itself and the body politic to deal with increased social services, redistribution of income, questions concerning the quality of life vis-à-vis the need for continued superfast economic growth. Nor can the government easily confront a major reorientation in foreign policy. In Germany the government has thus far been able to handle the rates of inflation that have jeopardized governmental authority elsewhere, but it also confronts dilemmas as harsh as those of other governments. This is as true in foreign policy, where the government must continue the delicate balance between its frequently incompatible American and European ties, as it is in the domestic realm, where it too is unable to achieve domestic reforms because of the persistent lack of an operative majority in the Bundestag.

The Italian and British situations seem to be worst of all and represent, for some, portents for the future of all industrialized societies and, for others, exceptions which will give the others lessons concerning the dangers of wrong-minded policies. The overstaffed Italian administration suffers fragmentation in both organized political life and in informal institutions. The multiparty system remains unable to form a coalition on any major issue, including the role of the Communist party (the traditional unifier in postwar Italian politics). The British government, which is far more efficiently organized for social and political administration, suffers from a similar lack of consensus. Both societies, confronting national "bankruptcy" as a result of the increased price of oil imports and domestic economic mismanagement, also exemplify the tendency within modernized societies to undergo a new round of class warfare, which the age of abundance seemed to have called to an end. Unlike most of the other industrialized societies, both in Italy and Britain the governments seem to have renounced any effort to come to grips with their current dilemmas and have decided to muddle through. In Italy this takes the form of relying on her partners in the Common Market to bail the government out of any difficulties and of continuing to hope that a generalized European prosperity will spill over the Italian borders. In Britain it appears in the hope that the development of North Sea oil will turn into both an export boom and a means of facilitating an end to endemic class conflict.

If there is a particularity in each of these domestic situations, it ought not to obscure a common set of threads which run through each of the various circles. Throughout the industrialized world there is a pervasive sense of governmental inefficacy and loss of legitimacy which seems characteristic of the evolution of high mass-consumption societies. Many reasons can be adduced to explain this. One has to do with the rapid social change to which such societies are subjected and the way social change affects a highly politicized citizenry. Change, when coupled with economic growth, can create new opportunities for the gaining of wealth and for its more equitable distribution throughout society. Yet even a growing economy is disruptive of traditional ways of life and thus seems always to have the tendency to gore someone's ox and to set up resistance to change.[10]

Another factor in the decline in governmental authority relates to the recessionary phase that the economies have recently undergone. In modernized societies, which are based on continuous economic growth, any persistent or even any sharp and temporary decline in prosperity is bound to weaken governmental authority. Economic stagnation or recession obviously has this effect, since it reduces the purchasing power of individuals. Inflation, even in a situation of sustained growth, will also have this effect, especially when it reaches double-digit levels. The combination of economic stagnation and double-digit inflation is deadly, if it lasts long. The existence of this combination after the winter of 1973-74 is surely one of the major factors contributing to the current crisis in governmental legitimacy and authority. Moreover, it is one which has no easy solution, since the deterioration of governmental authority itself promotes increased inflation and the further withering of governmental control, as the history of Britain over the past few years so clearly demonstrates.

This leads to a third and well-discussed factor in the decline in governmental authority: the re-emergence of corporatism in highly industrialized societies.[11] A major factor in the decline of governmental authority as well as in recent inflationary spirals stems from the regrouping of social relationships around organized activities within primary social groups; in other words, the failure of people to spread their loyalties among a set of overlapping social units, which was supposed to pacify domestic society, according to some theorists of modernization. The bargaining power of these enlarged primary units of social organization has had a dual effect.

On the one hand, it has meant that bargaining power over the distribution of social wealth has become monopolized by bargaining units; for domestic societies have become interdependent as never before in history, and the ability of any of the new corporatist groups to blackmail society as a whole has concomitantly been enhanced. Different groups may have varying influence in the blackmail power they can wield, but if a police force, or coal miners, or garbage collectors decide to strike, society finds that it cannot substitute other groups to carry out their tasks, which are essential for society to function.

On the other hand, the same increased bargaining leverage of corporatist groups has made it virtually impossible for economies to achieve necessary adjustments. Groups within society are attempting at a minimum to tie their income to inflation and to increase their relative share of social wealth vis-à-vis other groups. They are also attempting in some small and open economies to tie real purchasing power to changes in the exchange rate of the currencies of their economy. This has a double effect when coupled with the search for guaranteed employment: it makes both domestic and international adjustments extremely difficult. It serves to prevent governments from phasing out outmoded industry and capital and also, by eliminating "money illusion," from adjusting purchasing power by changing exchange rates.

A *third* element in the current crisis can be described in terms of the Kantian problem of whether republics can join together to create a system of perpetual peace. Kant's argument had to do with the pacific nature of republics as well as with the belief that a natural harmony of interests exists among them, which is enhanced by increases in international commerce: trade creates a stake for all governments in increasing internationalism. This belief is predicated on the notion that commerce benefits all by increasing the wealth of all trading partners, thus reinforcing the pacific nature of republican governments.

The governments of the industrialized non-Communist world seem to fit this description. They are democracies and also share common traditions. More striking has been the common evolution of their social structures. They are all highly modernized societies, built on high levels of sustained economic growth and oriented toward high mass consumption. Not only are they each subject to rapid social change, but they are highly urbanized and have similar problems related to maintaining viable urban environments and planning new ones. They face similar social goals, which are oriented toward a higher standard of living, since economic growth has been a requisite of maintaining social coherence. Most important in their common evolution, however, has been the development of similar structures for economic management. This has had a dual set of effects which impinges on both the desirability and the feasibility of international harmonization of economic policies.

On the one hand, the various national economies are administered according to what Theodore Geiger has called the "neo-national rule of experts," who see their own personal advance intertwined with the economic growth of their own societies.[12] This interweaving of personal and general welfare puts an emphasis on the desirability of national autonomy in decision-making and therefore on the isolation of the society from external events. "National economic policies," as Richard N. Cooper has argued,

> rely for their effectiveness on the separation of markets. This is true of monetary policy, of income taxation, of regulatory policies, and of redistributive policies (whether the last be through differential taxation or through direct transfers).[13]

Even when national goals are best achieved through international cooperation, there remains a built-in governmental incentive toward reliance on second-best solutions in which the risk of sacrificing national autonomy does not arise.

On the other hand, the convergence of domestic economic structures has meant that the governments are now pursuing similar goals. Paradoxically, this pursuit of the same or of similar objectives may well create difficulties for international cooperation. If we can assume that cooperation is based largely on the ability of different governments to strike satisfactory bargains with one another, we could also argue that successful bargaining usually requires that governments trade off different sorts of goals.

Successful political negotiations in Europe or between the Europeans and Japanese on the one hand and the United States on the other have generally involved bargaining between divergent but complementary goals.[14] Thus, for example, a number of the post-World War II institutions, including NATO and the structures of the international economy, were based at least implicitly on the ability of the U.S. government to obtain military bases in Europe and Japan and of the latter to gain economic benefits (preferential access to the U.S. market for Japan, trade discrimination through the establishment of a customs union for the Europeans).[15] The bargain began to become unglued precisely at the time when the original implicit bargain became explicitly too costly for the participants, and also when they simultaneously began to pursue similar goals.[16] The growth in common Soviet-American interests (in preserving their joint nuclear preponderance as well as their common interests as opposed to those they shared with their respective cold war allies) thus made the Atlantic as well as the Pacific security relationship less worthwhile. This was true for the Americans, who found the stationing of troops abroad less necessary for security, too costly for the rewards that were achieved, and perhaps too risky in an emerging and new nuclear logic. It was also true for Japan and Europe, where governments were decreasingly willing to see their security sacrificed by an American government whose strategic concerns evolved away from theirs. In the economic sphere, the apparent decline in the American position also led the American government to realize that economic sacrifices made to its Asian and European security partners had become too costly. Indeed, the United States by the late 1960s began to pursue the same kind of foreign economic policies as its major partners, and the upshot of this was an increased incompatibility in their collective objectives.

A similar logic can be used to explain political cooperation within Europe. European cooperation has been at its highest when its rewards have been different and yet complementary for each of the major European partners. It has been low, paradoxically, when the major governments have been pursuing the same goals. Thus, in the period 1969-73, when the European communities reached an apogee in political cooperation with the decisions to form a monetary union, to foster foreign policy cooperation, and to seek enlargement, the goals of Britain, France, and Germany were essentially different but complementary. The German government's major priority had been the successful implementation of its *Ostpolitik*, for which it had to assure itself of the support of its European and Atlantic allies. It thus fostered the decisions reached at The Hague summit in 1969 and implemented thereafter. The

French government, under the newly elected Georges Pompidou, was attempting to achieve progress in Europe in order to bolster the government's domestic popularity. It also fostered the monetary union in order to preserve the Common Agricultural Policy from dissolution under the global movement toward flexible exchange rates, and it looked upon the Community's expansion to Britain and other EFTA members as a means of preventing German economic dominance of the Six in the aftermath of the economic woes that followed the May events of 1968. Soon afterward, a new conservative government in Britain was amenable to plans put forth at The Hague insofar as Europe now became the centerpiece of Heath's "Gaullism." The consensus of that period broke down by late 1973, in part as a result of the successful fulfillment of the complementary goals of Britain, France, and Germany, and in part because of the incompatibility of new goals that had become higher in the priorities of these governments by that time. Each was now facing domestic problems which could not be resolved by attempts to foster the European construction. But each was also confronting similar problems and pursuing similar economic goals—including the attempt to secure their supply of energy resources—which seemed mutually incompatible.

There are a number of sources of international conflict in the kinds of economic goals that the advanced industrialized societies are now pursuing which make the international coordination of policies highly desirable but also extremely difficult. Some of those stem from confusion that has accompanied the rapid shifts in economic power which have occurred during the past five years. Others have been labeled "neo-mercantilism" in recent discussions of foreign economic policy and stem from the various reasons why governments pursue policies oriented toward the achievement of a current account surplus in their balance of payments. Such policies inevitably lead to conflict since it is impossible for all to achieve a surplus simultaneously—at least one must be in deficit if the others are to achieve that goal. Moreover, the situation is complicated by the divergent reasons for which the different societies pursue current account surpluses.[17]

One factor fostering the pursuit of a current surplus is government's desire to finance other foreign activities. For most of the advanced industrialized societies, a current account, or trade surplus, enables them to implement policies toward the less developed world, including the granting of foreign aid. In the absence of a trade surplus, governments would find it economically and politically difficult to grant aid to less developed countries on a continuing basis. In the case of the United States, external security and economic interests are also involved. Trade surpluses facilitate the financing of troops stationed abroad as well as the fighting of wars. There was therefore validity to the argument of Europeans in the late 1960s that they were helping to finance American participation in the war in Vietnam. A trade surplus was also seen as a requisite for the continuing ability of the United States economy to provide liquidity for world trade—a policy which also irked Europeans insofar as it meant continued American dominance in the international financial system.

A second source of the new mercantilism is related to the macroeconomic policies of all governments, and in particular to the policy which aims at full employment. The more open an economy and the more that output and employment are related to world market conditions, the more likely does it become that full employment policies will involve production in export industries. While it may be doubtful that, as some left-wing economists argue, full employment policies in market economies inevitably involve neo-mercantilist policies, it is clear that this is sometimes the case.

Policies related to advanced technology provide a third source of contemporary neo-mercantilism, especially for governments whose domestic markets are insufficient to assure adequate returns on investment or economies of scale. Governments of both middle-sized economies (e.g., Japan, Germany, France, or Britain) and large economies (e.g., the United States) find it necessary to invest in advanced technology for a variety of reasons, including national defense, fear that to do otherwise would inhibit long-term economic growth, and the desirability of maintaining national autonomy. If investments in advanced technology are to prove economically feasible, markets far larger than what is provided in the domestic sphere must be sought in order to maximize production and to lower costs. Thus in areas of advanced technology one also finds an incentive to achieve trade surpluses.

An additional set of factors also carries neo-mercantilist implications. One is rather traditional and relates to the need that governments have to prevent the emergence of protectionist interest groups. These groups are normally powerful when import competition is severe and when they cannot be counterbalanced by strong interests in export sectors. If a government fosters a current account surplus, it is thus likely to find its best means of preventing protectionist legislation. Another factor relates to the current international situation and the need to find any means available to finance imports of energy resources. The OECD countries have to date been relatively successful in obtaining pledges against the pursuit of neo-mercantilist policies to meet this need, but the future of this effort remains under serious question. An additional factor relates to what Ernest Preeg calls the "conflict between the economic gains from trade and competing national objectives":

> It reflects the growing economic role of governments in all industrialized countries.... The policy objectives could include regional development, a higher degree of self-sufficiency for particular sectors of the economy—from agriculture to computers to fuels—or environmental standards. To some extent, these objectives are pursued through the use of protective tariffs but they are also

affected by a variety of nontariff barriers from quotas to public financial support to preferential procurement policies.[18]

These issues of domestic legislation affecting international trade are so much a part of contemporary governance that many observers have called for a continuing process of international negotiation to avoid their detrimental concomitants. There is, in short, a need for international cooperation to deal with common problems that arise from interdependence, which is paradoxically impeded by the growth in neo-mercantilism; and the latter is itself a creation of the same processes which have created the interdependence.

A *fourth* major element in the current crisis results from the evolution of relations among the advanced industrialized societies. This system is one in which the economies have become highly integrated with one another, where joint decision-making is required to bring interdependence under control, but where the political systems responsible for joint decision-making remain fragmented. The implied contradiction has been long obscured by a stable tension in which the major industrialized societies have found themselves, as they have been unable to reassert their autonomy to act in a highly interdependent world and also unwilling to develop the institutional mechanisms to control that interdependence, except through *ad hoc* procedures adopted in periods of crisis. The events of the winter of 1973-74 brought that stable tension into graphic relief and in the process also made it clear that the tensions had assumed critical proportions.

The growth in interdependence is unprecedented in several respects. In some areas, like the integration of financial markets, the interdependence is historically unique in terms of its scope and the institutionalization of procedures for intergovernmental decision-making. Its management is also unique insofar as the governments involved have formed a security system, which when coupled with the consequences of a world of nuclear weapons has meant that one instrument of state-craft—the use of force or threat of force—has been closed off as a means of adjusting conflict. At the same time, all other instruments of diplomacy are potentially opened up to the governments as means of adjusting conflicting goals, but these too have proved somewhat ineffective.

An additional problem associated with the growth of interdependence has to do with the open nature of the system of interactions which it characterizes. The highly industrialized non-Communist societies do not form a closed system which is amenable to rational internal organization. The system is itself characterized by conflicting tendencies.

First, it involves one global power, the United States, whose interests both within the system and outside of it diverge *ipso facto* from those of the others.

Second, the growth in system-wide interdependence in financial affairs has been offset by a conflicting trend toward tripolarization in commercial matters.[19] Regional interests in commercial affairs are strikingly divergent. Japan remains the one government or regional power with a clear interest in continual progress toward a multilateral, universal, and liberal trading system. The European governments have an equally clear interest in a regional rather than a global framework. Now constituting the world's largest trading bloc, they require further tripolarization of the international commercial system as a means of fostering eventual political union. At the moment Europe wields great clout in the commercial system, but given its complex internal decision-making structures, it remains a system with great disruptive power—a hydra-headed monster with no mind. The United States interests are somewhat mixed. It probably no longer desires further international and universal trade liberalization, but also would like to see a system in which backsliding is prevented. If the Japanese government wants trade negotiations to progress, and if the European governments want to avoid trade liberalization lest it impede the growth in European unification, the United States desires to negotiate simply to enable the commercial system to stay where it is, with no further progress, but also no retreat into the environment of the 1930s.

Third, there remains the continued fragmentation of political interests across a set of issue-areas, in which different governments have divergent interests from one another, or joint interests with one or more governments in other regions of the system. In security matters, for example, the German-American connection remains basic to German national security and will continue indefinitely to impede the growth of a West European security system. In energy matters, Britain, Canada, and Norway, with potentially large oil or gas exports, have divergent interests from other states. Holland and the United States, which suffered most from oil embargoes in 1973, have the greatest interest in some automatic mechanism for sharing resources in the next crisis; and most consuming countries continue to look toward bilateral relationships with individual producing countries to secure sources of supply. The coexistence of these cross-cutting trends serves both to balance each other and to impede policy coordination in any single issue-area.

The growth in interdependence is a double-edged sword. It is clear that the major problems associated with international interdependence can be solved only by policy coordination or international institutional arrangements insofar as all of these governments have a major interest in preserving the general framework that has provided economic growth and security during the past thirty years. At the same time, each has conflicting interests as well and an unprecedented ability to harm each other where it hurts most: the implementation of domestic economic policies. This results from the unintentional effects of policies carried out by governments within their own domestic sphere when they impede domestic goals being pursued elsewhere. It is this reciprocal effect of domestic policies on one another that makes the control of interdependence both urgent and difficult. It is also the effect which has led Hassner to argue the following:

> Perhaps, then, a state of agitated immobility rather than either revolution or integration is characteristic of the post-cold-war system. . . . The essential characteristic of this state is neither force nor cooperation but the constant influence of societies on one another within the framework of a competition whose goals are less and less tangible, whose means are less and less direct, whose consequences are less and less calculable, precisely because they involve activities rather than strategies and because these activities are important as much because of their effects on what societies *are* as on what they do.[20]

Hassner concludes:

> The real race may be less to increase one's comparative power than to decrease one's comparative vulnerability, to manipulate not only an opponent's weaknesses but one's own, to encourage exported erosion or to control contagious explosions, to modify or maintain not so much territorial borders or even diplomatic alignments as what might be called the balance of will and the balance of expectations.[21]

From the onset of the cold war until the beginning of the 1970s most of the problems associated with the management of this system of interdependence could be resolved as a result of American predominance in defense, commercial, and monetary affairs. While elements of this asymmetry persist, American predominance has been weakened and, at any rate, was never viewed by the partners of the United States as a wholly desirable state of affairs. The rules of the game in the three basic issue-areas began to break down just as the decline of United States predominance reached critical proportions. This has made it especially difficult to reform the system of interactions in such a way that the conflicting and common interests of the states in the industrialized world could be reconciled and accommodated to one another.

Even the persistence of asymmetries does not solve this dilemma, and this is only partially the case because of the loss of will in Washington to provide leadership. It has often been alleged that the renunciation by the United States of the rules it had established in monetary and commercial affairs after World War II was the result of growing lack of interest in those rules. Others have alleged that the partners of the United States were the ones who first turned their minds away from those rules and who wanted to end what General de Gaulle has called the "exorbitant privilege" of the United States in international economic matters. Both points of view ignore certain critical elements in the recent evolution of the industrialized societies. The first group failed to see that the United States was among the last of these governments to have recognized that the old rules of the game no longer worked and has been far less disingenuous than American critics have alleged in arguing for reform and in making constructive proposals. The second group failed to see the degree to which America's exorbitant privileges served by the late 1960s to constrain far more than to benefit the United States. Unable to change its rate of exchange under a system of fixed parities and blocked by Japan and Western Europe from increasing access to their markets, the U.S. government had little choice after August 1971 but to force the others to accede to American demands by threatening them with domestic economic harm. The latter critics also overstate the degree to which a preponderant power has an interest in institutionalizing multilateral mechanisms that benefit it principally. In most instances, multilateral institutions benefit smaller states far more than larger ones. They serve largely as constraints on the use of national power by those who have the most of it. Thus, as Preeg has noted:

The GATT commits the powerful United States not to raise almost any of its tariffs on imports from a country as small and weak as Chad without affording compensatory trade concessions, or face commercial retaliation of comparable magnitude from Chad.[22]

Moreover, in an asymmetrical world in which relationships are highly interdependent, relative power tends to be equalized. Thus part of the current crisis certainly relates to an equalization of power and a concomitant inability of the United States government to influence events as much as its residual power would indicate it can. Several factors are responsible for this, including the increased cost of exercising power in an interdependent world. As the linkages among societies are increased, all, including the great powers, lose control over their environments. Lesser powers have an enhanced freedom to maneuver against them, knowing that the greater powers will not likely use instruments of disproportionate scale to achieve their ends. In the monetary crises after August 1971, the U.S. government confronted a situation where both economically and politically it had to achieve a turn-around in its trade balance. To do this the rest of the world would have had to accept higher levels of American imports at lower relative prices. But the trading partners of the United States did not want to revalue their currencies or to accept decreased surpluses or larger deficits in their own trade with the United States. The American government, while it was tied to the fixed exchange rate standard, could not unilaterally devalue the dollar since it would not be certain that its major trading partners would accept this alternative. In the end the U.S. government acted by threatening its partners with harm and by negotiating from the strength of its position in the security field.

The kind of action taken by the United States during the monetary crisis of 1971 was an exception to accepted and acceptable behavior. The principal power possessed by the American government—that of threatening to inflict harm—

can rarely be utilized, lest American credibility and reliability be severely damaged. And, should the psychological ambiance required for confidence in the United States be weakened, few of the remaining American goals could be realized. Moreover, the movement into a world of flexible exchange rates has served both to minimize the need for the American government to repeat the actions it took in 1971 and also to deprive it of the instruments of leverage that it possessed then. At any rate, not all of the relationships between the United States and its partners in the industrialized world are asymmetrically balanced in America's favor. In trade matters, the growth of the European Community into the largest trading bloc in the world, and one that the U.S. economy depends on as a market for agricultural products and high technology goods as well as for returns on direct investments, has injected a growing equality in transatlantic relations. This has served to deny the United States the ability to achieve its goals vis-à-vis the Europeans, just as the United States has the power of denial with respect to European and Japanese goals.

Interdependence has above all meant the need to foster generally accepted norms or rules or principles of behavior, especially, but not only, in economic matters. Two obstacles, however, persistently arise to prevent or to impede common decision-making and policy coordination. One is economic and the other political.

In economic terms, a major obstacle to international policy coordination has been the emergence of a situation in which the economies of the industrialized world have been in phase with one another. Policy coordination can be most successful in periods when the diverse economies are out of phase, and preferably in periods of rapid growth like that characterized by the two or three years before the winter of 1973-74. It is extremely difficult when the economies are in phase and in recession simultaneously, since none is then in a position to induce growth elsewhere by increasing its imports from the others.

In political terms, elections and electoral campaigns tend to have several adverse effects on policy coordination. They tend most obviously to turn the full attention of governments toward domestic problems and by that fact to a context in which policy coordination, particularly involving domestic sacrifices, is anathema. At times, electoral campaigns turn governments into exponents of internationalism, especially in the European context. Thus in 1972 both France and the Federal Republic of Germany not only became leading advocates of Europeanism in the preparation of electoral campaigns, but also tended to inflate the rhetoric of plans for political unification to a degree that later resulted in a loss of governmental credibility. The rhetoric of the Paris summit in October 1972 and later pronouncements in 1973 with the Community's expansion certainly were inflated beyond any realistic political projections and, by the summer of 1974, opinion polls conducted by the Commission indicated that more realistic policy pronouncements would better serve governments. Electoral politics, in short, also impede policy harmonization, yet do not eliminate the need for it.

Finally, interdependence serves directly as an element in the current crisis insofar as it tends to breed crises. A system of interdependent relations which lacks an overarching structure of political authority or a mechanism for policy coordination is inherently a crisis system at the international level. Just as the growth in interdependence knits societies closer and makes the domestic politics in one society subject to events that occur in the domestic systems of other societies, so too does it tend to spread crises from one portion of the system to the rest of it. A paradox exists here. The governments of the industrialized world have developed a rather effective tradition of joint decision-making in times of crisis, but are generally unable to reconcile their divergent goals in noncrisis situations. Several reasons can be adduced to explain this contradiction. There has so far been a recognition by all governments in times of crisis that if the whole network of interactions is jeopardized, so too would be their individual economic and political security. Fear of the system's collapsing, in short, serves as a motivation to prevent it from happening. Additionally, governments find that their freedom to maneuver is enhanced during crises. Governments in modernized societies have been unable generally to cope with the increasing demands that are placed on them, and, aware of the undermining of their authority, they are also concerned with the costs of making effective decisions when hard choices might further wither the support of their domestic constituents. They have, however, been willing to see crises erupt as a means of shortcutting their decision-making processes, since during such circumstances they can take forceful actions that can be valued by their citizens.

If crises are bred by interdependence, they tend also to result in *ad hoc* decision-making which is oriented more toward the patching up of a system under stress than toward fundamental reform according to universally accepted principles. This has perhaps served to permit the system to evolve in a way which reflects the divergent trends in monetary, trade, or security affairs. But it has also undermined the prevalence of generally accepted universal rules of behavior which are necessary not simply for the sake of equity, but more importantly as a means of preventing the governments from unintentionally harming one another through unilateral actions. Here interdependence carries with it the need for generally accepted principles for orderly collective economic management, but also brings a process of *ad hoc* decision-making which impedes it.

A *final* set of factors in the current crisis has to do with the failure of political leadership to emancipate itself from the outmoded rhetoric and grand designs of the past. If the system of relations with which we are concerned is undergoing change, and if governments have universally recognized this fact, their orientation toward the future has been deeply rooted in past debates, which serve to exacerbate tensions and to avoid a confrontation with the choices which governments realistically have.

All of the major powers in the industrialized world have been guilty of the sins associated with both inflated and outmoded rhetoric. In Europe, the goal of preserving all vestiges of European union as the basis for creating a common identity and eventually a common political system has resulted in a failure to accept divergent trends, either toward continued integration across the Atlantic or to the common interests that incorporate Japan as well. Especially with regard to Japan, there is the prevailing attitude that it is a Pacific power and an American, but certainly not a European, "problem." Discrimination against Japanese exports or direct investments has served to fragment the industrialized world in ways that impede recognition of the need to incorporate Japan into a system of common rules that all accept. With regard to the United States, there has been a persistent European fantasy that the use of the term "Atlantic world" by American statesmen implies an inevitable American hegemony. The difficulties encountered by the Europeans in responding responsibly to Henry Kissinger's call for a new Atlantic Charter represented European politics at its silliest. An invitation to the Europeans to suggest rules of common good behavior was understood, especially but not only in France, as a device to manipulate the Europeans to the American advantage and to prevent the further emergence of a European identity.

American policy has been no less sinful in this regard. The use of the term "Atlantic Charter" in the Kissinger Year of Europe speech was both an unnecessary provocation and a misnomer, stemming from the rhetoric of the past. The rules and principles which Kissinger was attempting to have the industrialized world jointly accept were by no means limited to the U.S.-West European connection. They were oriented to Canada, Japan, and the other OECD members as well. Moreover the Nixon-Kissinger diplomacy, with its intimations of a five-power balance, was another example of rhetoric that did not match the fundamental problems. As critics have pointed out, balance-of-power diplomacy is hardly a key to global stability in the latter part of the twentieth century. There remain but two, not five, major military powers and three, not five, major ecomonic regions that have interacted and will continue to interact with one another. And these are not the same powers.[23]

Any attempt to deal with the current crisis ought to focus on a diagnosis of reality rather than a reformulation of old myths. But here too there are dilemmas. The tendency to rely on the rhetoric of the past has, after all, reflected a dual problem. On the one hand, it has reflected the relative absence of an understanding of the evolution of the industrialized world, of the sources of disturbances within and among industrialized societies, and, therefore, of the means of dealing with them. The theoretical gap which apparently exists with respect to these problems is not one which political will can overcome. It is, however, something that can be jointly recognized and acknowledged. On the other hand, the rhetoric of the past has disguised the loss of direction in governments in the industrialized world. Neither in Japan nor Europe nor America do governments find it easy to orient themselves toward the future or to determine the sorts of societies that they wish to mold. The lack of a coherent set of priorities either within or among governments certainly impedes international negotiation, especially when all seem to fear any changes from an increasingly precarious status quo. It also impedes the enunciation of new grand designs and the sorts of common principles that interdependent societies seem to require.

The Future of the Industrialized World

It would be pretentious to attempt to predict how the current crisis will evolve or be resolved. If the analysis argued in this essay is substantially valid, it would appear that the current set of tensions in the industrialized world reflects long-term trends, which are both inescapable and intractable. This is especially the case if the whole spectrum of security issues, which were not discussed in this essay, are brought into the analysis. At the same time, one must recognize that the quadrupling of oil prices, joined together with endemic inflation and the more immediate need to handle unemployment, lower productivity, and the recycling of oil revenues, requires immediate and joint governmental action. The immediacy of these problems poses its own dilemmas. It is by no means clear that any short-term action can be taken without its precluding certain desirable long-term arrangements. This is readily seen, for example, in the way in which recycling facilities are established. A set of arrangements that involve only a few industrialized societies, rather than all of them, would severely narrow future European options for political unification. It is important, however, that the governments of the industrialized world do take holding actions with respect to their immediate problems until such a time when other issues begin to sort themselves out. These efforts are more likely to be successful if governments begin to assume the habit of accepting a set of rules for short-term actions.

(1) It is already clear that pragmatism has begun to predominate over ideology and inflated rhetoric in dealing with problems, and that this ought to be the case. The greatest evidence for this has been seen in the effective change in the French government's policy toward cooperation among oil-consuming countries. A pragmatic orientation toward policy and decision-making would enable governments to deal in the respective arenas as required. Some of these might well involve the entire industrialized world, where some "trilateral" formula might be desirable. Others could well pertain to the relatively unique problems of Western Europe or to North America or Japan. Pragmatism on the part of all would, moreover, probably result in the recognition that the achievement of narrow regional goals might well be enhanced in a more general decision-making framework. This is as true

for Japan as it is for Western Europe. One of the failings of the West Europeans in recent years has been the myth that the development of a European identity and a basis of a common European decision-making system require a separation from —indeed a confrontation with—the rest of the industrialized world. Intra-European cooperation and a European identity is, however, obstructed by confrontation politics, given the various cross-cutting ties of the European governments with the United States. Dealing with the rest of the world in a common and general framework can afford the West Europeans the opportunity to lobby together when necessary in a way that would encourage the growth of the European connection and also permit the cross-cutting ties across the Atlantic to take their own course. General cooperation, in short, does not inhibit divergent trends toward tripolarization and indeed may foster them.

(2) In dealing with one another, the governments of the industrialized world ought to attempt systematically to develop a set of "negative" principles orientated toward the goal of at least limiting economic damage in the absence of an ability to achieve agreement on positive rules of behavior. Any set of "thou shalt not" clauses ought to include recognition that many of the problems of industrialized society involve the mutual ability of governments to harm one another, either intentionally or unintentionally.

One set of damage limitation agreements should apply to problems associated with balance of payments adjustments. The massive deficits of the industrialized societies, and the concentration of these deficits in a small number of countries, naturally create incentives for the limitation of imports as well as for aggressive programs of export expansion. Agreements ought to become more widespread, such as those adopted in the OECD ministerial meeting in 1974, which commit governments not to limit imports as a way of making adjustments to the oil crisis. Such agreements are especially important because this kind of practice enhances the dangers of the current world recession without simultaneously easing the problems associated with the distribution of deficits.

Another set of damage limitation agreements should apply to problems associated with export controls. As Bergsten has argued, a regime of export controls is now urgent and ought to orient itself to the following goals:

1. To deter producing countries from erecting export controls except in clearly defined and justified circumstances.
2. To reinforce that deterrent by providing a basis for concerted response by the world trading community.
3. To limit the scope and duration of those controls which are actually applied.
4. To provide an international framework into which disputes triggered by export controls can be channeled when they are actually applied, to reduce the likelihood of unilateral reactions and emulation/retaliation cycles.[24]

In a world of "natural" and manipulated shortages in an array of commodities, such rules would clearly enhance the ability of governments to limit economic damage to others, even when actions are taken for purposes of domestic economic security.

(3) A special set of "thou shalt not" clauses should be focused on abuses or potential abuses of interactions among the industrialized societies. This is particularly the case within recent years of the attempts of governments to tie together negotiations in different issue-areas. In the modern world all issues are potentially or actually interrelated with the others. A government attempting to achieve its goals in one issue-area can thus always attempt to blackmail others by tying together various different issue-areas. Such manipulation can result in total inaction, as it did in Europe in the winter of 1973-74 when all governments used a unit veto against the others in

their attempts to achieve a year-end package compromise. If it is desirable to prevent the manipulation of issue-areas by blackmail, it is not desirable to prevent the linkage that exists among them from being worked out. Thus the general admonition against blackmail through linkage should not result in the establishment of different mechanisms of policy coordination in each separate issue-area. To isolate these would impede satisfactory reconciliation of differences.

(4) Of equal importance is the recognition that the persistence of the problems outlined above will require that a permanent framework for continual negotiations be created in what Harald Malmgren has called "International Peacekeeping in Phase II." The continual legislation in all nations of new regulations for domestic economic and political management carries with it a set of international implications since these domestic regulations are a concern to other societies as well. The establishment of international mechanisms of surveillance, or simply of information-sharing, seems necessary in an era of continuous negotiation and renegotiation. This may require the industrialized governments to commit themselves to the habit of international consultation in ways that they now do not. But information-sharing is necessary not only for dealing with issues of economic peacekeeping, but also for the resolution of inevitable crises.

It should be obvious that these suggestions for statecraft in a crisis-ridden interdependent world do not preclude any European option over the long run. They do, however, reveal that it is extremely difficult at this juncture to conclude that the governments of the Nine can act by themselves on major issues. They do have the ability to lobby together and to make proposals which will require acceptance by the United States, the oil-exporting countries, or other outside parties, if they are to be feasible. But there appears to be no major issue of immediate concern to the Europeans in which the European region is an appropriate and autonomous unit. This need not at all be the case over the long run. Certainly by the end of the twentieth century it is conceivable that energy resources will be available that will permit Europe to develop economically without the danger of economic blackmail from the outside world. Moreover, in security, monetary, or commercial matters it is also possible that a system will emerge in which an autonomous European region would make sense. For the moment, however, short-term actions must be taken that can deal adequately with immediate problems and, at the same time, not preclude an eventual European option.

It is still unclear as to whether any of the feasible options available to the governments of the industrialized world will be capable of meeting the current crisis. While the governments have proved themselves capable of handling crises in the past and have already taken measures in both the domestic and international realms to deal with this one, two fundamental problems remain. On the one hand, there is the continued lack of political leadership and willingness for self-sacrifice that seem requisite to handling the crisis. On the other hand, there is a need for sensitivity which would recognize that the actions or inactions of some governments, both domestically and externally, are of interest to a wide spectrum of foreign governments, just as the actions of others are of interest to them. There is also the need for awareness that major actions will have to await a time when the disruption of relations associated with the current crisis have settled down. Whether such sensitivity and awareness can be developed in the bureaucratic systems which deal with governance in the contemporary world is certainly an open question. Without their development, however, no effort to bring the current crisis under manageable limits will work.

NOTES

[1] See, for example, Walter Laqueur, "The Idea of Europe Runs Out of Gas," *The New York Times Magazine*, January 20, 1974, pp. 12 ff.

[2] This theme is stressed in a wide variety of articles and books. See, for example, the essays in Robert E. Osgood and others, *Retreat From Empire? The First Nixon Administration* (Baltimore, 1973); and Harold van Buren Cleveland, "How the Dollar Standard Died," *Foreign Policy* 13 (Winter 1971-72): 41-51.

[3] See Wilbur Monroe, *Japan: Financial Markets and the World Economy* (New York, 1973), pp. 3-17, 167-83.

[4] This complaint is forcefully made in François Perroux, Jean Denizet, and Henri Bourguinnat, *Inflation, Dollar, Eurodollar* (Paris, 1971).

[5] Yet the causes of global inflation remain the subject of a serious theoretical debate. Europeans have a tendency to see its basic origins in the breakdown of the international monetary system. Others focus on both real and artificial shortages in raw materials, which have resulted in the manipulation of supplies. Still others argue that intransigent labor demands in the absence of collective social compacts between labor and government are its source. See the summaries of the debates in *Problèmes Economiques*, No. 1373, May 22, 1974, and No. 1388, September 18, 1974.

[6] See C. Fred Bergsten, "The Threat from the Third World," *Foreign Policy* 11 (Summer 1973): 102-124; and "The Response to the Third World," *Foreign Policy* 17 (Winter 1974-75): 3-34.

[7] This point is made forcefully by William Diebold, Jr., "U.S. Trade Policy: The New Political Dimensions," *Foreign Affairs* 52, No. 3 (April 1974): 472-96; and by C. Fred Bergsten, *Completing the GATT: Toward New International Rules to Govern Export Controls* (Washington, D.C., 1974).

[8] Pierre Hassner, "The New Europe: From Cold War to Hot Peace," *International Journal* 27 (Winter 1971-72): 8.

[9] Ibid.

[10] See Marion J. Levy, Jr., *Modernization: Latecomers and Survivors* (New York, 1972).

[11] This issue is explored in Philippe C. Schmitter, "Still the Cen-

tury of Corporatism?" *The Review of Politics* 36, No. 1 (January 1974): 85-131.

[12] Theodore Geiger, *The Fortunes of the West: The Future of the Atlantic Nations* (Bloomington, Ind., 1973), pp. 13-57.

[13] Richard N. Cooper, "Economic Interdependence and Foreign Policy in the Seventies," *World Politics* 24 (January 1972): 164.

[14] Whether one emphasizes the complementarity or similarity of governmental goals is a question of level of analysis. At the extreme, goals which are too divergent are likely to lead to international conflict rather than to cooperation. And cooperation also requires that, at some level, there is a coincidence in governmental policies. My emphasis here is that currently the industrialized societies are pursuing similar goals, some of which require joint efforts for their achievement and others of which appear to be within the reach of some at the expense of others.

[15] This argument is elaborated in Robert Gilpin, "The Politics of Transnational Economic Relations," in Robert O. Keohane and Joseph S. Nye, Jr., eds., *Transnational Relations and World Politics* (Cambridge, Mass., 1972), pp. 48-69.

[16] See Benjamin J. Cohen, "The Revolution in Atlantic Economic Relations: A Bargain Comes Unstuck," in Wolfram Hanrieder, ed., *The United States and Western Europe* (Cambridge, Mass., 1974), pp. 106-133.

[17] This discussion is based on analyses found in Harald Malmgren, *International Economic Peacekeeping in Phase II* (rev. ed., New York, 1972), Chapters 1 and 2; Ernest H. Preeg, *Economic Blocs and U.S. Foreign Policy* (Washington, D.C., 1974), Chapter 10; and, especially, Hans O. Schmitt, "The International Monetary System: Three Options for Reform," *International Affairs* (London) 50 (April 1974): 193-210.

[18] Preeg, *Economic Blocs and U.S. Foreign Policy*, p. 152.

[19] Ibid., pp. 55-73.

[20] Hassner, "The New Europe: From Cold War to Hot Peace," pp. 12-13.

[21] Ibid., p. 13.

[22] Preeg, *Economic Blocs and U.S. Foreign Policy*, p. 139.

[23] See especially, Zbigniew Brzezinski, "The Balance of Power Delusion," *Foreign Policy* 7 (Summer 1972): 54-59; and Stanley Hoffmann, "Will the Balance Balance At Home?" ibid., pp. 60-87.

[24] Bergsten, *Completing the GATT*, p. 23.

Chapter 8
AMERICA FACES WESTERN EUROPE
IN THE 1980s:
ATLANTICISM PRESERVED,
DISENGAGEMENT, OR DEVOLUTION?

Andrew J. Pierre

Central to the transatlantic tensions existing at the three-quarter mark of this century is the lack of a clear vision—or organizing concept—of what should be the overarching political relationship between the United States and Western Europe from now until the year 2000. (Lest the reader be distracted by expectations of esoteric futurology, I would remind him that the remaining time until the end of the century is equal to that since the beginning of the Korean war, when most of the present Atlantic framework was put into place.) The first half of the 1970s has been marked by ungainly disputes among the Atlantic countries which have weakened the fiber of the present Atlantic relationship and opened its continuation to serious question. In the economic realm, the unilateral beggar-thy-neighbor initiatives undertaken by John Connally in 1971 upset the widely accepted assumption that major adjustments in the international monetary and trade system were to be undertaken only by nations acting in concert through a process of consultations. In the security realm, fear of unilateral withdrawal of U.S. troops from Europe and squabbles about "burden-sharing" have poisoned the atmosphere of the NATO alliance, while bilateral negotiations between Washington and Moscow have threatened to undermine it. And in the political realm the attempt to codify relations and to formulate rules of behavior in the much vaunted "Year of Europe" exercise served only to irritate relations, create tensions, and exacerbate differences of interests and priorities.

The energy crisis, in all its dimensions, which engulfed the Atlantic nations following the Yom Kippur War has had a critical impact upon the Atlantic relationship. The greater vulnerability of Western Europe, as contrasted with the United States, has been underscored and some see in this a reassertion of American "hegemony." The drain in the balance of payments and the transfer of wealth to the oil-producing countries increased already high rates of inflation and helped bring about recession. A deepening economic slump threatens social and political stability in a number of European states. Progress toward European unity through the European Economic Community suffered a severe setback and the first priority of statesmen came to be the prevention of the collapse of the Common Market. Moreover, the "new" issues on the international agenda—food, raw materials, environment, population, etc.—have made global approaches and solutions more necessary, thereby seeming to diminish the relative importance of not only the Atlantic relationship but of all bilateral and regional relationships.

Relations with Europe will, however, remain a central component of American foreign policy. Many of the global problems before us cannot be successfully handled without close cooperation among the advanced, industrialized countries. This is one clear lesson of the oil crisis. Moreover, the issues of peace and war, which will concern the United States and the Soviet Union as long as both have nuclear arsenals trained on each other, cannot be separated from the continuing political and military confrontation in Central Europe.

To be prescriptive about a desirable European-American relationship for the 1980s, rather than descriptive of the present and past, is a peculiarly difficult task because of the transformations in international politics which are under way in the mid-1970s. Europe is increasingly fragmented, and uncertainty pervades the domestic politics of many states. Nevertheless, if we are not to repeat the errors of the past, we must learn from them and we must think creatively about the long-term future. The underlying reasons for the dismal failure of the Year of Europe merit deeper examination than they have received thus far. We know that the lack of consultation prior to Henry Kissinger's initiatory speech led to much confusion and misunderstanding. We know that the unexpected Middle East war and the Arab oil embargo created divergencies between Europe and America. We suspect that the Year of Europe, in promising a round of summit diplomacy, was not unrelated to the Year of Watergate. But to this day Washington has failed to understand the primary reasons for the miscarriage of the initiative: first, *the lack of a clear vision of how we would prefer to see Europe evolve*; second, *the inability to imagine and work towards an overall, long-term, stable relationship between the societies on the two sides of the Atlantic.*

The question of what is to become of "Europe," whether it is to advance toward further integration, is, of course, a matter for Europeans to decide and act upon. But Americans should not underestimate their own very considerable influence on the content and character of the decisions involved. If European statesmen believe that the United States supports the further construction of Europe, and that we are willing to stand behind this support in action as well as in rhetoric, sometimes foregoing direct economic advantages for the indirect political benefit, an enormous psychological and political boost will have been given to the European cause. If, on the other hand, Europeans come to believe that the United States basically resists the emergence of a European political identity, many will be reluctant to move in this direction with any alacrity or enthusiasm. This will be the case for as long as Western Europe remains fundamentally dependent on its North American ally for its security.

Until recently—for most of the years since the Marshall Plan and the creation of the European Economic Community —there was little open questioning that a central component of United States foreign policy was to encourage European unity. A viable and strong Western Europe was seen as essential to the well-being of the European peoples as well as necessary to help the West balance the increasing power of the Soviet Union. Any economic disadvantages to the United States stemming from European unity were seen as secondary to the political benefits which it would bring. In recent years, however, perceptions have changed and there have been growing doubts about whether Washington still supports European unity. The economic recovery of the continent led to new competition in trade. With détente and the opportunities it presented for bilateral Soviet-American negotiations ranging from arms control to trade, it was feared that the freedom and scope of American action could be susceptible to limitation through concerted European action.

Accordingly, the Year of Europe initiative came under a cloud of suspicion. Some Europeans saw it as an attempt to make evident, and perhaps take advantage of, the present lack of European unity. Many took umbrage at Kissinger's assertion of Europe's regional interests and role in contrast with America's global responsibilities. The Secretary of State was in large measure accurate, but the statement was nevertheless seen as an intentional attempt to underscore Europe's weakness. When the Europeans responded with an unparalleled declaration of European identity, affirming the goal of a united Europe, Washington's attitude was less than enthusiastic. Kissinger chose to accentuate the negative, complaining in his speech before the Pilgrim's Society in London that some Europeans had come to believe that their very identity should be measured by its distance from the United States.

This suggests a fearful attitude toward European unity, one with little sympathy for European aspirations as well as an erroneous and incomplete understanding of European intentions. The same judgment can be made concerning the complaint that America should be fully consulted before the EEC makes its decisions. Having long regretted that Europe was incapable of taking a common approach in foreign policy, when it did more or less achieve this in the Middle East in November 1973, Washington was mildly horrified and had difficulty in acknowledging that Europe's legitimate interests may not at all times and in all ways converge with its own.

Thus there is no clear notion, either in the perceptions of Europeans or in the minds of Americans, of how the United States would like to see Europe evolve. Past support for unity has been thrown into question, and the remaining lip-service support, as in Nixon's State of the World messages, is belied by some actions and not fully believed. In my own view, the United States should continue to support European unity and will do so despite momentary lapses. But until this is loudly proclaimed and widely accepted, there will be little coherence in transatlantic relations.

The corollary question, and the principal subject of this essay, is the form and content of the overarching political relationship between Europe and America. The old Atlantic concept of past decades is shopworn and seems increasingly irrelevant to the new political and economic conditions. There is a growing disparity between the NATO of the past and the European Economic Community of the future. A broad consensus exists today that we are in a new phase of the postwar era, one in which the direct military threat to Western Europe has greatly diminished. Economic and resource-related issues appear as those most in need of early attention, and Western governments are highly susceptible to transnational forces and domestic pressures. The corrosive impact on NATO is taken as self-evident; the "unraveling" or "disarray" of the alliance has been announced for over a decade.

What remains altogether unclear, however, is the future structure of the political-security relationship. If NATO is to disappear, what, if anything, is to replace it? If the alliance is to continue, in what ways should it be altered so as to reflect changed conditions? And what should be the proper role for the nascent political Europe in the Atlantic relationship? Much of the failure of the Year of Europe exercise stemmed from the belief that it was an attempt to tie the future to the patterns of the past; it sought more to restore the "stable structure" of the 1950s than creatively to seek a concept applicable to the 1980s. The suspicions that the United States sought to restore its past "hegemony," or wished to gain greater freedom of movement so as to give priority to superpower relations by limiting European options, may not have been justified. But neither was there much indication that the United States was prepared to adapt to a changing balance of power and influence *within* the alliance.

The need, therefore, is for the articulation of an American vision of what it is that we seek for the 1980s and beyond. In this essay we shall examine three alternative approaches to European-American relations. We shall concentrate on the political and security dimensions as they are still likely to set the framework for the future relationship. Economic questions are more diffuse and in many ways more global in content; they are also discussed elsewhere in this volume. Our three visions—Atlanticism Preserved, American Disengagement, and Devolution of the U.S. Role and Power—are not the only possible options. No doubt Herman Kahn could multiply them tenfold. They do represent, nevertheless, the most clear-cut alternatives as I see them, and are useful for purposes of analysis. Moreover, they illustrate through their diversity and distinctiveness that the range of American choice is wider than is usually assumed.

Atlanticism Preserved

The United States could seek the continuation of Atlantic institutions in their present form, with only relatively minor modifications being made as they become necessary. This would involve little change in the existing structure of NATO. The preponderant American role in NATO would be retained; for example, the position of Supreme Allied Commander (SACEUR) would remain in U.S. hands. In general, the emphasis would be on the shoring up of the status quo.

The preservation of Atlanticism would presume the continued dependence, on a substantial scale, of the European countries on American political and military leadership. The views of Washington would be dominant in the management of East-West détente and the orchestration of policy toward the Soviet Union. This would apply to a wide spectrum of issues on the agenda of détente, from arms control in Central Europe to economic and technological interchange with the East. In some areas, such as the limitation of strategic armaments, American relations with the Soviet Union would remain on a separate bilateral track.

Although individual European countries would continue to have distinct national policies on most of these subjects, they would be urged to discuss them with Washington on a bilateral basis before in-depth consultations took place within Europe. The United States would consequently give only token support to West European endeavors to reach a common point of view, much less an agreed policy. In its public statements the United States might welcome the cooperative exchanges of ideas within the Eurogroup or the attempt to reach a common foreign policy through the Davignon Committee of the European Economic Community, but in private, American diplomats would maintain their present skeptical and disparaging attitude toward these European institutional innovations. Support for the emergence of a European political identity would, therefore, remain lukewarm.

In such circumstances there are not likely to be any new initiatives with respect to American nuclear sharing policy. Any arrangements for the possible coordination of the British and French nuclear forces, or some type of collaborative research and development effort between the two countries, would come under the most careful scrutiny in Washington to see if it contravened the terms of existing Anglo-American nuclear accords. Although the United States may not actively resist such efforts, it would be unlikely to increase European independence by new offers of nuclear assistance to France, or to an Anglo-French arrangement, for the modernization of the European strategic forces. This would make the acquisition of highly sophisticated technology, such as MIRVs, too costly or difficult for the Europeans to be worth the effort, thereby maintaining and, over a period of time, worsening the technological gap in armaments within the alliance. A similar policy might apply to tactical nuclear weapons in Europe, thus discouraging European efforts to develop a nuclear escalatory ladder of their own for the defense of the continent. Given such a perspective, Washington would not be inclined to expand SALT by bringing the two European nuclear powers into the negotiations.

American forces in Europe, especially in West Germany, would continue to be at the heart of the military balance. Some technical adjustments might be made, such as the rationalization of support elements, thereby freeing manpower and resources for combat units. The Seventh Army might also be redeployed northward in order to be better positioned for the most likely invasion route. But a *major* reduction of the level of U.S. forces would not occur; nor would there be a revision of NATO's flexible response strategy. American Presidents would put great efforts into persuading the Congress and public of the continued necessity for something like the present level of 300,000 U.S. troops in Europe. It would be accepted that the size of the American contingent, and the ability of NATO to match the Warsaw Pact, were of as great importance for European security as the fundamental political commitment which might be credible with far fewer forces.

The continuation of NATO's present military structure would diminish the chances of France's return into the fold. But this would be judged preferable to the alternative of a European defense community which was, or could become, French-centered. The Pentagon and American arms manufacturers would continue efforts to persuade European ministries of defense to buy armaments "made in the U.S.A." There would be no inclination to forego lucrative contracts, much helpful to the U.S. balance of payments, for the purpose of encouraging European weapons cooperation.

The preservation of Atlanticism would be the most comfortable policy for many persons in the United States as well as in Europe. The above policies may be somewhat more rigid in description than is likely in actual practice under future Atlanticism, but being well-known policies they would be the easiest to follow. Atlanticism is by far the preferred policy of Department of State and Pentagon officials, who would otherwise be engaged in an awkward process of adjustment to a growing—and therefore more demanding—European identity. To suggest that Atlanticism has lost its adherents, as one often reads in academic literature, is therefore quite misleading. For many Americans, especially those whose intellectual formation occurred in the 1940s and 1950s, Atlanticism is a familiar and therefore "safe" concept. To move away from it would be psychologically difficult. There is no doubt that the alternative of a more cohesive and forceful political Europe, underpinned with some type of European defense community, would present complex and difficult problems for the

United States. Similarly, the maintenance of the status quo is
the preferred policy of many Europeans. Sizable numbers of
politicians and officials fear that movement toward a European defense community would stimulate the withdrawal of
all U.S. conventional forces; they are also concerned that it
could lead to a "decoupling" of the U.S. strategic deterrent
from the defense of Western Europe. Atlanticism is also seen
as the best insurance against the massive power of the Soviet
Union and the risk of the collapse of détente. Increasing
numbers of Europeans, especially the younger generation, are
drawn to the European concept and see the need for its expansion from the economic sphere into the political realm.
They wish to maintain the American connection but do not
feel that it must necessarily take its present form. Others,
however, are more satisfied with the status quo and give
priority to maintaining roughly the present level of U.S.
forces, including the whole panoply of the U.S. military presence.

The principal difficulty with the preservation of Atlanticism
is that its structure fails to deal with fundamental—and increasing—instabilities in the European-American relationship.
For the short run, drifting along with the present framework
may be the easiest and perhaps most likely course, but it fails
to provide a solution to the complex problems on the European-American agenda. Indeed, the longer we permit the
drift to continue, and neglect to come to grips with the problems surrounding us, the more difficult will be the solutions
—and the more traumatic the process of reaching them.

Most of the sources of instability which would plague an
attempt to maintain status quo Atlanticism in the 1980s are
not novel, but in many cases the passage of time is likely to
aggravate them. The nature and characteristics of the American security commitment would be open to constant questioning and debate. Can our nerves afford still another decade
of uncertainty about precipitate unilateral force reductions

mandated by an ever-changing Congress? Yet this is what is likely to occur if the U.S. executive branch attempts to cling to present levels of troops without some timetable for orderly reductions. A subtler, but even more significant, element of instability in the security equation would be concern about the credibility of the U.S. nuclear guarantee under conditions of parity as the SALT process goes on. Current changes in American strategic doctrine, in emphasizing limited and controlled nuclear response, may come to be seen as downgrading the automatic response, thereby weakening deterrence in Europe. Related to concern about the strategic "decoupling" of the European security from America would be tactical "decoupling" through the placement of so-called mini-nukes in Europe designed to keep a nuclear war from escalating by limiting it to the continent. The broadening and deepening of Soviet-American bilateral relations would strengthen European anxieties regarding a "condominium" world. Even if this can be avoided through closer consultations than have existed thus far, the United States is bound to play a world role which will not be matched by Western Europe in the next decades. Differences of interests and priorities are therefore bound to surface with respect to political change in the Middle East, Far East, and elsewhere. In the economic area, many differences have already become manifestly evident in the past years. The danger of attempting to preserve the Atlantic partnership in its present form is that it will too readily tempt statesmen to create bargaining linkages between economic and security issues, which will complicate and risk worsening already delicate and complex relationships.

Finally, the process of American adjustment to a changing and slowly uniting Europe in the economic and political realms would create instabilities if a simultaneous attempt is made to preserve Atlanticism in the security relationship. The gradual emergence of Europe's political identity will inevitably create a psychological sense of community within Europe and separateness from the United States. European dignity will thus require a greater sense of independence than the old Atlanticism would allow.

American Disengagement

With the diminution, some would say disappearance, of the Soviet threat to Europe and the postwar recovery of Western Europe to a level of economic prosperity approximately equal to that of the United States, the belief that the United States should disengage itself from its outdated "cold war" role in Europe has gained considerable currency. This view is reinforced by the widely felt need to give greater attention to American domestic problems and by the assumption of many younger Americans that the postwar containment role is in any case "hegemonic" and in economic terms "imperialistic."

In thinking about disengagement, it is important to distinguish among the military, economic, and political dimensions of America's present engagement. The historical, cultural, and psychological bonds that cross the Atlantic, based on shared experience and values, are so deep and pervasive that *political* disengagement does not seem plausible. Almost equally remote is the possibility of *economic* disengagement, given the pattern of investment, trade, and monetary interaction in an increasingly interdependent system encompassing the advanced, non-Communist, industrial nations. Thus the *military* dimension is the only one in which American disengagement is really conceivable.

What, in practice, would American military disengagement from Europe consist of? The total withdrawal of U.S. air and ground forces from Western Europe would be the first, and most important, measure. This might then be followed by the withdrawal of the Sixth Fleet from the Mediterranean, an action which could have as grave consequences for the Middle East as for Europe. The final step would be the folding of the

American nuclear umbrella which presently covers the continent. The latter could be accomplished as simply as by a presidential statement. One can conceive that U.S. forces stationed in Europe might be withdrawn but that the United States would continue the nuclear guarantee. It is doubtful that this would be effective, however, for some level of U.S. forces must remain in Western Europe to perform a hostage function if the nuclear umbrella is to retain any of its remaining credibility for either the Soviets or the West Europeans.

Disengagement would only be an acceptable policy, in my judgment, under one of two circumstances. The first would be the evaporation of any political and security danger to Western Europe from the Soviet Union. This would have to include not only the disappearance of a military threat, but also the presently more germane risk of the gradual political manipulation of governments and societies which individually are no match for the U.S.S.R. The second circumstance would be the creation in Western Europe of a defense entity capable of providing for the security requirements of the member states. Such a defense community would, in effect, have to provide a sufficient military balance to the Soviet Union and the Warsaw Pact to sustain political confidence. It would, therefore, require its own instruments of nuclear deterrence which, although they need not be fully equivalent to those of the United States or the Soviet Union, would have to be on the scale of a superpower if they are to be credible. This would also require a high degree of political integration since some individual—a President of Europe—would have to be authorized to make a nuclear decision on behalf of all of Europe at a moment of crisis. Neither of these two circumstances which would permit American disengagement is now within the horizon or likely to occur in the coming decade.

One must therefore consider the consequences of premature disengagement. One possibility would be the rapid and forced coalescence of Western Europe after the American rug was pulled out from underneath. A defense organization with a nuclear component and with no links to the United States could be created outside of NATO, which would then collapse. This could bring to power a conservative, militaristic leadership—a European junta if you will—which would be essentially antithetical to the United States. Another possible, and more probable, consequence of premature American disengagement would be the subjection of Western Europe to subtle but not insignificant political blackmail. Over a period of time this could lead to its neutralization. Clearly neither of these two contingencies would be in the American interest. The first would be undesirable, the second would be unacceptable.

Devolution of U.S. Role and Power

The most attractive alternative for the future European-American relationship would, therefore, be an orderly devolution of the preponderant American role existing since the close of World War II, a devolution designed so as to bring about a redistribution of present roles and responsibilities. In contrast to the second alternative of disengagement, there would not be a total withdrawal of the American military presence in Western Europe. The emphasis on orderliness would, moreover, preclude the use of "shock" tactics which could have serious, undesirable political repercussions.

Devolution would involve a process which would take place over a number of years, perhaps as long as a decade. But rather than progressing haphazardly, almost as a consequence of drift, it should be initiated as a matter of political will and be given conscious direction. The aim would be the maintenance of the American engagement in Europe, within the Atlantic alliance, but at a lower level. For their part, the Europeans would accept a greater role for themselves in the making of decisions involving the defense of Western Europe and in their implementation. The United States would give political support and encouragement to movement toward greater European autonomy within the Atlantic alliance. The endpoint would be the creation of some type of European defense community which would give substance to a "European identity."

Devolution would obviously involve a fundamental reorganization of the present structure of NATO. A new European defense grouping could take several different forms, each of which has advantages and disadvantages which would have to be carefully weighed. The easiest course might be to develop the present Eurogroup more fully; but this might not give an adequate sense of a break from the American-dominated past, and would probably prove to be unacceptable to France, which has been absent from the Eurogroup since its founding. Another possibility would be to use the Western European Union as a base, an idea favored by Michel Jobert when French Foreign Minister. One of the problems with the WEU, however, is that when the organization was founded in 1954 it had a discriminatory aspect with regard to West Germany, requiring its permanent renunciation of atomic, biological, or chemical weapons. Although Bonn has never indicated interest in these so-called ABC weapons, it can be excused for not wanting to build a European organization for the 1980s on such a reminder. A third alternative would be to build up a defense component of the European Economic Community. A start could be made with the extension of the generally successful Davignon Committee process for foreign policy consultations to problems of security, perhaps through a new committee specifically focusing on defense. Given the still fragile nature of the EEC, however, one should hesitate before adding the immense burden of defense. The best solution for the long run might, therefore, be a new European Defense Commission, closely associated with but still separate from the EEC, and still within an overarching Atlantic framework linking it to the United States.

The question of the functional ways in which Europe might

organize itself for defense is an exceedingly complex one, consisting of a host of seemingly technical problems which are actually embedded in a minefield of politics. There is no doubt that a great deal could be accomplished through the standardization of conventional weapons, collaborative research and development, joint procurement, etc. In the area of defense planning, the national military establishments could have in-depth consultations in order to coordinate their deployments and mobilization plans, have joint training exercises, seek similar reserve policies, and develop common logistic systems.

The nuclear area is the thorniest. For the reasons referred to earlier, an integrated full-scale European nuclear deterrent is simply not in the cards during the 1980s. But what remains feasible is the coordination of the British and French strategic forces underpinned by a European Nuclear Committee. Such a committee, which would include the non-nuclear states along with Britain and France, would help formulate political guidelines for the use of the forces, be involved in contingency strategic planning, and assist financially and otherwise in the development of future generations of nuclear systems. Apart from the initial question of whether, or when, London and Paris might agree to such coordination, the usual objection involves the secondary role of Germany and assumes the disapproval of Bonn. It may be wrong to assume such objections in the future, however, now that *Ostpolitik* has about run its course and as the need to build up the European pillar of the Atlantic system becomes more evident. The time for an Anglo-French force has not yet come, and to raise nuclear politics in Europe prematurely could create tensions now better avoided. The obstacles, however, are often overstated and it is difficult to see how the nuclear question can fail to come to the forefront at some stage as Europe proceeds toward unity.

What might the United States do to enhance European defense cooperation as part of a policy of devolution? The single most important action would be a clearly avowed policy of political support and encouragement for intra-West European defense consultations and coordination of defense policies. The importance of such public support cannot be underestimated. It is the fear of many Europeans that European defense cooperation would be negatively perceived in Washington—and therefore lead to a U.S. loss of interest in European security and a corollary rapid withdrawal of forces from the continent—that restrains and discourages some of their own movement toward defense cooperation. And given the tenor of official American statements about Europe in recent years, and our present ambivalence about the desirability of a united Europe, such European anxieties are quite justified. A clear American indication of our willingness to restructure the European-American relationship and of our encouragement for the strengthening of the European identity, including its defense dimension, would give the many Europeans who are inclined to follow this road, but remain cautious, a "green light." A meaningful nod from America at an appropriate moment when economic and energy issues are quiescent might well catalyze a great European debate on the subject. Concrete proposals must, however, be left to European initiative.

Beyond this, there are some specific actions by which the United States could demonstrate its support of a new European role. Many NATO commands could be turned over to European officers and the first European SACEUR could be appointed. Past European objections to this would disappear as the American involvement in Europe became stabilized for the long run through the process of devolution. As American troops are gradually reduced, down to perhaps two divisions or to 100,000 soldiers, the Congress might well agree to a long-term compact maintaining such a level indefinitely as a recognition of the new Atlantic relationship. The United States could greatly assist the development of joint European armaments production and procurement of conventional weapons by imposing upon itself some restraint and self-limitation in the selling of U.S. weapons systems to European ministries of defense. In past years just the opposite has occurred as the United States government has encouraged U.S. industry to outbid European manufacturers for sophisticated fighter aircraft, such as the replacement for the F-104, and battle tanks sold to European NATO countries. The Pentagon might even conceivably agree to buy European armaments in order to help our allies develop their own military-industrial base! Finally, the delicate question of nuclear assistance to France could be resolved through a policy of equity with Britain. Having recently renewed the nuclear assistance agreement with the United Kingdom, Washington could offer assistance to Paris and declare its support, under certain circumstances involving targeting arrangements, for an Anglo-French coordinated nuclear force underpinned by a European Nuclear Committee. Nuclear assistance might also be expanded to cover European-controlled tactical nuclear weapons, especially once some of the 7,000 U.S. tactical nuclear weapons are withdrawn along with the reductions in U.S. ground and air forces.

For Europeans there would be a number of advantages in a process of U.S. devolution and the simultaneous coalescence of European energies. First, inflation and other economic trends, combined with the widespread desire for détente, are putting strong pressure on defense budgets. Cooperation in defense would permit more efficient use of existing resources. Rather than leading to increased defense expenditures, or to larger manpower levels, as is sometimes argued, European defense cooperation would be a way of rationalizing *decreasing* resources while avoiding a parallel increase in insecurity. Second, if the European concept is to progress, a way must be found for France to be a full participating member. The creation of a European Defense Commission might open the way for France to re-evaluate its position vis-à-vis the Atlantic alliance, as Giscard d'Estaing may in time be inclined to do.

Paris is unlikely to return to NATO in the organization's present form, but would probably accept some degree of military integration if it were accomplished within a new West European structure.

Third, European coalescence would be a way of avoiding potentially dangerous fissures within Western Europe. As negotiations on arms control and force reductions within Europe proceed, there is the risk of a wedge being created between Britain and France on the one hand, and West Germany on the other. Mutual Force Reductions may take place essentially on German territory. As forces are reduced in significant quantities, London and Paris could come to have perceptions of European security quite different from those of Bonn. The former might emphasize their nuclear deterrents, whereas the latter might make its security more dependent on a new phase of *Ostpolitik* and accommodation with the East. A European Defense Commission could therefore be a way of enhancing West German confidence and maintaining the Federal Republic's close links with the rest of Western Europe.

Such a defense organization, in providing a new substantive policy area for coordination and implementation, might help harmonize the foreign policies and governmental procedures of the West European states. If this proved to be the case, defense could in time become a powerful driving motor on the road toward greater unity. This has already been recognized in the MFR negotiations in Vienna where the West Europeans have made a major issue of rejecting any Soviet proposal which could foreclose options for a future common defense organization.

The most important advantage of orderly U.S. devolution combined with European coalescence may, however, be of a subtle, psychological nature. Europe's greatest need in the 1980s will be to maintain its political confidence. A number of trends will exist which could tend to erode it: within Western Europe, the reduction of American forces, competition and probably conflict over economic and resource issues, and an increasing sense of separateness from the United States; facing the East, limitations on the growth of détente with the Soviet Union, the constant risk of instability in Eastern Europe, and the continuation of an oppressive Soviet military presence on Western Europe's borders; in superpower relations, the continuation if not acceleration of Soviet-American bilateral diplomacy in arms control and other areas of foreign policy in such a way as to lead Europeans to question whether their interests are being adequately protected. If these conditions come about, and many have already begun, Europeans could have good reason for concern. The development of a European political and defense identity could then become an indispensable symbol of strength and source of political confidence.

A disadvantage of devolution often cited by its critics is that it would almost certainly be opposed by the Soviet Union and might seriously jeopardize détente. Moscow has already displayed anxiety about the eventual emergence of a politically and militarily united Europe and is particularly concerned about a European nuclear deterrent which would give West Germany a finger on the trigger. The somewhat crude, but often projected, image of a Soviet knee-jerk negative reaction requires more examination than it has thus far received. Much would in fact depend on how the Soviets perceive the gradual redistribution of roles within the alliance over a period of years and the process by which that redistribution is effected. The Soviet Union might see some benefits for itself in the creation of a European defense community as a way for the United States to withdraw some of its forces from Europe without a comparable increase, quite possibly no increase at all, in West European manpower levels or defense expenditures. Such a community might be seen by the U.S.S.R. as a means of placing some restraints on the independent nuclear forces of France and Britain, a continuing source of worry to it as made quite evident in SALT. It might also be viewed as a way of enhancing the influence of the allies of the Federal Republic over its internal politics and future course of action. The Soviets might come to understand that devolution within the alliance presents no new or additional security risk to them, although of course the stabilization of the European-American relationship would be an important plus for the West. Much would depend on the way any European Defense Commission is formed and how it is explained to the Soviet Union. In the final analysis, however, one can question whether Moscow should be given a veto on a matter of such consequence for Europe and the United States. It is well to remember that the Soviet leadership became reconciled to the European Economic Community, was prepared to accept the MLF if necessary, and today appears to prefer the retention of some level of U.S. forces in Western Europe.

Devolution has been presented as providing the best structure for the overarching European-American political/security relationship of the 1980s. Inevitably, however, there is a tension between desirability and feasibility. A look at the economic ravages on the European landscape following the initial consequences of the quadrupling of oil prices does not offer an overly bright prospect for an early period of political creativity. Clearly still missing is the European "basket" or "receptacle" into which the United States would devolve some of its Atlantic role. Such a basket can only be put in place through European initiative.

Although forward movement toward the construction of a European identity will have to be resumed before devolution becomes feasible, it is nevertheless not too early to think creatively about it. Recent years have been ones of breakthrough in East-West relations. The "era of negotiations" in SALT, MFR, the Conference for Security and Cooperation in Europe (CSCE), Berlin, and *Ostpolitik*, alongside the American preoccupation with ending the Vietnam war, resulted in West-West relations being placed on the back burner. But most of the advances in East-West negotiations possible at the present juncture of history have now been achieved, and what remains is a period of slow and difficult consolidation rather than rapid change. The coming years may therefore be the right moment to begin quiet but serious consultations on the restructuring of the old Atlantic relationship. At this moment East-West tensions are comparatively low, no U.S. troops have yet been withdrawn from Europe in this decade, and the headlines are focused on seemingly more pressing issues, from money to the Middle East. Preventive thought and action now may avoid more serious instability later. By starting now, might not devolution become the Atlanticism of the future?

Chapter 9
ALLIANCE DISSOLUTION AND AMERICAN DISENGAGEMENT

Earl C. Ravenal

Most makers and analysts of foreign policy share a certain vice, which is at the hinge of policy and methodology. It is the proposition that "policy" is the enumeration of certain national "interests," and the specification of the objects and programs necessary to preserve or enhance those interests. It all sounds straightforward enough—until we examine it closely and skeptically. Applied to methodology, it can be called "requisite analysis"—lists of things that "must" be done. Applied to policy, it is wishful thinking—lists of things that we would like to happen.

Both approaches err in two important, related respects: first, they ignore, systematically, the cost side of the equation—or even the fact that there is always some equation, or trade-off, that limits potentialities and imposes costs and sacrifices for every effort and every gain; sometimes the costs and sacrifices might be justified by the effort, but then again they might just equal, or even exceed, any gains. Second, they consider situations infinitely malleable—that is, they refuse to take the world as it is, and as it is becoming; specifically they fail to reckon with the fact (a fact, moreover, of increasing significance) that vast parts of the international system are often

205

beyond our prudential interference, and sometimes beyond the reach of our efforts at all. In short, the interesting questions are not What do we prefer? but What would we *do?* and How much would we invest to preserve certain situations and keep others from occurring?

It may well be that such "requisite"—that is, wishful—thinking, by both policymakers and academics, is more than normally prevalent in the consideration of the Atlantic relationship.[1] Why this should be—if indeed it is the case—would be an interesting study, but not one that I shall undertake here. It may suffice to say that I do not think that hortative and hopeful rhetoric about common purposes is a necessary badge of affection for Europe. It may be an illusion or a set of blinders.

Therefore my analysis does not proceed—as does the usual Atlantic literature—by citing ideal conditions for European unity and Atlantic harmony and then deploring lapses and deviations from these ideals. There would probably be a congenial and manageable range of opinion, in virtually any gathering of Atlantic statesmen or scholars, about an ideal formula for Atlantic cooperation and NATO security. The serious problems and the differences arise only when the comparative costs and the various constraints are introduced into the equation.

The critical questions about alternative policies and strategies are less what they will achieve than what they will cost, less what we would like to bring about than what alternatives are actually available. Thus this analysis concentrates on possible American strategic responses to perhaps inexorable and not altogether constructive or encouraging developments; and it is more influenced by the net costs of the situation than the gross opportunities. Moreover, since not only situations themselves are often beyond reach, but intelligence about situations is insufficient and unreliable, I am more interested in strategies that are broad enough and "blank" enough to be pursued unilaterally, if necessary, and in the absence of articulate information about the responses of other parties—particularly without reliance on summits and understandings between adversaries and the detailed "consultation" among allies that is incessantly demanded by publicists.

The Strategic Dimension

This analysis looks at the Atlantic relationship primarily as a *strategic* problem. This does not imply that political-military categories are the only, or even the "primary," categories of the Atlantic—or any—relationship. But I tend to reject the notion that we are in a "new era" of the "primacy of economics." Various factors or issues may be relatively salient at various times; but as dimensions of international situations, they are constant. Moreover, the basic structural relationships among nation-states—those relationships that constitute the shape of an international system—are almost by definition political-military. Other kinds of relationships are "transactional," and would continue, more or less on their own terms, over a wide range of political-military conditions. In the particular case of the Atlantic relationship, it is in the strategic area—even more than in the partially contentious economic area of trading blocs, monetary noncooperation, investment restrictions, and resource policies—that the latent and overt contradictions are likely to be most sharp and most corrosive. The Atlantic relationship may fail—or wane—because of factors affecting the security situation (changed balances or threats) or the security logic (contradictions in interests and priorities).

In general, strategic dilemmas ultimately admit of little compromise; strategic doctrines and dispositions sooner or later are tested by the events—actual, threatened, or just imagined—they were devised to meet. And strategic problems have a more rigid logic; the range of choices is severely limited, and each choice has its requisites and its consequences. Also, though the quest for security, particularly when manifested in alliance, ought to cause the greatest extension of community, it turns out to be the activity that engenders the greatest inherent distrust, the activity in which supranational attempts to transcend more parochial and organic communities will founder. The delegation of security responsibilities is the supreme *political* act of delegation, and is often too severe a test of the legitimacy of authorities to compel common sacrifices and of the credibility of authorities to promise common protection. The Atlantic community is certainly *not* a "security community" in this critical sense of the term.

Solutions and Nonsolutions

Over the long future, American foreign policy might, I believe, have to be oriented toward strategic disengagement.[2] For such a strategy, Europe is the most consequential and the most difficult case. A consistent national policy of disengagement would indicate total withdrawal from Europe—though this almost certainly would be the last commitment to crumble, and the process might take a decade or more. But the argument here does *not* turn on any abstract desirability of American withdrawal. Rather, it rests on its eventual necessity, as a matter of choice among unsatisfactory alternatives in deteriorating circumstances.

The projected situation in Europe is not the encouraging fiction of the Atlanticists: increasing regional integration, political as well as economic, and increasing willingness to share defense burdens and diplomatic responsibilities with a still-dominant partner, the United States. Two things are wrong with the Atlanticist projection: first, even the ideal formula contains contradictory elements; a more united Europe would enhance European autonomy and impair U.S.

control, and since control is the necessary condition for involvement, its diminution would prejudice the automaticity and strength of the U.S. commitment. And second, one can in fact project, from many current indications, the disintegration of the Atlantic alliance. One might more accurately say "further" disintegration; it is not a matter of the United States' abandoning NATO, since NATO is already in a state of dissolution. It is also important to realize that, in both logic and fact, the United States has *already*, implicitly, "decoupled" from the defense of NATO, in those cases that are the precise objects of the alliance. The alliance has not only ceased to function wholly for both parties, America and Europe, but it has done this in divergent ways: Europe's interest, in the center, is to avoid being caught in a quarrel between the two superpowers. America's interest, at the periphery, is to avoid being drawn integrally into a conflict that could otherwise be localized in Central Europe. These divergent attitudes and interests produce a normal condition of alliance instability and a crisis condition of military and political unreliability.

Actually, it was the Gaullist thrust—still a pervasive French attitude—that precipitated the disintegration of NATO, widening fissures that were inherent in the alliance from its inception, and extending cracks that were introduced when the Soviets achieved effective nuclear deterrence of the United States. Gaullism also sharpened certain dilemmas: on the nuclear side, the question of shared protection versus sovereign will; on the conventional side, the question of dominance versus partnership.

The nuclear argument is classic and familiar, though it has not lost its logical pungency: in an extremity, under the present circumstances of strategic nuclear parity, would not both superpowers tacitly seek to limit the battleground to Central Europe? An indication of the answer was provided by the American shift in the early 1960s from initial nuclear defense to flexible response, and U.S. pressures that resulted in the nominal adoption of this strategy by NATO in 1967.* The United States demonstrated that it would hesitate to risk North American cities to repulse a Soviet conventional probe of the defenses of Western Europe, yet it preserved the option of a tactical (theater) nuclear war limited to Europe. Thus the defense objectives of the Americans and the Europeans, always latently divergent, became openly divergent; and this divergence has been extended by the Strategic Arms Limitation Talks (SALT),** by the proposals for Mutual Force Reductions (MFR), and by the declaration on the "Prevention of Nuclear War," signed by President Nixon and General Secretary Brezhnev in July 1973, all of which further prejudice the assurance of American involvement in Europe. American strategy already does not defend Europe as the Europeans prefer to be defended. And despite the rhetoric about historical association and cultural affinity, in the nuclear era this state of affairs is an objective strategic fact. To the Americans, Europe is an early warning of Soviet intentions in the world, and a temporary barrier; but to the Europeans, of course, it is all there is.

The alternatives for American policy that are precipitated by this situation consist of two responses at the extremes, and a series of intermediate courses. Of the two extreme responses, the first is improbable, and the second seems improbable now but may eventually be more likely: (1) a tighter, *more* elaborate American protectorate of Europe, or (2) a unilateral, unconditional American withdrawal from responsibility for the protection of Europe. The several intermediate courses

* The earlier American-proposed Multilateral Nuclear Force (MLF), which provided for a "credible" nuclear response confined to NATO, though with an indefinite American veto on the trigger, represented for Europeans the worst combination of conditions.

** The SALT limitations on the offensive and defensive forces of the superpowers also have the effect of perpetuating the life of European national nuclear forces.

are, for various reasons, nonsolutions: (a) the present policy, which, despite the official hope for an agreed mutual force reduction and the rhetoric of "a new Atlantic Charter," is a pragmatic consensus around the status quo, with only minor adjustments in either direction; (b) true partnership, with the sharing of burdens, responsibilities, and command; (c) the perennial Mansfield initiative, which can be characterized as redeployment without decommitment; (d) a planned and orderly devolution of capabilities, including nuclear weapons and the authority to use them, by the United States to a European entity or individual European guarantor nations; or (e) Mutual Force Reductions (MFR), now being discussed with the Soviets, which would be asymmetrical in numbers in order to be equivalent in overall effect.

We can narrow the field of alternatives by contemplating two of these intermediate courses: (a) maintaining the status quo and (b) establishing true partnership. Both of these approaches are revealed as vulnerable when imagined in their characteristic moments of truth.

The moment of truth that tests the status quo is a Soviet attack on NATO. Though extremely unlikely, this is a valid test since it is, after all, the central threat which NATO is designed to deter or repel. What would be the American reaction, assuming (as do the preponderance of technical critiques and even some official statements of a succession of American administrations) that NATO conventional forces were not adequate? Would the United States risk a Dunkirk by reinforcing with American conventional units? Or escalate to tactical nuclear weapons? Or expose American cities by attacking the Soviet Union with strategic nuclear weapons?

Doubts about the conventional capability of American and allied forces in Europe, though not conclusive, are too widespread, and affect too many facets of defense, to ignore. Even such a former advocate of extended conventional defense as General Maxwell Taylor now doubts [3] the conventional strategy to the point of advocating a return to the nuclear "trip wire" which he previously anathematized. In doubting a conventional defense, General Taylor cites the small American forces in being and deployed, the slowness of U.S. mobilization, and the denial of the French line of communication, with the resulting lack of maneuver depth and vulnerability of supply lines. Other military analysts reinforce this diagnosis of the present incapacity of U.S. forces in Europe, warning of a tactical nuclear Dunkirk or a sudden collapse.[4] There is also evidence that the ability of the U.S. Navy to resupply and reinforce the army in Europe with convoys and sea-control forces against the Soviet submarine threat would be inadequate to sustain an extended conventional war.[5] Aside from the strategic "trilemma" that it presents (conventional improvement, nuclear reliance, or the risk of collapse), the status quo position fails on other grounds: the American public and Congress will not permit its indefinite continuance; and the European allies will not permit its remedy on American terms.

The deficiencies in the present strength, posture, and strategy of NATO have been recognized in recent statements of the U.S. government. But the operational thrust of U.S. proposals is to perfect the military status quo, rather than change the strategy or abandon the alliance. The U.S. government, when it calls for anything specific, talks about the effective implementation of the decade-old policy of flexible response and the equitable sharing of the burdens of defense, and pledges no unilateral and unbalanced reduction of U.S. forces in Europe.

The Kissinger approach, reflected in his Year of Europe speech, is not cynical, only self-serving; not brutal, only subtly coercive. Its characteristic feature is the suggested linkage between the American commitment to European defense, on the one hand, and European concessions on the sharing of defense costs, the relationship of European and American currencies, and the access of American products to the European market, on the other. It is not surprising that European reactions to this proposed linkage were unfavorable and even resentful. The mere mention of "settled" issues, such as the U.S. defense commitment, in the same context as other, "unsettled" issues cannot fail to place the "settled" issues in doubt, despite verbal assurances. (In fact, verbal assurances, in this context, tend to have a false ring—old axioms suddenly become conditional hypotheses or negotiable propositions.)

Though the Kissinger approach candidly projects real American interests, it has not worked. Its concept is *reverse* linkage, in several respects: it threatens allies and friends (rather than offering incentives to adversaries); and it threatens to withdraw or devalue something (American protection of Europe) that has heretofore been considered an item of independent value and concern to the United States. Such an approach, though immediately formidable, invites a calling of the U.S. bluff in the longer run. It encourages the Europeans to be unresponsive in both areas: to conduct their own bilateral diplomacy and construct independent forces, and to arrange their economic business to their own narrow advantage.

The establishment of true partnership (the second intermediate course) is tested by a moment of truth that, ironically, some would welcome as the fruition of the alliance: the attainment by Europe of the capacity and the will to make an equal contribution, sharing control with the United States and having a larger voice in devising strategies and allocating benefits. But at that moment NATO is more likely to founder on psychological and bureaucratic issues of decision-making. As the European share of the alliance burden increased, the Europeans would demand at least a commensurate role in the command of NATO. This would imply at least a European Supreme Allied Commander (SACEUR). But who? A German? And failing that, a Dutchman? An Italian? It is even more difficult to envisage an acceptable European substitute than a continuing American overlord. The point here is that the American military, and the American Congress and public, would almost certainly refuse to commit U.S. forces to a true allied command.

The prospects for the other intermediate solutions are also doubtful. One solution that becomes less convincing after an inspection of its premises is the Mansfield proposal (either a resolution or an amendment, offered for eight years, until 1975), calling for unilateral reductions, up to two-thirds, of American troops in Europe.[6] The problems are (1) that, in most of the Mansfield proposals,* these forces are simply to be redeployed to the continental United States, not deleted from the active force structure, and (2) that the U.S. commitment to the defense of Europe is to remain in full force.

First of all, the Mansfield proposal deals only with U.S. deployed forces. But the approximately five divisions, plus support troops and air contingents, including eight tactical air wings—altogether some 320,000 men—that the United States keeps in Europe are only roughly half of the forces it maintains in its baseline force structure in support of NATO (the total annual cost of these forces *for* Europe, deployed in Europe and in the United States, is about $47 billion in 1976 terms).[7] Simply redeploying some fraction, or even all, of U.S. visible forces in Europe would save nothing unless the withdrawn units were deactivated. It is even doubtful that a proportional saving in balance of payments—$800 million to $1 billion a year—would materialize from a 50 percent reduction in U.S. deployments in Europe. The United States might realize only $200 to 300 million in foreign exchange savings,** after discounting the fact that troop reductions might not produce proportional dollar savings, and the fact that Europeans, particularly Germans, would probably spend less in the United

---

* Senator Mansfield's proposed amendment of June 1974 for the first time included the provision that the withdrawals from abroad must be matched by a demobilization of troops from U.S. active forces.

**Philip Odeen ("In Defense of the Defense Budget," *Foreign Policy*, Fall 1974) places foreign exchange savings from removal of American troops in Europe at "only $100 to 200 million annually."

States if the United States spent less in Europe.[8] If Congress is unwilling to consider eliminating the redeployed divisions from the force structure—something that would, if consistently pursued, require the diminution of the U.S. commitment to Europe—then the case for redeployment should not be pressed with such conviction.

Another solution that has been much elaborated is devolution—a deliberate, orderly, and militarily adequate effort by the United States to confer defensive capability and responsibility, including nuclear technology and the authority to use it, on Western Europe, either as a unified political entity (perhaps including West Germany in some capacity) or as separate nations. But it is unlikely that such a planned devolution will work, from either the U.S. or the European end. The United States will probably be reluctant to accord the necessary technical advice and financial assistance, especially to France. And there are other inhibitions on the U.S. government, among them the strictures of the Nuclear Nonproliferation Treaty and the reluctance, during a period of cooperation in controlling nuclear arms, to arouse hostile Soviet impulses which might lead to countermoves in the next stages of the SALT negotiations.

In any case, there probably is not sufficient political trust between Paris and London—let alone between those two capitals and Bonn—to create a truly effective (because truly common) nuclear force, not a mere bag of ill-joined national nuclear forces. Simply adding up the damage potential of the several forces proves nothing. And just pooling peripheral technical, financial, and logistical items is not sufficient. The allies must share strategies, decision-making, and targeting. And the advent of joint targeting would produce mistrust rather than mutual reliance, because of the lack of homogeneity of the political will involved in the decision to strike the targets or withhold fire.

A truly independent European nuclear force—whether perfected or not, whether joint or a series of national nuclear forces—would at best be useless to the United States, and at worst a considerable embarrassment. The United States could not credit such a force to its global advantage. And if the United States suspected that such a force might trigger its own deterrent—even if this were not the intended function of that force—it would not *want* to be committed.

The main point about devolution is that it is a sensibly motivated choice—and perhaps an eventual likelihood—but it will not quite take the course or lead to the end state that its proponents foresee. First, devolution, if it occurs at all, is likely to be a messy and partially unintended, rather than a neat and deliberately managed, process. Second, it is likely to be inspired more by European sentiments of separatism, verging on distrust of the United States and restiveness toward American dominance, than by truly cooperative and consultative motives. And finally, even if it "succeeds," it is likely to precipitate—or formalize—American decoupling from the fate of Europe (particularly in those worst cases that might be generated by European diplomatic sequences no longer under tight American control). Without true and irrevocable delegation of power and concession of strategic and diplomatic autonomy, devolution would be a meaningless charade—just another mask for American efforts to shift the burdens of alliance. But with these, the prior and automatic American commitment that is a necessary condition of alliance would be severed.

How much, then, can be expected from the last intermediate solution, Mutual Force Reductions (MFR)? This is the proposal to negotiate a meticulously equilibrated reduction of NATO and Warsaw Pact forces in Central Europe. It is an American initiative, endorsed by NATO in 1968 and accepted by the Soviets in May 1972 as an item of negotiation, separate from the talks on European security. The official talks began in Vienna in October 1973, and have continued without result.

The talks snagged early on technique and procedure. After

the first five months of preliminary bargaining, the term "balanced" had been dropped from the official title of the talks, and Hungary, where 39,000 Soviet troops are stationed, had been designated only a peripheral participant, with the Soviet troops there excluded from the comparative calculation of forces. More serious is the divergence in the basic approaches of the two sides. NATO has insisted on unequal cuts, resulting in balanced opposing forces; the Warsaw Pact has insisted on equal cuts, resulting in unbalanced opposing forces.

The prognosis for substantive agreement is dim, even though both sides have reasons for preparing elaborate proposals and floating them tediously in this international forum over the next several years.

MFR will probably be defeated by asymmetries and details of geography and types and functions of forces, and by the incommensurate interests of the parties. First, the forces that both sides keep in Central Europe now have more political than military significance. Thus, reductions would have different meanings and effects for each side. This factor alone obscures the objective calculations that could lead to productive results.

Second, the calculations relating to the complexity of forces and factors embodied in a conventional military confrontation (in contrast to the simpler and more symbolic calculations involved in strategic nuclear bargaining) are too numerous and detailed for meticulous negotiation.

Third, the forces involved are too unlike, in numbers, nature, and above all in remoteness and readiness for re-entry in a crisis. Since the Soviets will not even consider correcting the disparity of numbers, prospects are not bright for compensation for the other asymmetries.

Fourth, there is too much mutual suspicion about motives and advantages, and the uses to which advantages might be put, to allow the amount of good faith necessary to bridge the obscurities, ambiguities, and apparent inequities that must characterize any negotiated agreement. In SALT, motives have been clearer and factors more comprehensible, so some trust could be generated as negotiations proceeded. In MFR, suspicions are likely to be heightened, rather than allayed, in the course of the negotiations.

Fifth, there is too little commitment by any of the parties to the success of these negotiations. European allies—notably France—are less than enthusiastic. The Soviets, at best, are cynical. Even the Ford Administration, as did its predecessor, considers them more as a ploy to spike premature congressional pressures for unilateral withdrawal.

All these negative indications emphasize one point: if significant withdrawals are really wanted, they must be initiated *unilaterally*, and will probably be *un*balanced.

All the intermediate solutions are intended to maintain American involvement and alliance with Europe at a more tolerable cost that might better ensure the longevity of the American commitment. But all run into dead ends or reveal contradictions. If the United States wants to enhance its confidence of never having to face a choice of disasters in Europe (putting aside the universal question-begging argument that if deterrence works, nothing will ever happen anyway), it is driven to the extreme solutions: (1) Stay in Europe, confirming and even strengthening its commitment, maintaining its forces there, improving their capabilities, and paying the cost of higher confidence. But if the United States stayed, it would have to continue to dominate the diplomacy and decision-making of the alliance. Or (2) insulate itself from the consequences of conflict in Europe, disengaging its forces and attenuating its commitment.

Of these extreme alternatives, the first is not tenable over the long run. The American public and congressional mood is already hostile to the indefinite postponement of troop redeployments; it certainly would not support an American initiative to infuse the alliance with *greater* capability and commit even more resources. Nor would European allies accept continuing or even enhanced American control, though they value U.S. contributions of money and manpower.

The remaining alternative for the United States is a policy of measured—but irreversible—disengagement, with few illusions about maintaining American political weight, or replacing American force with equal European force, or preserving the efficacy of the American defense commitment. What would have to be decided is the timing of military withdrawal and diplomatic revelation, and the choice of occasion. Some such occasion *could have* been provided by the Conference for Security and Cooperation in Europe (CSCE). This conference was first proposed by the Soviets in 1954, and finally took place in Helsinki in July 1975. Even an American administration that was far from embracing isolationism might have viewed this conference as an opportunity to explore the conditions for withdrawal from Europe. But the European security conference was viewed by the West more as an opportunity to promote the "freer movement of people and ideas." Of course, expanded human contacts, such as travel, education, access for journalists, and the penetration of ideas, are valuable as ideals, and should be pursued as normally as possible; but they may be elusive and even self-defeating as bargaining points, because they are hard to enforce and appear subversive to the other side.

If the United States were to choose a course of disengagement (or any alternative policy), it must accept the whole range of consequences—certain, probable, possible, and improbable. The scenario of a calculated large-scale Soviet invasion of Western Europe is close to zero in probability. But if the worst happened and the Soviets attempted to exploit some opening by force, the United States would no longer be prepared to defend effectively. More cognizance must be taken of the argument that the withdrawal of the U.S. presence might lay Western Europe open to Soviet pressure and influence; that, because of its sense of impotence and exposure, Western Europe would lose its will and would become malleable to Soviet manipulation—in short, that Western Europe might be "Finlandized." The function of this range of scenarios is to force the United States to confront the ultimate question: what is the nature of its interest in Europe?

The fact that European allies, severally and perhaps eventually jointly, want U.S. help and protection is not a sufficient reason for giving it to them. The United States, with its different scale of interests, its peculiar geography, its diplomatic traditions, and its domestic constraints, is not situated to look at Europe through the eyes of European statesmen. Not that the European perspective is invalid; it is simply and inevitably different. The United States should be neither surprised nor influenced by the efforts of West Germany or France to keep the United States steadily committed in Europe, while they engineer separate accommodations with adversaries and maneuver for position within the alliance and the Community. It is a perfectly proper object of European diplomacy to invoke the United States to redress the balance with the Soviets, for as long as the United States is willing to respond.

None of this argument is to deny that certain things *about* Europe are pertinent to U.S. security. Obviously, the world would change drastically—and this in itself would be the principal consequence for the United States—if the Soviets were to conquer or dominate Western Europe. But this would be true whether the United States did or did not initially defend or eventually counterattack. In any case, the very intention of a great antagonist, such as the Soviet Union, to perpetrate an act of violent alteration on such a scale would be enough to cause the United States, and almost every other power, to make drastic increases in defense preparedness (though the *specific* further purpose of these measures would not be entirely clear).

But this probable global response indicates two things: (1)

in itself it would be a profound reason for the Soviets to abstain from such actual or threatened behavior. And (2) the United States, and several other powers, would still be capable of second-chance reactions that would sufficiently conserve their strength and resources and protect their security. This argument suggests that the principal *function* of Europe for the security of the United States is as a massive early warning system of the intentions of its major adversary. But obviously this cannot be the case for Europe itself. So the strategic significance of "Europe" differs for the Europeans and for the Americans; and this residual fact must inevitably affect their respective perceptions and plans.

Nor does this argument deny the existence of certain less-than-vital U.S. interests in Europe. One would be a sentimental attachment, rooted in history, ancestry, culture, and shared political values. Sentimental ties are not insignificant. Quite the contrary: sentiment can transcend all other calculations and dictate the commitments of nations, starting with the often taken-for-granted defense of parts of their *own* territory that might in themselves be strategically useless and economically unviable. Beyond that, nations plan to defend themselves against take-over by even potentially constructive foreign masters, to protect their autonomy as national communities, and to preserve their own values—not as values, but as their *own*. Thus it remains conceivable—and always will be an item in the calculus of potential aggressors—that the United States, alliance or not, might respond in some potent way to pressures on Europe.

Other less-than-vital but still important American interests in Europe are economic investment, trade, and the possibility of travel and cultural exchange. But the fact that the United States enjoys an increasing measure of these benefits in Eastern as well as Western Europe indicates that these other functional relationships can be maintained without alliance structures. And in assessing and pursuing these nonstrategic interests, the United States must keep them in perspective. It is entitled to ask: at what costs, with what prospects, and with what alternatives?

The proposition of disengagement is not designed to destroy the fabric of transatlantic respect and cooperation, nor is it designed—as are so many measures conceived on this side of the Atlantic—as a bargaining bluff to stimulate the Europeans to make a more substantial contribution to the common defense. Rather, it must be seen as an attempt, partially predictive and partially prescriptive, to adjust to diverging conceptions of security and to unalterable desires for autonomy of decision and flexibility of diplomatic maneuver—as an attempt to choose realistically among several contingent alternatives, none of them "first best."

The thesis of disengagement prompts the question: what should the United States do if things do not work out in a way that is ideal? Americans do the Europeans no favor by refusing to answer that question—or by failing to ask it.

NOTES

[1] See, for example, the article by "Z," "The Year of Europe?" *Foreign Affairs,* January 1974, p. 246: "Provided goodwill is present, there is nothing particularly insoluble about the present difficulties in American-European relations. . . ."

[2] I elaborate this point of view in my article "The Case for Strategic Disengagement," *Foreign Affairs,* April 1973, and in my book *Beyond the Balance of Power: Foreign Policy and International Order* (forthcoming). Strategic disengagement, it should be understood, is not a rigid program, but a general orientation.

[3] Speech at the U.S. Army War College, June 19, 1972 (reprinted in *Parameters,* the Journal of the Army War College, Vol. 2, No. 2, 1972).

[4] See Lieutenant Colonel Zeb B. Bradford, Jr. and Lieutenant Colonel Frederic J. Brown, U.S. Army, "Army Support of Coalition Security," *Military Review,* May 1972. See also Steven L. Canby, "NATO Muscle: More Shadow Than Substance," *Foreign Policy,*

Fall 1972. But both articles propose radically redesigned forces, which they consider potentially effective.

[5] On this point, see Captain Robert H. Smith, U.S. Navy, "Toward a Navy Second to One," *U.S. Naval Institute Proceedings*, November 1972. After a detailed analysis, Captain Smith states: "The requisite number of ASW [anti-submarine-warfare] escort forces do not now exist nor are we going to have them. . . . It can no longer be a realistic part of U.S. strategy to plan to deliver large amounts of surface-borne supplies across a hostile Atlantic. . . . It follows that the nation, and hence the Navy, should drop the pretense that it is possible to do so."

[6] In May 1971, the Mansfield amendment to the draft extension bill, calling for a cut by December 31, 1971, of troops in Europe to 150,000 (from about 320,000), was defeated by the Senate. On February 3, 1973, in a news conference, Senator Mansfield called for a 50 percent reduction in U.S. forces in Europe within five years. In early 1973, Mansfield called for a two-thirds cut in troops abroad, but modified his proposed amendment to call for a "substantial reduction." More recent versions have called for a one-half reduction in the (600,000) American troops abroad, worldwide, within three years (statement before the Senate Committee on Foreign Relations, July 25, 1973); a 40 percent worldwide cut over three years (defeated September 26, 1973); and an amendment requiring 125,000 troops (out of 437,000 then deployed abroad) to be pulled back by December 31, 1975 (defeated June 6, 1974).

An alternative approach to reducing the U.S. burden of European defense is the Jackson-Nunn amendment, which was approved by Congress in late 1973. This legislation requires European allies to offset the entire adverse balance of payments due to U.S. troop deployments in Europe, and makes mandatory a troop reduction proportional to any shortfall. On May 16, 1974, President Nixon declared that the terms of the Jackson-Nunn amendment had been met: balance of payments costs for FY 1974 were estimated to be approximately $2.1 billion; bilateral offset payments by Germany would provide approximately $2.2 billion over a two-year period, and the balance would be made up by arrangements with other countries. (*Department of State Bulletin*, June 10, 1974.)

[7] All official public estimates of the costs of European defense to the United States, and almost all unofficial estimates, vastly under-

state the full costs; they are commonly throught to be on the order of $4 billion to $14 billion a year; even some of the largest estimates run about $36 billion (see Barry M. Blechman et al., *Setting National Priorities: The 1976 Budget*, Washington, D. C.: Brookings, 1975, p. 143).

One way of trapping these costs is to take the FY 1976 defense budget of $104.3 billion (requested total obligational authority), initially identify the portions for strategic forces ($18 billion) and general purpose forces ($76 billion), adjust these to include retired pay (this yields $19.3 billion and $81.7 billion, respectively), multiply the general purpose force figure by a fraction 10-2/3 over 19, representing the portion of active ground units oriented primarily to Europe (this yields $45.9 billion), and add military assistance for that region's allies. The resulting figure is $47 billion. (I am assuming that 2 of the 3 Army divisions recently added to the force structure are oriented primarily to Europe, and the third is part of the strategic reserve.)

[8] "In 1972 the United States spent about $2.1 billion in other NATO countries to support our NATO deployments. Allowing for NATO military spending in the United States, mainly for equipment and training, our net military deficit was about $1.5 billion." Richard Nixon, *U.S. Foreign Policy for the 1970's: Shaping a Durable Peace* (fourth State of the Union Message), May 3, 1973, p. 83.

Chapter 10
THE AUTONOMY OF "DOMESTIC STRUCTURES" IN EUROPEAN-AMERICAN RELATIONS

Nicholas Wahl

Current economic troubles and domestic political changes are straining the conventional wisdom about European-American relations. The usual view of these relations, as expressed in articles in establishment journals and repeated by governmental spokesmen, can be summarized in a kind of syllogism. Common national interests, increasingly interdependent economies, and shared political and social beliefs have drawn Western Europe into close cooperation with the United States since World War II. Yet occasionally selfish nationalism, misguided leadership, and errors of judgment have caused temporary estrangement between the United States and one or more of its European allies. Therefore, verbal reaffirmation of common interests and beliefs, a rational—perhaps institutionalized—effort at resolving momentary disagreements, and a periodic review of mutual responsibilities are all that is required to recreate what is a natural and potentially permanent alliance of basically like-minded states. Reasoning together, rejecting irrational and unattainable objectives, making mutual concessions have been the operative goals of this frequently recommended process of Atlantic "jawboning."

Observing European-American relations principally from the perspective of domestic politics, I have often wondered why these periodic calls to reason, responsibility, and realism have assumed the existence of a universal logic in political life an automatic sense of responsibility, and a common view of the real. From my vantage point the failure of Europeans to achieve greater unity among themselves has been due to their conflicting outlooks on what is reasonable, responsible, and realistic *in terms of their internal political situations*. Why shouldn't the same hold for the Atlantic community? What Kissinger and Nixon saw in 1974 as reasonable solutions to the oil and monetary crises in terms of their own domestic interests was not perceived as such—on the contrary!—by Messrs. Jobert and Pompidou; just as General de Gaulle's initiatives within the Common Market in the mid-1960s—often motivated by concern for the peasant vote—were not always perceived as reasonable by the Dutch or Germans.

And yet why do commentators and leaders on both sides of the ocean continue to call for a return to a kind of alliance morality that never really existed and that they know cannot exist today? Indeed, economic crisis may make things worse as far as reason, interdependence, and mutual understanding are concerned. Still the rhetorical calls for a return to the old-time Atlantic religion of reason, responsibility, and realism continue to be uttered, especially by Americans. But even European leaders are loath to admit in public that internal political considerations have been the principal causes for strains in the alliance because, *pari passu*, the same can be said of the Common Market. At at time of increasing *de facto* autarky no one wants to add to the gloom and, anyway, in diplomacy nothing is to be gained by stating the obvious.

II

The fact is that the same domestic forces that limit progress toward European unity also limit the margins within which

European governments can change their attitudes toward the United States and its Atlantic policies. Poor governmental performance in economic matters, fragile if nonexistent governing majorities, the consequent preoccupation of building or maintaining coalitions for the next election, and offsetting economic reverses by gestures in the more manipulatable area of foreign policy—these are the overriding realities of domestic politics in the major European states. When faced by a decision pertaining to Community policy, European leaders inevitably consider the implications it may have for these realities. In electoral terms—that is, staying in power—this means taking a decision perceived in one of three ways: Community interest over that of a vocal national pressure group; or national interest (the pressure group's) over the Community; or seeking a judicious compromise, which may or may not be so perceived. How you tilt is important to who is with you and against you at the next elections.

Similarly when faced by an American initiative such as the 1973 Year of Europe, America's allies were obliged to react at least partly in electoral terms: what votes are to be gained and lost by seeming more "European" than "Atlantic," or vice versa, or—as the Germans often do—by steadfastly refusing a choice between postures, maintaining that one can't be European without being Atlantic—and vice versa? No doubt European leaders have long understood these constraints imposed on their margins of action by internal politics. They have realized years ago that their supposed common problems, emerging from supposedly convergent societies and cultures, were really quite different in terms of domestic political costs and benefits. In the same way, the Europeans know that their attitudes toward the United States can never be completely harmonized. Schmidt's opposition does not afford him the flexibility in relations with America that Giscard's opposition offers. The German Christian Democrats are fervently pro-American and Schmidt, therefore, can never threaten that after him comes the deluge of neutralism. Giscard's majority does not allow him the elbow room on European unity that

Schmidt's political situation affords. Gaullists remain relatively hostile to supranational trends, and the pro-integration
elements of Giscard's cabinet are in the minority, as they are in
the country. Italian options in foreign policy may well open up
as the need to accommodate the Communists becomes a
condition of effective government. British choices vis-à-vis
Europe may narrow once again if anti-Market forces in Labour
take over the party while it is in power. But they may also open
toward a more positive attitude toward the Common Market
if the Conservatives were to return to power in coalition with
the Liberals.

All this suggests to me that notwithstanding the occasional
integrationist rhetoric and denunciations of French self-interest, European leaders have surely accepted long ago the near
standstill in progress toward unity as a fact of their domestic
political lives. The "differentials" of internal politics, combined, of course, with serious conflicts of national interests and
frequent direct and indirect interference by American diplomacy, are the real obstacles to the development of supranational institutions. And if they usually fall back on the
European version of the conventional wisdom, it is for reasons
similar to the American habit of calling for more cooperation,
consultation, and responsibility from their European allies.
American officials know that there is a standstill in the Atlantic relationship and that progress is not likely in the near
future. What else is there but to hope for change?

More important, in both cases there is a gloomy home truth
that must be cloaked in traditional alliance rhetoric: in Europe it is the poor prospects for further integration; in America
it is that the U.S. government prefers a relatively disunited
Europe and, at any rate, does not see its way clear toward a
more equal relationship at the present time. Our official
statements, therefore, alternate between pious calls for mutual
understanding and angry complaints over the Europeans' inability to speak with one voice. Yet we know that the one voice
is not only impossible at this stage of European unity but that

its existence is not really in our interest as presently conceived. Nor do we have any real interest in mutual understanding, if it is to mean making concessions of our own in regard to our global vision. American domination of the Atlantic area in an international system of sovereign states is justified for its own sake; it is also justified by the need to approximate relations with our allies that are as symmetrical as possible with those the Soviets have with their bloc.

III

These are all conscious, if privately held, motives for the extreme reluctance American policymakers and their scholarly and journalistic commentators show toward raising the question of whether or not the Europeans can actually do what the U.S. urges on them. There are also less conscious, habitual, indeed "systemic" reasons for American reluctance to give adequate weight to the domestic political factors constraining our European allies.

American foreign policymakers became accustomed to denying autonomy to European internal politics in the years after World War II. In Marshall Plan and early NATO days it was dangerous to admit such an autonomy, for it meant leaving open the possibility of anti-American governments coming to power and thus offering hostages to latent neo-isolationism in Congress. To suggest that internal politics in Europe should be taken into consideration in the formulation of American demands seemed to carry the risk of losing important votes as a consequence of pressure group reactions. The only domestic factor regularly invoked in official explanations of American policy toward Europe was the threat of Communist take-overs or the drift toward anti-American neutralism. Although the realities of European domestic politics were faithfully reported by our diplomatic and intelligence services, they were often ignored by policymakers simply because taking them into account implied that specially favored policies were unrealizable. In the 1950s John Foster Dulles pursued a European Defense Community in the face of warnings that European political support for it was on the wane. In the early 1960s Dean Rusk sought to create a "multilateral force" (the famous MLF) within NATO, again in the face of reporting that solid European interest in the scheme was minimal. In both these cases there was something of an obsession with the magic properties of pet "solutions." This obscured American official understanding of European domestic structures of opposition that were ultimately to upset American foreign policy planning.

Furthermore, professional analysis of European-American relations has left little role for a separate, autonomous weight to the internal dimension. Deterministic, rational-model explanations of interdependence, both economic and political, have served to produce a theory to justify the power political goals of American policy toward Europe over the past decades. Even a more traditional student of foreign policy like Henry Kissinger, who explicitly deals with "domestic structures" as a factor, has carefully chosen the "structures" to emphasize: those which place the least restraint on the choices available to American policy. In his essay on domestic factors [1] he chose to stress two "structures"—the bureaucracy and the leadership group. Transcending the scope of his essay, he said, were factors such as "historical traditions, social values, and the economic system." Unless he meant them to be subfactors of the aforementioned, he might also have listed party politics, electoral and group competition, ideologies, and national belief systems. In any case, Kissinger chose not to deal with those "structures" which have a specially influential role in the foreign policymaking of the democratic states with which he has been least successful.

Obviously the Secretary, as well as his predecessors, was aware of the importance of these other "structures," but he, as his predecessors, has been bewildered by how to deal with them ever since they became structures of resistance to American policy domination. When the American government lost leverage over these structures, it tended to forget them. Yet it should not be overlooked that for the ten years after the war the United States *did* pay considerable attention to European domestic structures of historical tradition, social values, and economic systems. Both openly and covertly America made a huge effort to change any traditions we thought weakened our allies against the Soviet threat. We attempted to alter social values that appeared to promote our domestic enemies in Europe, and we aided economic and social forces that cooperated with us and shared our views of the common danger. The Marshall Plan, subsidies to pro-American political parties and leaders, "free" trade unions, vast information programs favoring European unity and the free enterprise system, all bear testimony to our vigorous postwar concern for domestic structures impinging on the foreign policies of our allies. But as our European "partners" recovered, prospered, and ceased to fear a Soviet invasion, our leverage on these structures diminished. Direct economic aid was suspended, our information programs were curtailed, and our covert operations became severely restricted when not eliminated.

At this point—in the mid to late 1950s—our official thinking about domestic structures should also have undergone a change. Rather than thinking in terms of influencing European domestic politics in a direction favorable to us, we should have thought more about accommodating our attitudes to European policies now affected by new structures over which we no longer had influence. After all, we have accommodated to the policies of the Soviet Union, over whose domestic structures we have had little influence. But instead of drawing this conclusion, American foreign policymakers, including Kissinger, have chosen simply to neglect those domestic factors which they could no longer manipulate. The basic assumptions about relations in the Atlantic area were reaffirmed no matter what changes took place in the internal politics of our allies. For the U.S. government Adenauer never died, de Gaulle was a bad dream, the Christian Democrats would rule Italy forever, and it didn't matter who was in power at Westminster.

When government figures were asked why domestic political changes were not given more attention, the official reply usually was the conventional wisdom: permanent and overriding common interests, a community of values, the continued Soviet threat, all obviated the need to give the internal dimension of our friends' societies the kind of study reserved for the internal politics of our enemies. When pressed harder, those arguing the American case admitted that it really didn't matter whether or not these interests and values were shared or were indeed operative. Given economic interdependence, the American defense of Europe, the divisions of the European Community, a natural American domination was both rational and inevitable.

Another, less evident reason for systematically neglecting European domestic structures is the nature of the relatively stable group of people who have dealt with European relations over the years. If its membership has been rejuvenated recently, the ideas of the generation which launched the Marshall Plan, created NATO, and encouraged Europe to unite (in the 1950s) continue to inspire this group. Whether Republicans or Democrats, scholars or officials, lawyers or businessmen, they were united in their faith in the conventional wisdom. They remained dedicated and passionate "friends of Europe"—all the more dedicated and passionate since their understanding of American national interest coincided with the conventional wisdom about the purpose of the alliance.

For many years this group had its counterpart within the "domestic structures" of the European allies. Today this continuity has disappeared in Europe. For not only have changes in policymaking personnel been radical as a consequence of governmental shifts and the retirement of the war and postwar generations, but also the ideas about the alliance have been submitted to a far more rigorous debate in Europe than has been the case in America. Thanks to the contributions to this debate by neutralist and Communist parties, the European discussion has not only been more continuous but it has also explored more radical alternatives to the alliance. Whether or not this debate was "rational" or "responsible" is less important than the fact that it took place in Europe and that it hardly existed in the United States. For in Europe, even anti-Communist and formally pro-American parties and leaders have had the chance to reflect on alternatives to the traditional American-dominated relationship. It is inevitable that some of this debate has rubbed off on the generation of leaders now in command.

American debate, however, has not progressed very much even though Kissinger is more a "realist" than was Rusk and even if conflicts of economic interests between the United States and Europe are more openly mentioned as causes of tension. Those involved in making American policy continue to affirm the traditional litany of Atlanticism: the common danger requires a close-knit alliance in which the leading power sets goals and priorities for the good of all. Nor has there been much of a challenge from Congress or the political parties. Republican and Democratic "friends of Europe," long won to the litany, have sat on the private and public committees and study groups which could have raised questions about the relevance of the conventional wisdom to a changing European scene. Only from the press and the universities have there come suggestions—and these quite modest—to modernize the traditional American assumptions about the alliance.

The continuity, homogeneity, and conformism of the Americans responsible for European policy are hardly an accident—but neither is it a conspiracy. Superpower status (also referred to as global responsibility) has had the consequence of maintaining elite thought about Europe relatively intact. To rethink the alliance meant allowing other parts of the puzzle to become unstuck. But even more important, to recognize changes in Europe that suggested recasting Atlantic doctrine meant to the "friends of Europe" that the Pandora's box of debate in American public opinion over the European connection might have to be opened, and out might pop the reincarnations of Burton K. Wheeler and Gerald Nye—the famous prewar isolationists.

Fear, suspicion, even contempt for Congress and for middle-American attitudes toward Europe continue to inhibit the traditional "friends of Europe" to a degree that is not justified; even American "domestic structures" have evolved in this respect since the war. To admit that change in Europe required revision of American policy implied to the "friends of Europe" the need to re-educate Congress and public opinion about the new and more troublesome European scene. The memory of past efforts of this kind was not encouraging; and since Europe had lost its salience for both Congress and opinion, leaving well enough alone was deemed both prudent and preferable. Telling Congress that a more independent Europe suggested a more flexible relationship could well have unfortunate results, as experience with the troop reduction issue seemed to suggest. Congress could raise the "price" for a new relationship with a more independent Europe by insisting on impossibly larger contributions to the common defense, or punitive concessions from Europe on trade matters—both of which could drive Europe into a posture of further independence which policymakers wanted to avoid. On the other hand, in a full-scale debate Congress could also react by asking the embarrassing question of why Europe should not be given its head, thus allowing the relationship to become less one-sided. On balance, the "friends of Europe" have seen little benefit in raising publicly the subject of how internal factors in Europe are altering relations with the United States and the meaning of the alliance.

Moreover, for American Atlanticists a theological cast of

mind on the question of the relationship has either prevented them from noticing the changes or, if they have, has caused them to divert their eyes. To look hard at the Europe emerging in the 1970s is to admit that the basis for the theology is much diminished. Explicitly pro-American parties have disappeared, Communist parties are legitimate candidates for sharing power, and the groups and classes Americans once counted on have absorbed at least some of the critical thinking about the United States that has become so widespread. The ostrich reaction of the theologians has been encouraged by the conceptual modes of professional writing and discussion of foreign policy and international relations. Prevailing theoretical approaches have tended to subordinate contingent domestic factors to the overriding influence of "national interest," defined in abstract and rationalist terms. American commentators on foreign policy have stressed the objective factors of self-interest and material power, playing down ideological, historical, and psychological factors. Policy is analyzed in terms of its rationality or irrationality (that is, cooperative or irresponsible, furthering or hindering the common Western purpose as defined by the principal power). The question never raised in the literature is: given agreement on a rational course of action, can their domestic situations allow European leaders to comply with the agreement?

Obviously an advantage in dealing with China and the Soviet Union is that their governments more often than not *can* execute agreements without fear of domestic veto groups. That our European allies have more trouble in "delivering" agreements both among themselves and with the United States is not due to the parochialism of European perspectives; or the absence of something Kissinger termed, in pique, "legitimacy"; or the disappearance of "giants" such as Adenauer or even de Gaulle, who did "deliver" on occasion—for example, during the Cuban Missile Crisis of 1962. It is due, above all, to something American policymakers have forgotten since we have become a superpower: democratic politics limits the choices available in foreign policy as well as the ability to "deliver." Yet when Congress threatens to limit the "delivery" capability of American leaders, it is *force majeure* that is invoked and not parochialism, lack of legitimacy, or an absence of leadership.

Global interests and the conditioning of the cold war have given the American Executive greater room for maneuver in foreign policy than the logic and even the law of its political system allow. From this the nation has recently suffered morally as well as materially. As a consequence of Vietnam it may be that in the future, American foreign policy will be submitted more closely to the constraints of domestic structures. But until now much of the official impatience with Europe has been due to American refusal to acknowledge the growing autonomy of domestic politics over European foreign policies, while at the same time the hope has been maintained that cold war habits would keep American domestic politics from intruding too much into the decisions of Presidents and Secretaries of State.

IV

Unfortunately, the recognition of the autonomy of domestic structures in European-American relations will not come easily. As has been argued above, the denial of this autonomy by both American leadership and opinion stems from a complex of psychological, historical, and generational factors as well as from the conscious calculation of national interest. But it is also traceable to a vastly underestimated problem of communication between Europe and the United States. This requires an examination of factors such as mutual perceptions, national stereotypes, value conflicts, and ignored differences of custom and habit—an examination I would like to attempt no matter how tentative and incomplete the conclusions must necessarily be.

Communications on all levels between allied nations are affected by the "static" of cultural differences—no matter how old the alliance and no matter what the conventional wisdom of traditional alliance rhetoric is made to say. Here I will limit my observations of the cultural obstacles to a mutual understanding of the internal dimensions of foreign policy to an admittedly extreme case—that of French-American relations. There is an advantage in this choice precisely because of the tensions and interest clashes of the recent past. The greater overlap of American national interests with those of the other European powers has, in my view, tended to veil and, in the case of Germany and Britain, actually to sublimate cultural differences that have implications for communication and the perception of domestic constraints on foreign policy. In the case of relations between France and the United States, a sharper conflict of interests has long focused more attention on a wide range of obstacles to agreement, including problems of communication. In any case, relations with France are the most difficult aspect of the European-American relationship, and unless France leaves the Atlantic alliance, she will continue to require considerable attention.

It is in the realm of mutual perceptions that Franco-American communication has undergone the greatest changes since World War II. These changed perceptions have not been shaped by the will of governments, social groups, or individual leaders, but, rather, by the psychological needs of the two nations. Indeed, one can say that communication between our countries has actually been hostage to the changing self-images of the two peoples, subordinated to the problems of redefining national identity that have confronted both countries over the past twenty-five years. For communication between us is not today, nor was it ever, simply a matter of transmission of information about American reality and American motives to the French people and government—and vice versa. Rather, the central problem of communication lies in the fact that the French stereotype of the United States has helped to maintain a vision the French held of themselves, while our view of France—and Europe generally—has helped us maintain a self-image that we have found both useful and comforting. In these terms, neither the French nor the Americans have really wanted to understand each other: they did not want true communication, for they only "heard" what they wanted, indeed needed, to "hear."

From this point of view it can be argued that no amount of additional or "truer" information could have made much of a difference to French perceptions of the United States. The old French stereotype of America as being efficient, dynamic, generous, yet lacking in "culture," subtlety, and a sense of measure, served a vital purpose down to the late 1950s. It helped the French to live with a nagging and humiliating consciousness of their decline as a world power and the shabbiness of their war-torn social fabric. At least, they could think, France still has her culture, her wit, and her safe hierarchical society. Similarly, the old American stereotype of France as being civilized, sophisticated, and stylish, yet economically backward and politically unstable, helped us to bear our guilty worries about our materialism, puritanism, and dehumanizing economic life. In both cases the stereotype allowed the self-questioning to arrive at the same conclusion: "But just look at the price *they* must pay!"—the French for their culture, the Americans for their material abundance.

Stereotypes break down when the needs which produced them change. By the 1960s the French no longer needed to balance their economic backwardness with a flourishing traditional culture—nor could they. French reference to a mythical America that was paying the price of a provincial culture for its great economic progress was no longer needed nor possible. They no longer needed the old stereotype because they no longer saw themselves as a great power in decline and they knew full well that American culture had become the metropolitan culture of the West. But being no longer so self-critical about their society and so self-touting about their own

culture did not make the French any easier to communicate with
—quite the contrary. Without complexes about their economic
and social progress, the French actually became more acces-
sible to critical analyses of American society—just as Americans, no longer suffering a cultural inferiority complex,
became more susceptible to critical views of sclerotic French
customs and culture. Thus changing self-images led to a
demystification of mutual perceptions. The victims of this
process have been: the myth of the "oldest ally," the myth of
common values, the myth of complementary economies and
national talents.

In other words, communication between France and the
United States worsened as a consequence of the breakdown of
the old stereotypes, for they had really served as a kind of
common language. New stereotypes were being created, to be
sure, but they had yet to develop to the point where they
facilitated communication. Today signs suggest that the
emerging new self-images will continue to make communication difficult, for they seem to lack the complementarity and
symmetry of the old stereotypes. Again, it is important to
recognize that real understanding is not the purpose of
stereotypes: *misunderstanding* is necessary if the self-image is
to be reinforced. Thus, if we are to maintain our self-image as
the generally disinterested and benevolent leader of the "free
world," we must see the French as irresponsible, nationalistic,
self-concerned, and regionally oriented. If the French are to
maintain their self-image as the emerging leader of a European
bloc that will avoid the excesses of both the Soviet and
American systems, then they must see us as domineering,
manipulative, and adventurist. Clearly, French leaders vastly
prefer the United States to the Soviet Union and know that
France is well within the Western capitalist camp. Yet they
also know that the idea of the *juste milieu* is still important to
the French self-image and hence Giscard as well as Pompidou
has renewed the old Gaullist claim of a France pursuing a
course midway between excessive Soviet socialism and exces-

sive American capitalism. For France to be the *juste milieu* in terms of self-image, American society must be cast into the polar position of "savage" capitalism.

This example shows that stereotypes would not be any less a problem for communication were political leaders, at least, free from their impact. Quite the contrary, politicians become successful in large part precisely because they are skillful and articulate spokesmen of national self-images. De Gaulle was a success, not because he rationally convinced the French to change attitudes—including their traditional friendship for the United States—but because he voiced effectively a long-maturing critical attitude toward America. This has been one reason why both Pompidou and Giscard have refrained from altering French foreign policy. And similarly American leaders—even one so basically pro-French as Henry Kissinger—must continue to insist that were it not for French vanity, vainglory, and unrealistic national goals, there would be no clash of interests and France would resume her traditional role as the "oldest ally."

The fact may well be that French society is becoming more like the American every day, but the French don't want to admit it and their self-image as well as their leaders' interpretation of this image rejects the possibility. This, I think, is true in varying degrees for all of Europe. On the American side, the fact may well be that we wish to maintain France within our "system" and to minimize the growing diversity of interests between our governments and societies, yet we don't want to admit our imperial urges and accept our estrangement from our "oldest ally." Our self-image and our leaders' voices reject these "facts" and continue to insist that the fault lies with the French in their pursuit of an unattainable role in the world. On both sides the newly emerging stereotypes serve the needs of the self-image. In order that the French may continue to believe in an independent mission for their country, it is necessary that they see the United States as an imperial power. In order that Americans may continue to prize their mission as a disinterested free world leader, it is vital to see France as an irrational actor in world affairs.

Thus in the case of French-American relations these relatively hostile mutual perceptions and stereotypes have warped communications and prevented an understanding of the domestic constraints on foreign policy on both sides. To maintain the official view of France as an irresponsible "spoiler" in the European-American relationship, American foreign policymakers have been obliged to avert their gaze from Gaullist strength in parliament and from how a united left opposition limits the possibilities of change open to Giscard. To maintain their official view of the United States as a vaguely domineering ally, which is useful to their internal strategy vis-à-vis the left, French leaders refuse to see that in American opinion there is little support for treating Europe as an equal partner.

V

The ultimate obstacle to a correct assessment of domestic structures, however, is a kind of cultural ignorance. This is not an ignorance of information or even trends in other societies —although that cannot be excluded even on the policymaking level. It is rather an ignorance of the correct weight and relative importance to assign to crucial patterns of political belief and behavior that are different from your own. In some cases this ignorance also involves a stubborn unwillingness to recognize the foreign policy implications of vast societal differences between two formally allied and traditionally friendly nations. Again the French-American relationship offers an example of this problem.

A nation's customary and traditional political system is a paradigm for its society as a whole. The basic structures of French politics are a monistic outlook on what constitutes the public good and a highly centralized administration destined historically to pursue this objective public good. The basic structures of American political life are almost diametrically different: a pluralistic view of the public good and a diffused power structure operated by actors who consider themselves in a market situation, and not in a command hierarchy. The monism and centralization of French political life is replicated in business, culture, family, and voluntary associations. While real change in all these realms has taken place in recent years, France is still very much a land of monistic thought and hierarchical organization. Anyone who has attempted to explain to French students the reality of American federalism and the way in which different levels of public authority negotiate over policy outcomes in the United States knows how true this is. The problem results from the vastly different national experiences which have reinforced very different values, expectations, and senses of what is the right way to pursue the public good. For the hazards of the market to dominate this pursuit and for the execution of policy to be "up for grabs" in a negotiating process appears thoroughly illegitimate to the French.

Political discussion and, indeed, all debate and controversy in America proceeds on market assumptions: all parties have equal access, the adversary mode of discourse prevails, the best argued and documented case becomes policy. In France the paradigm of the State and its historic mission to pursue the objective public good conditions discussion, bargaining, and negotiation in all fields. The French remain skeptical of the possibility of a true marketplace of ideas, for they fear that selfish and particularistic points of view may marshal superior resources and win out over both truth and the objective good. They believe that for the objective good and the "ideal" policy to prevail, a third-party judge is essential in all discussion. Hence instead of a loose, adversarial confrontation in a market situation involving plural interests, the French prefer an informal airing of differences among the parties, with an ultimate decision coming from a source outside the disputants—or appearing to be independent of them, at any rate. The State—guardian of the objective public good—is the model arbitrator for almost all Frenchmen, no matter what they may feel about the leadership currently presiding over the State machine.

Clearly, the American faith in the clash of interests in a market situation as ensuring the "right" policy for the country is far removed from this French model of determining the good. And as noted previously, the political model applies to an amazing degree for decision-making and organizational behavior in other spheres as well.

Obviously, the value systems of the two countries remain very different. The traditional catalogue of differences still is largely current, and oddly enough, it has been artificially invigorated by the strained relations of the governments in recent years as well as by the dismantlement of old stereotypes. For as Frenchmen perceive their country moving into an adversarial, competitive relationship with the United States—whether as part of the European Common Market or simply in terms of resisting "materialism"—many of them unconsciously see the confrontation as a zero-sum game in basic values. Thus, if U.S. monetary, energy, and security "demands" are met, or if American business continues its "invasion" of the French economy, it means the decline of the French way of life. To dismiss these views as hysteria or nonsense is to underestimate the importance of the questions of identity and self-image which continue to dominate French perceptions of other countries and of their own place in the world.

This brings us briefly to present-day policy differences and the legacy of past relationships. The greatest obstacle to improving communications is to continue our old, hypocritical assumption that no serious divergence of interests exists between our two countries. Fortunately, this assumption is articulated less frequently today than in the past. The French have repeatedly shown in opinion polls and at the ballot box that they approve the broad lines of current French foreign policy by a large margin. That policy is based on the assumption of divergent interests between the United States and Europe. For us to deny this divergence by insisting on the conventional wisdom of "shared" interests is to suggest to many Frenchmen that the United States wishes to reimpose its old domination of Europe and thus block France's search for a relatively independent destiny in the world. American policymakers' interest in "packaged" Atlantic solutions to monetary, energy, and commercial problems are cases in point. No matter what the "rational" and objective solution to these problems may be, the French—and, to a lesser extent, other Europeans also—will continue to have a Pavlovian reaction to any moralizing, utilitarian formulation that, in their view, shields a narrowly self-interested and strictly national policy.

Whether they are right or wrong about this is not relevant: that's what they believe and must believe if they are to maintain a rationale for at least an apparently autonomous course in foreign policy. In other words, if the bad old days of U.S. dominance over Europe had not existed, they would now have to be invented by the French in order to serve their present foreign policy objectives. But the fact that they did exist historically makes it all the easier for any French government to invoke the bogey of American domination. As long as France continues to slowly reconstruct her national identity along present lines, the memory of past inferiority vis-à-vis the United States will continue to be a factor to be reckoned with in our relations with her. For under present circumstances it is this memory that is inscribed on the French side of the coin, as far as the Atlantic alliance is concerned—no matter how generous and disinterested the United States believes its motives to have been and to continue to be.

VI

In the years to come it will be increasingly difficult to maintain the conventional wisdom about the Atlantic rela-

tionship. During the Vietnam war and the first years of détente it may have been inevitable that American policy should
ignore changes in Europe. There were more pressing problems,
and to acknowledge deterioration or even serious change in
relations with Europe meant opening yet another "front" in
an embattled foreign policy. When relations with the Soviet
Union dominated American attention, the need to organize a
"tight ship" on the Western side argued against acknowledgment of new domestic conditions in the alliance.

Today changes in leadership and in party politics and
the economic and energy crises make the need to revise the
conventional wisdom very pressing. Inflation and rising unemployment have created a demand for high levels of governmental performance in Europe. Among the conditions for
these high levels in parliamentary systems is the existence of
stable governing majorities which legitimize government action. Yet over the last few years the trend everywhere has been
toward fragile majorities, if not minority governments. The
coalition models and governing "formulas"—when not the
governing parties themselves—all appear to be worn out. They
are simply no longer credible in terms of promising high levels
of performance. Hence the talk in Britain of new parties or
coalition governments. Hence, too, the debate in Italy over
the "historic compromise" between Christian Democracy and
communism, seen by many as the key to more effective
government. In France President Giscard d'Estaing's narrow
victory in 1974 suggests the possibility of both a new governing
party, subsuming the diminished Gaullists, as well as a united
left, including the Communists, once again in power. Even in
relatively stable Germany the Socialist-Free Democratic
coalition is fragile and sensitive to spy scandals and economic
troubles.

It is conceivable that some changes in majority parties or
coalitions could consolidate the power of supporters of the
traditional relationship with the United States. But in most
foreseeable changes of majority, the conventional wisdom
would be challenged if not denied. Here are some relatively

mild possibilities: a Conservative-Liberal government in Britain decides to play the European card to the full; a Mitterrand government under a pragmatic Giscard decides to make some foreign policy concessions to its Communist members; a grand coalition of Christian Democrats, Socialists, and Communists in Italy does the same; and in Germany, a Socialist government, now ruling alone and with a large majority, feels free to "experiment" with its Atlantic policies. Almost every imaginable governmental alternative to those now in office would be more assertive of national or European interests.

A second development in European political life having implications for the alliance is the rise to public and private power of a new generation of executives. Whether Prime Ministers or presidents of companies, they are bereft of any sentimentality concerning the "old alliance," they are committed to a competitive posture both among themselves and vis-à-vis the United States, and they accept without passion a pragmatic vision of European unity as an ultimate goal. Schmidt and Giscard exemplify this development, and their personal friendship and determination to cooperate on economic matters suggest interesting possibilities. Any kind of serious cooperation between the two major continental powers would tend to give new dynamism to Community affairs which, in turn, might require review of the Atlantic relationship.

In both business and government the people in power in Europe have had their most formative experiences in the 1950s and 1960s. Neither the Depression nor the war is important in their memories. They are used to prosperity, detached from cold war rhetoric, disabused of American virtue and power, yet realistic about European economic and defense capabilities. This is a generation of hustlers whose competitive instincts are unencumbered by either residual feelings of inferiority or any real sense of debt or allegiance toward the United States or to the abstraction called the

Atlantic community. They are willing to go to great lengths to maximize profits or stay in power—including accommodation with trade unions, bringing Communists into power, and making the needed foreign policy adjustments.

Thus, objective factors such as the problem of fragile majorities and subjective factors such as the nature of a new generation of leadership both suggest that the restoration of the traditional relationship with Europe will be difficult. Yet if the old rhetoric has lost its charm, the possibilities for American *de facto* domination have increased. In a Europe floundering in economic troubles, preoccupied by faltering government majorities, and ruled by opportunistic and highly competitive leaders, eager to curry favor with the dominant power, the opportunities for American manipulation are many. However, it would be most shortsighted to exploit these opportunities. The message from the European domestic scene is to abstain from this temptation since the long-range trends will make the price very high.

In a sense this message from Europe is similar to the message from the domestic scenes of our adversaries: not much can be done about them, so it is best to accommodate them. But here the parallel ends, for accommodation with the Communist countries has meant reaching out and renewing relationships after long years of confrontation. To adapt to the changing domestic scene in Western Europe the need is to let go—not reach out—to let go and recreate the relationship on a new basis in which domination, implicit or explicit, willed or involuntary, is eliminated—above all in the perceptions of the Europeans. To recognize the autonomy of European domestic structures in determining their relations with the United States and to abandon the conventional wisdom of the alliance which rejected this autonomy will be a difficult effort since it depends on cultural and psychological changes that are still in process. The best we can hope for is more self-restraint from our policymakers when it comes to imposing American policy views on the Europeans. In relations with allies as well as friends, dependency is tricky: "letting go" is often the best way of holding on.

NOTES

[1] "Domestic Structure and Foreign Policy," in Henry A. Kissinger, *American Foreign Policy* (New York, 1974).

Chapter 11
EUROPE AND AMERICA: AZIMUTHS

Barbara Gibson Schwarz

A colloquium was held at Bellagio, Italy, in October 1974, between Europeans and Americans, with Barbara Schwarz acting as rapporteur. Participating Americans included the authors of the preceding essays with the exception of Seyom Brown, who was unable to attend. The Europeans, who had previously commented critically on the essays, entered into a general discussion of European-American relations, from which these excerpts are drawn. The European commentators are:

Christoph Bertram, Director of the International Institute for Strategic Studies, London; co-author of *Europe's Futures, Europe's Choices*

Miriam Camps, Research Committee Member of the Royal Institute of International Affairs, London, and Senior Research Fellow of the Council on Foreign Relations, New York; author of *European Unification in the Sixties* and numerous other works

Wolfgang Hager, presently at the Deutsche Gesellschaft für Auswärtige Politik, Bonn; during the conference, at the European Community Institute for University Studies, Brussels

Anthony Hartley, Deputy Director of the London office to the

European Community; author of *Gaullism: The Rise and Fall of a Political Movement* and other articles and books

Michael Howard, Fellow in Higher Defence Studies at All Souls College, Oxford; Professor of War Studies at the University of London, 1963-68; author of *Disengagement in Europe, The Franco-Prussian War*, and many other works

Giorgio La Malfa, Chairman of the Center for Studies in Economic Policy, Turin, and a member of the Italian Chamber of Deputies

Thierry de Montbrial, Chef du Centre d'Analyse et de Prévision, Ministry of Foreign Affairs, Paris; Professor of Economics, Ecole Polytechnique, Paris; author of *Le désordre économique mondial* and other works

Michel Tatu, Foreign Editor of *Le Monde*, Paris; author of *Le Pouvoir en U.R.S.S.*

STANLEY HOFFMANN: Reflecting on the discussion and the papers, I am struck by its Janus-like aspect—its old and its new face. Continuity of an old debate which has been going on for years on the nature of the American national interest is implicit in the suggestions of disengagement, devolution, and leadership. Divisions continue among the Europeans on what European identity should be: inward Europe versus outward Europe. As before in the old debate, the United States figures both as an integrative and a disintegrative force: integrative when it pushes for unity (and sometimes when it pushes too hard this can have the opposite effect); disintegrative in producing a collective habit of dependency in Europe's attitude toward the United States and of insufficient nationalism. However, in this conference and in the papers, there is a tension between the traditional focus of such conferences on U.S.-European relations and the very new rude intrusion of global interdependence. As a consequence of American foreign policy, disintegration of the economic system, and the energy and raw material crises, the outside world is intruding, bringing the Atlantic system to an end.

The new aspect has important effects. There is increasing discrepancy between the two sides of the dialogue. U.S. globalism is not new. The United States has needed to look at the problems globally, beyond the European scene, since the beginning; but the context is new. For West Europeans, the global problems and the end of the Atlantic coalition are new. Globalism reinforces the arguments of those skeptical of concentration on European identity first, since the problems are insoluble in a purely West European framework. And it increases the tensions among the Europeans, heightening the risk of European domestic structures evolving in very different directions from each other.

The intrusion of global problems diminishes considerably the value of the "old solutions." It devalues disengagement because of the problem of unraveling. The United States cannot disengage on a large scale because of its global involvement and responsibilities, and because engagement means some ability to control. Devolution does not have much of a receptacle and is not terribly applicable to the diplomatic-strategic front. The intrusion also devalues the older varieties of Atlanticism, of which trilateralism is the most recent form, for they neglect the problems of the North and the South.

This leads to points to consider here—empirical and normative, though they cannot be separated to any great degree. First the empirical. There is a tendency in times of crisis to cling to existing and tested relationships. Europeans are reassured about NATO since they are used to it and are given commands and some sense of participation; but there is an increasing sense of the irrelevance of Atlantic institutions in the monetary and economic fields. We must face more urgently the new dimensions of this problem of economic interdependence and also the East-West dimensions of détente. *Ostpolitik* seems to have run its course and European security appears somewhat deadlocked. The stress is not over; the impact of the whole area of East-West European relationships is not stabilized.

On the North-South issue, we have not done our work. Americans continue largely to ignore a major revolution, the ideological solidarity of the Third World. At the Conference on the Law of the Sea, even landlocked countries affirmed their solidarity with the coastal countries though it was not in their actual interests. On oil, even Fourth World countries are showing much more solidarity with the oil-producing OPEC countries than with the industrialized countries, whose plight they share. Europeans have for a longer time had an awareness of the importance of the southern dimension, and have developed different approaches.

Now for the normative. In the short run, the crisis makes the United States even more important for Western Europe, though in the long run globalization may have the opposite effect. The United States will remain very important, but Europe will have to take account of other actors; and Europe will become less central to American foreign policy. If there are to be initiatives, they will have to come from the Europeans themselves. What would be desirable European initiatives, given their domestic considerations and their wider situation? And what should American reactions be to those initiatives? If the United States stopped objecting—even in areas where harm could not be done to vital American interests—when Europeans get together, would there be improvement? If there are no European initiatives and Europe proves incapable of cohering, what should American policy be? We are faced with problems "leadership" does not cover. Leadership can mean anything from taking action, where everybody has a role, up to hegemony and total manipulation. If my gloom about the capability of Europe is justified, these are some of the questions we should ask rather than going back to the old scholasticism: devolution, disengagement, and the old Atlanticism.

WOLFGANG HAGER: One important aspect of leadership is the ability to come up with a good plan of action. Here the United

States continues to be way ahead of the Europeans. One sees this in the field of energy, where the United States provided most of the working drafts for the establishment of the International Energy Agency; and one sees it in the monetary field, especially as concerns ways of dealing with the recycling problem. The Americans do their sums quickly, and the Europeans are left to amend an American draft. Europeans, if they want to share in leadership, must learn to present policy proposals which are more than general outlines. One reason for their vagueness is, of course, the inability to agree among themselves on specifics; they do, however, agree on specifics in a negotiating context that includes the United States.

In the new context of world economic insecurity and bargaining, the Community has gained a new importance for its members. Should the world economy break down, the Community and its regional periphery may well provide an island of relative stability—as far as observance of the rules of the game are concerned—to its members.

Moreover, to the extent that this insecurity stems from Third World assertions of ideology, of new concepts of right and wrong, the Community, by its own economic philosophy as well as by its special vulnerability, will not always hold the same views in international forums as the United States. The intrusion of the South into the West-West relationship must be seen as a permanent structural element; compared to the East, the Third World is a more volatile as well as a more ambiguous adversary-partner for the Atlantic world.

MICHEL TATU: U.S. leadership is a fact. How it is advanced is new. If you assert it, it will necessarily be opposed by those people who are not in favor of abdication (and you would always find some governments not happy with that); if you assert it in the mistaken way of Henry Kissinger, even people inclined to abdication start to protest.

On the notion that problems are global, I would question or qualify that idea. Sometimes we call problems global simply because we don't see solutions. That the problem is global does not mean necessarily that the solution is global. There are different, multiple interests. If people meet with common goals in mind, they can come up with common solutions. If a European identity is asserted, Europe should not be ashamed of having regional interests. European unity must be an end in itself and Europe must tackle first its regional problems, and after that its more external problems. And defense is a part of the regional interest. This was also the way the United States was built—beginning with regional problems and regional goals.

On the situation in the East, détente is not a definite fact, but has its ups and downs. I believe we will see the Communist systems collapse before the end of this century. Many specialists in Soviet affairs see a profoundly serious situation, even an impasse. And a crisis in the East may be sudden and more dramatic than what we have in the West. There is, in effect, a race as to who will have their crisis first, the East or the West. If the West has one before the East, this will change the one in the East, reinforcing the system and delaying their crisis. If the Eastern crisis comes first, it will have important repercussions for the Western political situation, particularly for the Communist parties in France and Italy.

ZBIGNIEW BRZEZINSKI: I believe M. Tatu's warning is basically very right, and would merely note that the rivalry in competitive development between the East and West has now become that of competitive decay.

The global context introduces a novel dimension which tends to devalue the U.S.-European relationship. What we have been discussing is much less important than a few years ago when it was essential to stability, peace, and survival. The Atlantic relationship remains important, but important alongside other things that are more urgent.

In the past era the United States needed a united Europe for psychological reasons and as part of the competition with the Soviet Union. Today the United States needs a united

Europe less for those reasons. The United States now needs cooperation in the context of global concerns, either with the European Community or through bilateralism. But today Europe needs a united Europe for its own sake, at a time when political and economic developments make unification more important strictly for internal reasons.

In this context, trilateralism is not Atlanticism refreshed, nor is it a creed or a mission; rather, it involves a wider collaborative process among countries who have the highest stake in stability and change. To argue for that is not to avoid the North-South issue; rather that we must reform our institutions to include the South and to shape a unique cooperation with those countries. If the international system is collapsing, it is because the existing system is no longer broad enough to encompass all those who should be inside. The new arrangement—essentially devolution of power from the Western powers to the new—imposes on us the need for cooperation rather than competition.

CHRISTOPH BERTRAM: Global problems, however important, do not automatically and to the same degree affect all of the world's regions. Regional concerns and regional priorities will remain, not least in Europe, and there will be a strong tendency to try and ignore global problems if they should run against these interests and priorities. It is, therefore, not enough to state that there is a new powerful group in the Third World countries intent on changing the rules of the international game; what is required is a much more precise and concrete analysis of how the problems of "the South" will affect the European region as well as the Atlantic system, and indeed what the consequences would be for Europe of ignoring the global context by that favorite European policy device of survival by muddling through. The call for a redistribution of wealth among nations coincides with pressures for a redistribution of wealth within nations, aggravated by the economic recession experienced by all industrial countries.

Could there be, in dealing with the North-South issue, a

division of labor; or must there be, as Dr. Kissinger has advocated, a common front of the Western industrialized world? The limits of the superpowers have become all too obvious, and a greater autonomy of European action could become helpful to the solution of problems of international resources and equity by isolating them to some degree from East-West superpower rivalry. We cannot expect the United States, with its global interests, to wait for Europe to make up its mind in all areas, but there would be some advantage for the United Staes to keep a place for Europe in some areas. This could be a more powerful challenge to a common European effort and a more farsighted expression of American leadership than the insistence on a common front.

In Zbig Brzezinski's new Atlanticism, I think he is right to point out that the European-American relationship is less central than it was in the past. But what does this mean for the East-West problem, which in Europe will continue to create both stability and concern? To the Soviet Union, Western Europe will remain a matter of highest priority, for its traditional interest as well as its "hostage function," offsetting a perceived American global superiority by Soviet superiority in the European region. If Michel Tatu is right and there is a collapse of the Communist system, this will not come abruptly but in stages, and in the interim the importance of Western Europe to the Soviet Union, and the significance of European affairs for the definition of Soviet-American relations, will increase, not decrease.

We have discussed devolution and disengagement within the Atlantic alliance. The inadvisability of American disengagement will not, by itself, prevent it from taking place. The process of fragmentation in the international system will be delayed for the Atlantic region, but can it be totally stopped here? European political integration remains the most obvious reinsurance against the unpredictability of world affairs in a period where the traditional elements of international order, like alliances or arms control, are losing much of their relevance. This gives to renewed efforts for European defense cooperation a major political importance, not only for the sake of security, but for that of providing a measure of confidence in an increasingly uncertain world.

GIORGIO LA MALFA: I, too, do not believe the global nature of world problems will make European problems less central for the United States and the world as a whole. West European political integration is now more important for the United States than ever before. During the 1950s there was a military situation which kept Europe from falling apart: the contest with the Soviet Union. Now that the European countries are much less cohesive than in the 1950s, they are more open to troubles. I don't know whether the East European system will undergo an economic crisis, but their political system is such that they can resist longer. Western Europe will suffer a crisis first. It is going through a serious crisis now, which may well lead to "Finlandization" in Western Europe, and then the United States will have a problem; for Europe is still a field of contest with the Soviet Union, which is much more dangerous now precisely because of détente.

There is a tendency in these papers to ask whether European political unification is still necessary. Why not go on as before with limited political integration, mostly on economic matters? For the essential reason that, as a result of the changing prices of raw materials and oil in particular, there will be a redistribution of wealth from the industrial countries to the oil countries. To avoid political consequences, European political unification must be brought about if at all possible, so that no single European country will be able to shove the costs onto another European country. Otherwise political disintegration will follow. If nothing else, self-interest should dictate that the United States promote political unification and refrain from actions which inhibit it.

DAVID CALLEO: I would like to put my comments into the context of Stanley Hoffman's; in other words, to try to deal with the future, in particular with the long-range significance of the oil crisis. Moreover, I believe that things will get much worse before they get much better.

We are heading into a time when raw materials may well be more limited, and, in any event, growth gradually reduced. Such a world will obviously be more straitened, not only because of lower growth generally, but also because others, the Third World in particular, will demand more growth for themselves. Before the oil crisis, we had come to take the present distribution of world resources for granted and felt that it would last forever; it will not. Others are developing ways of demanding their share. In a straitened world, conflict is more likely, not only between the developing countries and the rest of the world, but among, and indeed within, the developed countries themselves.

Growth has been our solution to fundamental problems. As growth ceases, our societies will have to confront those problems more directly; we will no longer be able to use growth as a way to sidestep the problem of distribution, nationally or internationally. Our societies will have to plan the use of their resources a good deal more carefully.

Democratic planning requires a political consensus underneath it. We must hope that our Western societies can find the political and spiritual resources to solve the coming challenges in a democratic fashion. That democratic consensus must inevitably be primarily national. Among neighboring countries who share a common situation in the world, national consensus can conceivably be stretched to a regional dimension. But consensus cannot be reached on a global scale. Thus, while some problems may, in a manner of speaking, be called "global," they will never be resolved on a global basis.

My vision of the future sees a world which is much more of a multiple than a global system—a world in which each region comes to terms with its own regional problems. Such a view rests, not on the technical superiority of regional solutions as such, but on the need for consensus as the basis for any solution. You cannot engender consensus on a global scale; on a regional scale it is more reasonable. This is the real argument for European unity and for the European region. By the same argument, I don't think we can count on maintaining an Atlantic consensus built around American hegemony and European subservience or indifference. The consensus will break down—indeed, the system is breaking down around us, and we have been too slow to see it.

For example, my own paper explores the possible effects of the oil crisis as the taking-off point for more intensive European integration. To protect themselves, European states must try to link their regional system to a Mediterranean and African dimension. I find the prospects for such an arrangement not all that unpromising in the long run. It represents a rather grand historical movement, and I see no reason to feel its prospects are hopeless. At the same time, to succeed in its Near Eastern policy, Europe cannot link itself tightly to an American-dominated solution to the energy crisis—a hegemonic pattern which will strongly limit the prospects of a viable European-Middle East regional arrangement. Almost inevitably, the European states and the Americans will come into conflict insofar as Europe pursues its own policies.

For this reason, if the European bloc is to be formed, it must ultimately extend itself to defense. No European system will hold together if it is militarily helpless, for there will be a continuing American veto on European economic policies. And it is too much to expect the United States to renounce its hegemony without strong pressures from the Europeans, no matter how enlightened such a policy might seem. Europeans will have to take the initiative.

On the question of Europe's will, I am not as skeptical as most people. Their weaknesses are obvious, but they have nevertheless accomplished a great deal, and, in the comfortable postwar world, there hasn't been the need to go further.

Major shifts in policy disturb domestic interests, something politicians never do except when seriously threatened. But the time is coming when Europeans will have to do something or take a real loss in economic prosperity and security.

One final point: in the United States some of us who have long pressed for American devolution from hegemony and a more assertive Europe are sometimes accused of unrealistic sentimentality—of being more European than the Europeans. No doubt some of us do have a certain sentimental view of Europe. It is not surprising that any civilized westerner should love the nations of Europe, and wish them well. But for the Europeans to think that we are more concerned about European interests than our own is a mistake. It is a patronizing and rather cheap way to dismiss serious arguments, a misunderstanding that could be costly in the long run. The idea that it would be good for the world if there were a Europe is not a sentimental enthusiasm, but flows from the belief that only thus can world problems be solved in a fashion satisfactory to the West. It is not in the American interest to go on trying to manage all the world's problems on a global, hegemonic scale. We risk structuring our own society in a way that increasingly undermines a viable domestic order in the United States. And not only is American imperialism bad for America, but it will grow bad for Europe as well. It is unwise to imagine that the rich and defenseless Europe will forever remain unexploited, its interest looked after by others.

NICHOLAS WAHL: I also would like to stress the American national interest in a more united Europe, one that has greater responsibility for its defense and that, naturally, would pursue goals that are at least somewhat different from those of U.S. foreign policy. It has been said, quite rightly, that the initiative for greater European unity and increased political will must come, in the first instance, from the Europeans. But it has also been said that the United States must stop objecting to these initiatives when they are taken without consultation and when they appear to diverge from American interests. I think these two things are tied to one another.

In my view, the optimal conditions for effective European unity initiatives must include a necessary restraint and self-control on the American side, including a conscious refusal even to comment upon what Europeans may choose to do without us. Above all, we must abandon traditional insistence on subordinating European unity to the larger global concerns of the Western alliance as defined by us. Unless we let go in this respect, we will always be providing Europeans with an alibi for failing to progress toward greater political unity.

Of course, it is far from certain that the Europeans will take the initiative once we have abandoned our "globalism." But it is worth trying, for in the difficult times ahead a self-reliant Europe might be very useful to us. For the moment the United States is embarking on a stormy passage with Europe being hauled in our wake, unhappy with its dependence but unable to sail on its own. Europe attributes this weakness at least partly to the fact that we are keeping it in tow. But wouldn't our own voyage be safer if we were in convoy with a truly seaworthy Europe? To be sure, the possibility of Europe taking a somewhat different course would exist. But Europe would always be in sight and would at least be better able to help us in possible distress if it were a fully equipped vessel with a command of its own and an experience of unity and problem-solving upon which we could draw in the future.

If this future is one of economic crisis with the need for greater cooperation among industrialized nations, it is necessary that Europe become a unit with the potential of effective cooperation. One of the conditions for this unity and this potential is a greater degree of foreign policy autonomy. This in turn depends on the emergence of a European political will. Even if American "interference" is only a minor and partly mythical reason for the slow emergence of this European political will, it is worth taking a measure of risk to eliminate this factor of disunity and to give Europe every chance to join us as a full-scale partner in the effort at discovering solutions to our common problems.

MICHAEL HOWARD: On the question of a possible clash of interests between American-Soviet relations and American-European relations, and whether Europeans see this as a serious threat, we must make a distinction between tensions in the international system which can be handled and those that cannot. Europeans tend to have greater faith than do Americans in the ability of their professional diplomats to handle such problems. The difficulties which academics consider to be insoluble, professionals often take in their stride.

As to the relationship between domestic and global problems, it is no doubt correct in principle to maintain that domestic problems cannot be solved unless the global ones are solved as well. It is in principle quite monstrous that part of the world should be starving while we maintain our own very high standard of living. Yet the problems which really obsess cabinet ministers are inevitably those of their own people—the people who elect them. The maintenance of the standard of living of British workers is more important to the British government than starvation elsewhere, and it will become even more so as inflation increases and makes such domestic issues harder to deal with. The North-South question has for them been more one of how to get cheap resources from the South than how to redistribute wealth. Only if the Third World acquires political muscle will its problems become a serious issue for the rich nations of the North.

I accept that we can solve British domestic problems only within a European context, but in the process it is important for us to come to play a world role as well. As to whether Europe will be competitive, I think that in the long run we will do better than some think. But in the relatively short term, I am afraid that Western Europe will continue to be inward looking and unable to play its role on the global scene except in a lame and protesting manner. The problem for the United

States is how to handle Europe as long as we remain in this discouraging situation.

EARL RAVENAL: If I don't have much company in my prediction of alliance dissolution and my recommendation of American disengagement, I would suspect that part of the reason is that my propositions are not congenial and *therefore* do not sound like sensible "policy goals." But I submit that this has to do with a misconception of the nature of policy—specifically, the misconception that policy has more to do with interests than with constraints; and that interests can somehow be defined, and pursued, without reference to constraints.

Given a range of pure "choices," no one would opt for dissolution and disengagement. But that is not the point; it ignores the structure of the problem. We cannot get what we want. Situations—among nations and within nations—are intractable. In fact, the entire Atlantic relationship will be increasingly characterized, not just by the usual confusion of purpose, but by the extreme stringency of the parameters of the situations of states, and, most of all, by a lack of control by states over those parameters. These parameters, or constraints, are of two kinds: external, or systemic; and internal, or domestic.

Enough attention has been devoted here to external systemic factors that constrain the behavior of nations, and will constrain the actions of the United States and its European alliance partners. We must also consider the net effect of domestic factors on the foreign policy behavior of states, and in particular on American foreign policy. Like Michael Howard, I believe that governments—whether democratic or authoritarian—exist, *in fact,* to serve the needs of the people they represent. The consequence of this fact for the legitimacy of national governments is the critical problem, not only for their domestic survivability, but for their scope of action in the international arena. The minimum condition of legitimacy is that governments fill the peoples' needs—whatever the further

"requisites" of statecraft might be. Moreover, almost by definition, national governments have no mandate to legislate
and act for *other* nations' citizens.

These simple, even obvious, facts constitute a very powerful
set of constraints on the actions of foreign policy "makers," in
pursuing what they, and allies to whom they are oriented,
consider to be the common "interest," and also their own
ultimate self-interest.

But what is an "interest," anyway? First, an interest must be
objective: that is, the various outcomes of a situation involving
that interest must make a difference to a nation. Second, an
interest, to be asserted, must be enforceable (in a way that is
analogous to the law of blockade). Otherwise, it is a mere
wish—not "binding" on the nation itself, and not convincing
to other nations. In other words, a nation must be able to do
something about its "interests." And this is where constraints—particularly domestic constraints—come in. So the
real question, in all the prognoses and prescriptions offered
here, by Europeans and Americans, is the power of the United
States to make its writ run, in the face of rising centers of
countervailing power in the world, and in the face of increasing—or at least abiding—internal division.

It is in these terms—the increasing external and domestic
constraints on its behavior—that I question whether the
United States has the inevitable and permanent global interests that most of my colleagues here, European as well as
American, would take for granted, as an axiom of U.S. policy
and a given in international politics (though, of course, the
problems we face might be global in scale).

Of course, the United States is not without influence. At
the moment, American power—if we wish to commit it—still
possibly runs even with our pretensions to create and support
extensive order in the world. But it is increasingly likely that
American power will fall short of this universal scope, whether
through external opposition, insupportable cost, or insufficient domestic support. Our ability to "choose" indepen-

dently and effectively, over a wide range—and to make our choices stick—will be greatly diminished.

The question, then, is not directly whether we "choose" to continue to exercise a global reach and command global interests, but, indirectly and more fundamentally, whether we will continue to have the means and the competence to pursue such interests. In this context of international and domestic constraints, disengagement should be seen not as a kind of scholasticism, but as an indicated—perhaps necessary—retreat from a global role, and from pretensions to global leadership, that have become untenable for the United States.

ANTHONY HARTLEY: More than a year ago there was a great deal of talk about the possibility of American "disengagement" from Europe. There appeared to be major disagreements of an economic nature between the United States and the European Community—disagreements brought into prominence by Dr. Kissinger's speech of April 23, 1973—and, after the experience of Vietnam, there was doubt among America's European allies as to whether public opinion in the United States were not turning against permanent international commitments. Interpretation (or extrapolation) of the Nixon Doctrine seemed to suggest that there might be in the future a gradual reliance on "local balances" of power to replace an American military presence.

Now, so it seems to me, the position is rather different. The crisis in the Middle East has demonstrated that, when an international upheaval of this magnitude takes place, the United States will inevitably be involved, and that the solution—the safe solution restoring some degree of stability—will consist rather in an increased American presence than in a diminished one. Only in this way can the makers of American foreign policy remain in control of situations which carry within them a danger of global conflict. In the Middle East the United States under the auspices of Dr. Kissinger has taken on what amounts to responsiblity for peace in the entire area. It is not forward from the Nixon Doctrine. If anything, it is back to the Eisenhower Doctrine.

In addition, I should like to express my appreciation of what M. Tatu had to say about the Soviet Union. The most immediate threat to the peace of Western Europe would come from a crisis in Eastern Europe, and there appears to be an inherent instability in the relationship between the Soviet Union and its satellites which is often neglected in the discussion of international affairs. The greatest question mark in this area, of course, is that hanging over the internal future of the Soviet Union itself, and we should be conscious that much of what is said and anticipated may be proved false by the evolution of Russian government and society.

A final word on the so-called North-South problem. Here I think Michael Howard is right. The average European will not wish to make sacrifices for the sake of the Third World at a moment when he is having to adjust himself to the rising cost of energy. Disagreeable as the prospect is, the Third and Fourth Worlds may be left to fend for themselves, and the question will certainly be put: "Why shouldn't the Arabs do something? They have the money now." This is a field where it would be easier for the European Community to behave in a more humane and enlightened manner than for individual European governments.

ANDREW PIERRE: When in the fall of 1973 we started thinking about the desirability of a book such as this, giving various American views regarding the long-term European-American relationship, there was a growing tension between the two sides of the Atlantic. As our discussions have borne out, the Europeans saw in the Year of Europe initiative an attempt to constrain the development of a European political identity, while American policy did not seem to accept that European interests may not always be identical to ours, such as during the Yom Kippur War. It appeared that the old Atlantic relationship had become completely archaic and irrelevant.

Hence the attempt to develop in our papers and exchanges some "alternatives to Atlanticism" for the 1980s.

In this regard, a number of the contributions have portrayed Atlanticism as being an undesirable American attempt to maintain a "hegemonic" position and have advocated disengagement. Others, such as myself, do not believe that U.S. policy has been deliberately "hegemonic" but have nevertheless suggested new directions with a revisionist thrust in our policy prescriptions. Interestingly enough, the response from our European colleagues at this conference has been along these lines: "You Americans have not really been as hegemonic as some of you portray your government's policy to be. We rather like the overall Atlantic relationship as it is presently structured. Certainly there are difficulties, but they can be resolved; NATO is not likely to dissolve. True, we don't like the attempt to link the security benefits we receive from you with the economic concessions you want from us, but this approach is fortunately no longer being emphasized in American policy. For many reasons, now is not a very good time to make any significant changes in the Atlantic relationship."

In my view, neither maintenance of the Atlantic framework as presently structured nor disengagement will be practical alternatives in the next decade. Nor will the existence of new global economic and social problems, requiring a larger than Atlantic framework, negate the importance of European-American ties. Although North-South issues involving energy, raw materials, and a more just distribution of the world's resources will no doubt grow in importance, East-West problems will not disappear and the United States will continue to play an important role in the maintenance of European security. Western Europe will be evolving politically, and the European-American relationship will have to be adjusted accordingly. I doubt that we can attempt to simply muddle through in the next decade without creating new and unnecessary tensions and conflicts.

But, the initiative for a new Atlantic relationship will have to come from our European friends, since it is the form and velocity of European political construction that will be the critical variable in the creation of a new relationship. As to the United States, we should indicate our receptiveness to change when the Europeans are ready for it, and understand that this will involve some loss of American power if not of influence. A continuous dialogue between friends is needed, out of which in time may well emerge a mutually satisfactory solution. For we will deceive ourselves if we believe that the future can be nothing more than a straight-line projection from the past.

RONALD STEEL: There is a certain unreality, which this conference has brought out, whenever we try to focus the Atlantic alliance on problems of defense. Defense was, to be sure, the original stimulus that brought America so intimately into European affairs. And it has been the looming presence of the Soviet Union that has persuaded Europeans that a perpetual American military involvement on the continent is necessary. But the reasons have changed. It is no longer necessary because West Europeans fear a Soviet attack. Rather it is because they find it both cheaper and easier to rely on American protection than to create a credible—that is, a unified and nuclear—defense force of their own.

This is an understandable position. But it is a matter of choice. If the Europeans want to build a military force capable of deterring the Soviets, they have the means to do so. This is why cryptic references to "Finlandization" strike me as quite unpersuasive. Not because the Soviet Union does not represent a potential danger. No weak country is going to feel secure on the borders of a very powerful nation with a very different social system. Rather the dilemma is hypothetical since the Europeans have the means to avert it: either by maintaining the American connection or by building a deterrent force of their own.

The larger issue, which is masked by endless discussions of the military factor, is whether the economic and political interests of the Atlantic allies are sufficient to keep them bound in such wedlock at a time when the old reasons for their union have sharply diminished. To discuss areas of "devolution" is rather like a paterfamilias deciding which onerous chores he will allow his sons to take over. Dependency is written into the definition.

To mean anything serious, "devolution" would have to lead to some sort of "disengagement" in which the Europeans would emphasize their continental over their Atlantic, or their multinational, identity. For the moment this is too troublesome. Thus the more likely path is a little more sharing, a little more grumbling, and a self-conscious quest for a new "identity."

MIRIAM CAMPS: On the global-regional matter, I agree with David Calleo that there is likely to be more consensus and therefore more problem-solving at the regional than at the global level, but that does not abolish the need for global action. The relationships between the regions must be regulated in various ways. Moreover, there is a need for involvement of all groups of states in certain kinds of activities. With regard to Earl Ravenal's point that the United States does not have global interests, I should like to point out that we are in an interdependent world, in which nations cannot operate in the autonomous way implicit in such thinking.

Much has been said to the effect that the decision on European defense will define the structure of European unity. Although this seems logical, I doubt that defense will prove to be the key. The monetary issue is more likely to be the central structural issue in the next few years. Decisions will soon have to be made on how money is handled on a global basis. Basically the key decisions on money rest on decisions about how interdependent one wants to be and with whom. If the Europeans decide to be more interdependent with one another than with the United States, the global system will be constructed on that assumption. But if they do not move fairly soon to closer monetary arrangements among themselves, the global rules will be constructed accordingly and Europe will have foreclosed its choices.

A second global "structural" issue will be the distribution question. It is true today that the needs of domestic workers seem to most states to be more important, but there is a point, given TV and our interconnections, beyond which one cannot see people dying on the TV screen and do nothing: there comes a point at which something will have to be done about global distribution. Thus we need to think not in conventional "welfare" terms but, rather, how to build appropriate distributive mechanisms into the global economic system.

EDWARD MORSE: Very well then, it seems to be the case that global problems devalue the U.S.-European relationship. I am, however, skeptical about resource scarcity; natural resources are now far from exhausted. Rather, there seems to be a greater scarcity of knowledge of how to get and distribute what is available than there is a scarcity of supply. Ought the United States do something about it? the Europeans? together? Here there probably ought to be a divergence between the United States and Western Europe. I would myself prefer to see the United States do nothing active in the Third World at present, given the recent history of our involvement and our propensity to make things worse in the Third World than might otherwise be the case. In any event, any interest there is in doing something at the present time is European.

THIERRY DE MONTBRIAL: For my part, I should like to look at U.S.-European relations within the framework of a definition of a New World Economic Order. And in this respect, my first point is that the new order will have to recognize the necessity and the value of regional arrangements. This is so because we live in a world where the possibilities of integration are limited. It would be unrealistic, and possibly dangerous, to lay the foundations of a new economic order only on the two dogmas of free trade and of a monetary system based on fixed parities and unrestricted convertibility. The United States should, I believe, accept the ideal of a multipolar world, with highly integrated subsystems and a mutually agreed code of behavior to regulate the relations between the subsystems.

My second point concerns the North-South issue. I think we should regard the problem in a very constructive way, not only for moral reasons, but also because it is in the interest of the industrialized world. Thus my analysis can be summarized as follows:

(1) The rules of the game will have to be accepted by Third World countries. If they are not, these countries have means to prevent any system from operating properly.

(2) If we fail to define a new world economic order, the current economic crisis, in particular inflation, will probably continue.

(3) In the latter case, the democratic regimes, particularly in Europe, will be seriously threatened. After all, the Great Depression brought Hitler into power and was a major cause of World War II.

To have a chance of restoring a world economic order, it is therefore necessary to develop concerted policies among the industrialized countries, and between them and the Third World. This would not mean that industrialized countries should yield to unilateral action on the part of Third World countries. However, the best way to prevent such actions is to open a dialogue with the Third World.

JAMES CHACE: Before the conference some of us thought we would produce a prescriptive book on U.S. foreign policy toward Europe—what is likely and what is desirable. But diagnosis precedes prescription, and I think many Americans have learned to be particularly wary when it comes to offering one. For too much of the postwar era Washington has appeared to offer facile solutions or, to put it more kindly, and, I suspect, more accurately, solutions that were made-in-America. Such prescriptions did not sufficiently take into account European realities and European sensibilities.

In the post-cold-war era when global politics is no longer dominated by an ideological conflict between the United States and the Soviet Union, the relationship between America and Europe is changing markedly. Washington has become ever more preoccupied by the emergence of a world in which the poorer nations demand equity with the rich, and for this reason too often takes for granted the community of interests—both economic and political—which bind Europe and America together. In a world where ambiguity rather than order is the prevailing climate, where the struggle between the two superpowers has yielded not to a latter-day balance of power but to a randomness of power, where interdependence conflicts with independence, the European-American relationship remains both crucial and fraught with tension. For in this not-so-brave new world, interests clash as much as converge.

As the last quarter of the twentieth century unrolls, most of the Americans here perceive a Europe still slouching toward unity, yet too disunited to offer a coherent foreign policy, while chafing at the American yoke which—particularly in regard to security—continues to exert its power over any emerging European policy. Europe, in its turn, resents American predominance, realizing full well the knotty paradox: without a European political will, such hegemonic impulses are likely to continue; as long as this American attitude persists, a politically independent Europe will be hard put to emerge. Often those very Europeans who most cry out for independence from American hegemony demand that Washington take the first step in renouncing its predominant position in order to force Europe to make further headway.

In short, America must call the tune for Europe—exactly what many Europeans have been complaining of for the last quarter century. A different tune perhaps—but the same orchestra conductor. There are, as is evident from our own discussions, Americans who do indeed want a more independent Europe, not built-in hostility to the United States but also not a client-state beholden to America. Such a Europe would be a more reliable ally, if it knew and followed its own interests which at times will complement, at other times conflict with, America's.

Can relations between Europe and America, then, undergo a fundamental change without destroying the community of fate that exists between the two continents? I would like to believe they could. What is most hopeful is the fact that many of us on both sides of the Atlantic do finally perceive a new world emerging that makes many of the legitimate concerns of the past obsolete. But without acts of vision in the U.S.-European relationship there is more likely to be corrosion than renewal.